Giving to God

Giving to God

ISLAMIC CHARITY IN REVOLUTIONARY TIMES

Amira Mittermaier

UNIVERSITY OF CALIFORNIA PRESS

University of California Press, one of the most distinguished university presses in the United States, enriches lives around the world by advancing scholarship in the humanities, social sciences, and natural sciences. Its activities are supported by the UC Press Foundation and by philanthropic contributions from individuals and institutions. For more information, visit www.ucpress.edu.

University of California Press
Oakland, California

© 2019 by Amira Mittermaier

Library of Congress Cataloging-in-Publication Data

Names: Mittermaier, Amira, 1974– author.
Title: Giving to God : Islamic charity in revolutionary times / Amira Mittermaier.
Description: Oakland, California : University of California Press, [2019] | Includes bibliographical references and index. |
Identifiers: LCCN 2018041059 (print) | LCCN 2018045798 (ebook) | ISBN 9780520972056 (ebook and ePDF) | ISBN 9780520300828 (cloth : alk. paper) | ISBN 9780520300835 (pbk. : alk. paper)
Subjects: LCSH: Charity—Religious aspects—Islam. | Islam—Charities. | Charities—Egypt. | Arab Spring, 2010—Social aspects.
Classification: LCC BP170.25 (ebook) | LCC BP170.25 .M58 2019 (print) | DDC 297.5/40962—dc23
LC record available at https://lccn.loc.gov/2018041059

Manufactured in the United States of America

26 25 24 23 22 21 20 19
10 9 8 7 6 5 4 3 2 1

CONTENTS

ILLUSTRATIONS

NOTE ON TRANSLITERATION

When transliterating from Arabic texts, I have largely adopted the system outlined in the *International Journal of Middle East Studies*. I use long vowel marks, and mark the *'ayn* (ʿ) and *hamza* (ʾ), but I omit the dots. When transcribing from Egyptian colloquial Arabic, I modified the *IJMES* system slightly to convey a sense of colloquial speech, partly borrowing from the *Dictionary of Egyptian Arabic* by el-Said Badawi and Martin Hinds (1986). I do not mark long vowels in transliterated names, and the names of some well-known personalities, place-names, and terms with common English spellings, such as Quran, are preserved as such.

Unless otherwise noted, all translations from Arabic are my own. For Quranic verses, I generally use Muhammad Asad's translations. Plurals of Arabic words are in most cases indicated by adding an *s* to the singular form, such as *shaykhs*. All dates follow the Common Era. For the sake of privacy, I have changed the names of interlocutors except for those who wanted to be named.

ACKNOWLEDGMENTS

This book tells a story about *giving*—and so it is inevitably also about *receiving*. Alongside recipients who diligently perform their suffering and gratitude, we will meet others who purposefully do not thank the donor, who simply take and walk away. I spent much time in Egypt thinking about gratitude, its virtues and limits. I was, and continue to be, impressed by economies of giving that are organized around the idea of a "rightful share." But I was raised in Germany, in a culture suffused with "bitte" and "danke." Now, living in Canada, I say please and thank you even more often, and I teach my three-year-old to do the same. With these rules of politeness ingrained in my very way of being, I cannot but begin with a familiar gesture of gratitude: the obligatory acknowledgments.

Many of the people with whom I spent my days in Cairo are not merely "interlocutors" but have become friends over the years. My friendship with Madame Salwa has withstood more than the geographical distance. I first met her at Ibn Sirin's shrine about fifteen years ago; she turned out to be not only a gifted dreamer but also a committed giver. Her mark on this book is pervasive. Shaykh Salah and the woman I call Nura welcomed me into their *khidmas,* patiently put up with my questions, and enacted the very hospitality that they talk about abstractly and embrace spiritually. I learned far more from them than I could ever convey in writing. At Nura's *khidma* I also often saw the dervish Shaykh Mahmoud; I regret that it took me so long to realize how much I learned from him too. The charity organization Resala was a very different kind of space, but it, too, welcomed me in; dozens of volunteers shared their life stories, dreams, and frustrations with me and took me under their wings as we marched through the slums. Dr. Sherif Abdelazeem, the organization's founder and its current chairman, generously agreed to multiple interviews despite his busy schedule, and invited me to various Resala events. Trying to grasp even more bureaucratized forms of Islamic charity, I spent countless days at the Mustafa Mahmoud Association and am grateful to its employees, who shared their work space, tea, gossip, and boredom with me. As in previous years, Ramadan was marked for me by late nights with al-Ashraf al-Mahdiyya, followers of the late Shaykh Salah al-Din al-Qusi, who host a large Ramadan table (*mā'idat al-rahmān*) throughout the month of fasting. I keenly appreciate the ways this community has taken me in. Special thanks to 'Umar El-Gendy, who spoke to me with as much passion about the spiritual merits of serving food as he did about the promises and pitfalls of the revolution. To the woman I call Amal: thank you for the many strolls and conversations, and for bringing me back to people's real material struggles at times when I was at risk of getting carried away by the beauty of an Islamic ethics of giving.

I am grateful to the self-declared revolutionaries who showed me around Tahrir Square and indulged my questions about things that were sometimes deeply important and sometimes utterly irrelevant to them, as well as to those who sat down for extensive interviews with Mariam later on, at a time when remembering could be painful. More fundamentally, I thank all of Egypt's revolutionaries, who opened up a space of hope for so many of us, a space still reverberating despite the oppressive atmosphere, and currently merging, I believe, into entirely new spaces that have little to do with "politics" narrowly defined. Unexpected openings, unexpected conversations.

I was truly blessed with the research assistants I had in Cairo. Hassan Surour was more friend and mentor than "assistant." I don't know anyone who is able to move as gracefully across Egypt's starkly different social worlds. Hassan also brought on board two additional research assistants: Hana El-Rakhawi, who, through her meticulous fieldwork and photographs, helped me get a better grasp of a broader landscape of *khidmas* and Ramadan tables; and Mariam Abou Ghazi, who did countless interviews, patiently indulged my desire to put charity and revolution into conversation, and is now already thinking with me about my next project. I would also like to thank Mahmoud Bayomi for carefully sorting through media sources; Ahmed Sarhan for tracking political discourses related to social justice; Karim Khashaba for transcribing interviews; and Hana El-Rakhawi, Inger Marie Vennize, Yomna Magdi, and Hager El Hadidi for allowing me to use their photographs.

Generous research funding was provided by the Wenner-Gren Foundation for Anthropological Research and the Social Sciences and Humanities

Research Council of Canada. A Chancellor Jackman Research Fellowship gave me a break from teaching, a vibrant interdisciplinary community, and the necessary headspace to sort through my materials. My home departments, too—the Department for the Study of Religion and the Department of Anthropology at the University of Toronto—have been wonderfully stimulating environments for thinking and writing. Special thanks to John Kloppenborg, my Department Chair at the time, who agreed to give me a semester off when I was itching to get back to Egypt in 2011. Research assistance in Toronto was provided by Ayah al-Oballi, Hadear Shaheen, Khalidah Ali, Mourad Laabdi, and Dylan Shaul. To all of them I am grateful for their intellectual labor, their meticulousness, and also their humor.

The actual writing I had to fit in here and there, in my office, at Robarts Library, in neighborhood cafés. It felt frantic at times, and it took me a while to pull the strands together. I don't know if I fully succeeded, but much of what works about this text I owe to friends and colleagues who generously, carefully, and critically read and commented on drafts: Bill Christian Jr., Eva-Lynn Jagoe, Webb Keane, Hannah Mayne, Yasmin Moll, Nada Moumtaz, Kevin O'Neill, Samuli Schielke, Christian Suhr, and the students in my Anthropology of the Middle East seminar in 2016. Special thanks to Katie Kilroy-Marac, who read this entire manuscript not once, but twice. Our friendship began in Harmony Hall during our first year in graduate school; I could not have dreamed that the two of us, years later, would once again end up at the same university.

Critical feedback was also provided by the audiences at the various institutions where I have presented parts of this work: at Arizona State University, Northwestern University, Memorial University of Newfoundland, University of Toronto Scarborough, Queen's University, Johns Hopkins University, New York University, the Graduate Center of the City University of New York, McMaster University, McGill University, University of Michigan, Eberhard-Karls-Universität of Tübingen, Leiden University, Aarhus University, Yale University, Cornell University, meetings of the American Anthropological Association, and the "Anti-Gift" symposium in Oberbozen. For conversations and provocations that moved this project along, I thank Naisargi Dave, Julia Elyachar, Michael Gilsenan, Michael Lambek, Andrea Muehlebach, and Emilio Spadola. A brilliant workshop on creative nonfiction writing, organized by Elspeth Brown and Eva-Lynn Jagoe and run by Catherine Taylor and Alexandria Marzano-Lesnevich, encouraged me to move more boldly "up and down the ladder of abstraction" (Clark

2006). The very gifted editor David Lobenstine untied many knots in this text and pushed me to work more carefully on its flow and rhythm.

The University of California Press was a pleasure to work with, just like last time. Many thanks to Reed Malcolm for his continued support; to Kate Marshall, who took over as editor and nudged this book toward publication; and to project editor Kate Hoffman. Sue Carter carefully copyedited the text, and Basit Iqbal prepared my index.

There are people with whom I did not speak directly about this project but who were present for me whenever I was thinking and writing about my materials. Foremost among them is Saba Mahmood, whose death in March 2018 shook me deeply. Her groundbreaking interventions, ethos of critique, and commitment to thinking through and beyond one's visceral reactions, will continue to shape my life and my scholarship, and, I'm sure, those of many others. Her work was and is an inspiration.

Last but not least, my family: my parents, Raifa and Norbert Mittermaier; my sister, Mona Hein, and brother-in-law, David Hein; and the whole Gonzalez Jimenez family, all of whom have supported me for many years—mostly from afar but no less lovingly for that. Alejandra Gonzalez Jimenez has been there for me, for over fifteen years, in all the ways, big and small, that matter. She has encouraged me to keep going, reminded me to take breaks when I needed them, read multiple drafts, mulled over my ideas and arguments with me, and, most important, helped me keep it real. And finally, there is Felix, who, since October 2014, has turned my world upside down in the best possible way. I dedicate this work to him and Alejandra.

Introduction

"I DON'T CARE ABOUT THE POOR." Madame Salwa talks bluntly as we rush through the unpaved alleys of Islamic Cairo.

In a sentence, she disrupts my illusion of goodness and compassion.

It is August 2011. This year, Ramadan has fallen on one of the most difficult times of the year.[1] The sun rises a little after 5 A.M. and sets close to 7 P.M., making for almost fourteen hours of fasting. The days are long, and it is hot. But this does not stop us.

Three days a week, Madame Salwa and I meet early in the morning, take a bus to the Sayyida Nafisa mosque, head into a small alley, and take a narrow staircase up to a roof. Here, in a room on this roof, lives Abir, along with her husband and their four children. Abir has assisted Madame Salwa for several years, buying vegetables and meat for her at a local market and offering her kitchen, basic as it is, as well as her labor.

This day, like so many others, we spend hours with Abir and her children in their small home on the roof. We cook vast amounts of rice and *kufta*—meatballs in tomato sauce—which, about an hour before the sun sets, we will distribute downstairs in the alley. The people in the neighborhood are expecting us; they line up with empty bowls and plates. They take the food home, often after having collected more food from other donors. For many of them, ironically, the month of fasting is the only month when they have enough to eat, when they get to eat meat on a regular basis, and when they can save some money. Abir's family receives food from us too, and each day Madame Salwa gives them 20 Egyptian pounds (around $3) for helping us.[2]

Madame Salwa lives about ten kilometers to the northeast, in the middle-class neighborhood of Agouza. Her husband is a police officer who had to retire early because of an injury. They have no children. Generally on the conservative side, Madame Salwa was skeptical of the uprising that had exploded seven months earlier, in January 2011, and she was equally suspicious of the Muslim Brotherhood, the longstanding Islamist organization that, by the summer of 2011, was increasingly asserting its political presence and whose candidate Mohamed Morsi would win the presidential election in 2012. Later she would sigh with relief when, following the military coup in 2013, the former minister of defense, Abdelfattah el-Sisi, became president.

While skeptical of Islamist organizations, Madame Salwa is very pious. She fasts during Ramadan and, following the Prophet Muhammad's example, on most Mondays and Thursdays throughout the year; she prays five times a day; she wears a hijab; and she has long felt drawn to *ahl al-bayt,* literally the "people of the house," saintly descendants of the Prophet Muhammad, many of whom are buried in Cairo. Madame Salwa regularly visits their shrines, where she distributes bean sandwiches or small plastic containers filled with *ruzz bi-laban,* a sweet, sticky milk pudding that smells of rose water. She believes that giving is central to Islam. "It's what Islam is all about," she often explained to me, citing a hadith, a saying ascribed to the Prophet Muhammad, stating that you cannot be a good Muslim if your neighbor goes to bed hungry. "And there are so many people who don't have enough to eat," she said in the summer of 2011, "especially now." Food prices had been on the rise, and many were struggling to get by.

Madame Salwa is aware of the people around her who are going hungry. She seems to feel compassion for the poor, for the homeless who linger around the saint shrines, for the many people lining up with their bowls and plates during Ramadan; occasionally, she also seems to feel compassion for Abir and her children. She seems affected by the needs of other people.

But then, this: Madame Salwa and I are done for the day. We have distributed all the food, said good-bye to Abir, and are walking swiftly toward the bus station, hoping to make it home before the call to prayer announces it is time to break our fast. I'm exhausted, thirsty, and hungry. But at least we have done something good. Indeed, that sense of goodness is more pronounced than my seemingly trivial academic accomplishments. Collecting data always seems a bit overrated on such days. Yes, I will write fieldnotes in the evening, and yes, I spent the day with Madame Salwa because I am researching different manifestations of Islamic giving. And yet as we rush for the bus, it is the fact that we have given food to people—people who would otherwise be hungry— that seems more important. It is almost impossible to resist the self-congratulatory logic of charitable giving. We give because it is the right thing to do but we also give because it feels good. But then, walking by the crowded, decrepit homes of those who collected food from us an hour earlier, Madame Salwa flicks her wrist as if swatting a fly, and says, "I don't care about the poor."

This from a woman who gives to the poor throughout the year, and who cooks for them for hours while fasting. Who travels on crowded city buses to the busy outdoor market in ʿAttaba because there she gets a good deal from a Christian blanket salesman, and who then distributes the blankets in slums. A woman who has taken me to visit orphanages all over Cairo and who has led me through the hallways of a rundown children's hospital so that we can pat the backs of sick kids—"to make them smile," as she says—and so we can ask them and their parents if they need anything. Friends and relatives entrust their alms to Madame Salwa because they know that she will do something good with the money, and she will not waste a single piaster. Having known her for over a decade, I, too, have long been impressed by her tireless commitment to giving and, when I am not in Egypt, I send her money every Ramadan via Western Union.

On the surface, Madame Salwa is the quintessential charitable Muslim. She is all about caring for others, caring for those in need, caring for the poor. "I don't care about the poor," she says. "I do all this for God [li-llāh]."

BEYOND DEVELOPMENT, BEYOND COMPASSION

We live in an age of pervasive global inequality. The story is familiar by now: the richest 1 percent in the world have far more wealth than the rest of the world's population combined.[3] In Egypt, inequality has only increased in the age of accelerated neoliberalism since the 1990s, and more recently in the age of "military capitalism" (Amar 2018).[4] It is obvious everywhere you look. Many Egyptians—including people who self-identify as "middle class"—face job insecurity or unemployment, or they make a salary that cannot keep up with inflation.[5] Forty percent of Egyptians live in poverty, subsisting on less than $2 a day and often relying on the handouts that people like Madame Salwa provide. At the same time, the Forbes list of billionaires for the past few years has consistently included a handful of Egyptians. Since the uprising in 2011, the gap has become only more pronounced. Even more Egyptians have fallen below the poverty line while the elite and the military have managed to increase their wealth even further.[6]

Some fight to undo and remake this profoundly unequal world. Others give within it—the proverbial "drop in the ocean." My account of Islamic charity is set against, and enters into conversation with, a particular historical moment, a time of immense social inequality but also one of temporary revolutionary openings. When Egyptians took to the streets in January 2011, they called for "bread" and "social justice." As we will see, this does not mean that they would approve of Madame Salwa's efforts. On the contrary. The "progressive" common sense holds that free meals cannot change the social, economic, and political structures that sustain inequality; they do not eliminate poverty.[7] Charity, in this view, is a dubious practice that should be replaced by more effective forms of social and economic improvement. The revolutionary call for "social justice," then, can easily fall in line with an ethos of development. Following that same temporal orientation, over the past two or three decades, many NGOs in Egypt have shifted from handouts to microloans (Atia 2013; Elyachar 2005; Hafez 2011; Ibrahim and Sherif 2008). These organizations embrace a neoliberal logic of individual responsibility and entrepreneurship, while keeping their gaze firmly fixed on the future.

In this world, Madame Salwa's kind of giving can easily seem outdated, or ineffective, or even selfish. And yet, she still gives, and her gifts do make a difference, at least to that one person who receives that one meal in that one alley on that one day.

But then again, Madame Salwa does not give to "do good" or to "be good." She does not, I eventually realized, give out of compassion. She gives because she has no choice. As a pious volunteer in Cairo explained to me, compassion is not the right framework for understanding an Islamic ethics of giving: "Christians help those in need out of love and in order to do good; [Muslims help] because God told them to do so."[8] The givers in this book are a varied bunch, in age and class and religious practice, but they all share one essential belief: they give to the poor in order to give to God.

Giving to God is neither about building toward a better future nor about attending to the suffering Other. It is something different, a third way, and this third way collapses common critiques of charity—precisely because it is neither "charity" nor "charitable."[9] Rather, it is dutiful and directed at God. Placing God in the foreground, and the suffering Other in the background, disrupts both the liberal conceit of compassion *and* the neoliberal imperative of self-help. And in so doing, it protects the recipients from charity's condescending dimensions—from what Mary Douglas, in her foreword to Marcel Mauss's *The Gift*, calls charity's "wounding" character (1990:ix). It protects the recipients from having to be grateful and from having to reciprocate. As such, this giving is very different from the dynamic at play in other charitable contexts, such as when middle-class American evangelical Christians sponsor at-risk children in postwar Guatemala and expect of them the right kinds of thank-you letters with the right kind of content written in the right kind of penmanship (O'Neill 2013). It is different from humanitarian giving that responds to, and thereby demands, a "spectacle of suffering" (Boltanski 1999:3; Bornstein and Redfield 2011).

People like Madame Salwa give because God ordered them to do so, because they want to make it into paradise, and because a share in their wealth is the divinely ordained "right of the poor" (*haqq al-faqīr*).[10] Their practices look like charity while also enacting a profound critique of charity. Put differently, they invite a rethinking of *rahma,* or compassion, by reminding us that there is *rahma* in *not* pitying the poor.

My account of an Islamic *nonhumanitarian* ethics of giving helps unseat the very logic of "humanitarian reason" (Fassin 2012) and its focus on empathetic connection and compassionate care.[11] From Hannah Arendt's (1965) stance against a "politics of pity" to Miriam Ticktin's (2011) critique of an "antipolitics of care," many scholars have problematized a compassion politics. For one, compassion is never evenly distributed. Even though the "ethical grammar of philanthropy" holds that "one's primary and most enduring commitments should be to the whole, all humans" (Bornstein 2012:x), compassion never extends to everyone. Put differently, if you help, save, and care for only those toward whom you feel compassion, then your politics is contingent on your feelings (Berlant 2004). As such, it is unreliable, selective, and tends to exclude those who are simply too different from you. A politics of compassion displaces a politics of rights and justice (Fassin 2012).

While my account resonates with these critiques, my insistence on taking God seriously runs counter to a commonly proposed solution: the idea that it is best to approach structural inequality and injustice through the register of political economy. For all its value, I find that this register is too resolutely tied to a secular universalism and the rights-bearing subjects it produces. It is not good at seeing difference, let alone describing it. It leaves little space for God and other invisible actors.

KEEPING GOD IN THE PICTURE

It is easy to dismiss Madame Salwa's logic of giving as anachronous or insignificant or just, well, too religious. Indeed, activists and academics have long done just that and assumed that the more religious a person's motivations are, the more irrelevant they are to political reimaginings. But I believe that if we want to grasp the significance of Madame Salwa's giving, we have to do the opposite: we have to take God seriously.

The concept of *li-llāh* is central. The phrase—from the preposition *li* (meaning "for" or "belonging to") and the proper noun *Allāh*—is used in many expressions in Egypt, including when people speak about giving alms or food to the poor.[12] *Li-llāh* means "to God," "for God," or "for the sake of God." It can imply that the human donor is channeling God's generosity since what you give is never yours to begin with; all things belong to God and are merely entrusted to humans (*amāna*).[13] But *li-llāh* can also imply a trade-like relationship with God in which one's good deeds are an attempt to accrue points toward a place in paradise.

Of course one could read Madame Salwa's declaration "I don't care about the poor" in many different ways. For one, it is a self-effacing move, the pious refusal to take credit for being charitable and generous, in line with the moral imperative, found across the Abrahamic religions, that one should give without drawing attention to oneself. Another option is to think of it as an affective outburst, tied to the mood and frustration of a particular moment. Maybe the people lining up with their bowls and plates that day had rubbed Madame Salwa the wrong way. Maybe she had expected a little more gratitude. Maybe she found them annoying or repulsive and so she chose to turn away from them, reminding herself that her gifts are really not for them, but for God. Maybe the sentence emerged from her life history, from her feeling compelled to give while finding that people are often ungenerous and uncaring toward her. There are many explanations one can offer. But, having come to know Madame Salwa quite well over the years, I am convinced that the *li-llāh* matters more than as a rhetorical gesture that helps enhance one's self-image and social reputation or as a means for dismissing ungrateful recipients. Madame Salwa's continuous orientation toward God (and, by extension, toward the Prophet Muhammad and his saintly descendants) shapes who she is in the world, and how she is in the world. It makes her charitable efforts absurd from the perspectives of humanitarian reason, neoliberal models of development, and the revolutionary desire to overthrow the socioeconomic order.[14] But it also makes her giving persistent and provocative. Because she gives to God, she addresses immediate needs and responds to hunger and poverty. But equally, because she gives to God, her giving is not organized around the poor's suffering, the donor's compassion, or the hope for a better tomorrow.

Some scholars, particularly those more oriented toward texts, have described Islam as a religion categorically averse to immanence—a religion that "drained the world of divinity to concentrate it in a single transcendental God," a religion that "does not know the idea of a mediating instance . . . All bridges are torn down: there are no sacraments, no images to be worshipped, no church music."[15] In fact, in Egypt one finds both immanence and transcendence. At times God is far removed, an abstract lawgiver and judge. Other times God is intimately present. The emphasis can shift—in people's lives, from one moment to the next, and historically. For some, since the Islamic Revival in the 1970s, a more legalistic, abstracted form of religiosity has displaced the more intimate attachments of previous generations to the Prophet Muhammad and the saints, and through them to God.[16] As Samuli Schielke puts it, Islam has become a "perfect system that is all-encompassing yet pure and distinct, somehow located outside and above everyday life" (2015:14). The shift has not been absolute, however, and even Islam as a "perfect system," with its detailed ritualistic rules, is often about finding a way to embody the Prophet Muhammad's lifestyle and about drawing closer to God. At the same time, even a highly transcendent God can be very present in people's lives, precisely in His absence and remoteness. God, moreover, is continuously *made* present through rituals, such as prayer, sacrifice, and almsgiving, and through the very phrase *li-llāh* and the way that it relentlessly orients charitable gifts away from the human recipients.

And God is not only rhetorically present. God interferes in, and directs, believers' lives. Time and again, I was told that a *khidma,* a Sufi space of hospitality, was opened as a result of a dream or other divine signs. One of the largest bureaucratic charity complexes in Cairo, the Mustafa Mahmoud Association, allegedly goes back to a divinely sent dream-vision seen by its founder.[17] Conversely, Amal, a single mother of five who struggles to get by, insists that "God is on her side," and told me how God once punished a civil servant who had been rude to her. The civil servant's husband ended up in the hospital, and she somehow came to realize that she was being punished for having treated Amal badly; she apologized profusely. On a different occasion, a lawyer who used to say he would only help Amal if she paid him had a dream and heard a voice throughout the night telling him "to take care of that woman." By the morning he had decided to do all the legal work for free.

In these stories, and in endless ways every day across Egypt, God has voli-tion.[18] But God's will and agency do not displace human agency. Keeping God in the picture means looking all the more closely at how people act in the world. My interlocutors' practices are always about God *and* about humans and their material things; they are about the present *and* about para-dise, all at the same time. One purpose of this book is to think about how God, variously understood, constitutes, shapes, disciplines, and disrupts believers' subjectivities, relationships, and communities. By holding the vis-ible and the invisible in the same frame, I complicate Marcel Mauss's classical story line, in which almsgiving *secularized* the sacrificial act and brought it down to earth, replacing "God" with "the poor" (1967:15–16). More broadly, my account builds on and adds a twist to Mauss's *The Gift,* which since its publication in 1925 has become a cornerstone for anthropological thinking about social life.[19] Mauss argues that the reason why the exchange of gifts is crucial in cultures around the world is that it establishes social relations and binds people together. He describes the act of giving as dyadic: I give to you, and you will give back to me. When we keep God in the picture, we must think of the gift as triadic.[20] God is not made and sustained through gift exchange—parallel to "society"—but rather is an active player who trans-forms the relationship between giver and recipient. It is because of God that Madame Salwa is both utterly concerned with and utterly disinterested in the poor.

FROM SAINT SHRINE TO TAHRIR SQUARE
AND BACK AGAIN

It was during my earlier research on dreams that I first began to wonder about the many people distributing food around Cairo's saint shrines. Again and again, I heard the same story: a saint had visited them in a dream and they were reciprocating the visit by distributing food at the corresponding shrine the following day. I was interested in how a saint who died centuries ago could visit, speak to, and direct believers in the twenty-first century. But then something else grabbed my attention: I could not help but notice that the dreams' material effects—the sandwiches, *kufta,* rice pudding—were often received by people who were at the very bottom of Egypt's rigid and unforgiving social ladder. My curiosity about the invisible and the imagina-tion could not shield me from the extreme social disparities in Egypt.

I decided that my next research project would focus on an Islamic ethics of giving—religious encounters with, and responses to, poverty.[21]

I knew Cairo would be a good site for this project: poverty is omnipresent there, and the Egyptian state does next to nothing to help. Already in 1992, when a devastating earthquake shook the city, killing over 550 people and injuring nearly 10,000, it took the government over a week to provide any tangible relief; within hours, the Muslim Brotherhood and other Islamic charitable organizations had come to help, offering housing, food, clothing, and money (Sullivan 1994:xiii). At the same time, in Cairo one finds many different grammars of Islam, ranging from Sufi to Salafi to a "pious neoliberalism" (Atia 2013), from informal to highly bureaucratized, from ostensibly apolitical to proudly political. This abundant variety that defines Cairo is a fruitful reminder that Islam is not one fixed thing but is continuously made and remade, in conversation not only with the secular but also with its own many iterations.

I applied for research funding, began studying classical Islamic texts on almsgiving, and negotiated to take a semester off from my teaching. In the midst of my preparations, on 25 January 2011, protests erupted in Cairo and other Egyptian cities. Hundreds of thousands of people took to the streets, calling for an end to police violence and for bread, freedom, and social justice. After eighteen intense days of protests and sit-ins, with Cairo's Tahrir Square becoming the symbolic and physical epicenter, the country's longtime president, Hosni Mubarak—widely considered corrupt, oppressive, and autocratic—stepped down. As I watched the coverage on al-Jazeera, I was thrilled and hopeful. And my research project suddenly felt irrelevant, as the saint shrines and their pious visitors seemed far less important than the vibrant tumult of the revolution. It didn't help that the day after Mubarak gave up power, Madame Salwa texted me to say that she felt bad for him.

I arrived in Cairo in June 2011. In the months that followed, my days of fieldwork involved a constant back-and-forth between seemingly apolitical spaces of giving and highly politicized spaces of protest and debate. In a typical day I might attend a meeting where representatives of new political parties introduced their election platforms—including the obligatory but always vague-sounding program of social justice they would enact—and then I would take a taxi to a *khidma,* where food is served to whoever shows up. On another day I would go to a slum neighborhood with volunteers from the charity organization Resala, head home to shower and change, and then attend a so-called "Flash Hub" downtown, where young people from a more privileged background discussed their ideas for how to make Egypt a better place. Another day I would sit in the intake office of a charity organization, watching petitioners present their cases of poverty and need, and then join a protest at Tahrir Square, where mostly middle-class activists were once again fighting, at least in theory, in the name of the poor. In light of this temporal convergence and spatial proximity, I found it impossible to separate my thinking about an Islamic ethics of giving from the revolutionary moment (or what remained of it).

Outside of my own mind and heart, however, the revolutionary and charitable worlds I describe remained quite separate. There was a time, to be sure, when Egypt was home to a flourishing Islamic left. While Saad Zaghloul, the nationalist leader of the Egyptian Revolution of 1919, had used the phrase *li-llāh* in the patriotic liberal-secular slogan *al-dīn li-llāh wa al-watan li-l-gamiʿ* (Religion is for God; the homeland is for all), the early Muslim Brotherhood presented a radically different vision, one that refuses the distinction between religion and politics. The organization's founder, Hasan al-Banna, and Sayyid Qutb, its key ideologue, were both deeply concerned with social justice. The latter argued that Islam "labors to elevate the nature of both those who give and those who receive" by making giving a duty (2000:108).[22]

A number of Egyptian intellectuals in the sixties and seventies actively engaged with Marxist thought, some of them formulating a program of Islamic socialism, others eventually rejecting Marxism—but all deeply concerned with social justice. Many of these thinkers hoped to recover what they took to be Islam's revolutionary potential.[23] Yet by 2011, the idea that Islam could offer some kind of revolutionary path forward seemed to have faded. Although many of my secular, liberal, and even Sufi friends voted for Muslim Brotherhood candidates in 2012, simply because they did not want "more of the same," a common view held that the Muslim Brotherhood engaged in social service provision for purely pragmatic reasons. Many grounded their suspicion in the organization's entanglement with Egypt's business elite and the repeated assurance by its leaders, in the wake of the uprising, of their commitment to free-market capitalism.[24]

There may be an absence of loud Islamic leftist voices in Egypt today. But there is an abundance of alternative understandings of Islam, which we find in quiet lived everyday practices, in articulations of Islam that are widely framed—and dismissed—as "nonpolitical." Giving to God is not about an Islamic alternative in the form of a political movement or state model or global order, but it is about the making of selves, relationships, and life-worlds, and it is about relating to God.

Translating between quiet lived practices and the loud revolutionary moment is not easy. Often, the back-and-forth was draining. I found myself getting caught up in each side, in the collective fight for a better future, and in the stubbornly present-oriented practice of handing out meals in the slums. How could an activist with whom I felt allied be so dismissive of the pious givers, helping day after day just blocks away? I ended up arguing with activist friends about the value of food distribution. They said handing out meals distracts from, and prevents, real change. I asked, sometimes with annoyance: So do you think it is better *not* to give? Equally, I found myself arguing with my pious friends: Do you really think handing out meal after meal makes a difference? Do you care about what happens to these people after you leave, about whether they will have something to eat tomorrow? Don't you think this is a time for bigger fights and bigger ambitions? There were moments when the revolution felt essential and just, and religious charity felt problematic; there were other moments when I was fully consumed by the self-congratulatory logic of charitable giving and found the activists self-absorbed and disconnected from Egypt's harsh material realities. But most times these certainties about what was good and what bad were far less stable, and it is this sense of uncertainty, as profound as it was frustrating, that I hope to pass on.

Despite the seeming incommensurability, I aim to put these two spheres into conversation: the chaotic fury of the uprising—the aggravations of inequality, the cry for social justice, the Tahrir utopia—and the quiet everyday acts of giving that are oriented toward God. I am interested in such a conversation not because I think that all pious givers should drop what they are doing and take to the streets, or that all activists should start running soup kitchens, but because I think that these two spheres have something to say to each other. They share a commitment to justice (whether divine or social) and to a being-with-others (whether that includes God or not), and both these commitments have political and ethical implications.

In this spirit, I begin and end with the historical backdrop; the first chapter is about the uprising, the last about President Abdelfattah el-Sisi's ideology of sacrifice less than five years later. In between, I tell a story about men and women who give and receive, and their various orientations toward God. The pious givers include people like Madame Salwa, who hand out alms and meals of their own accord, far from all institutions and bureaucracies. They include volunteers who systematically prepare meals and distribute them to the urban poor. And they include Shaykh Salah and Nura, who run *khidmas,* Sufi spaces of hospitality, serving food to guests and strangers. Among the recipients is Amal, who lives in a slum neighborhood and seeks help from anywhere she can. And there is Shaykh Mahmoud, a dervish, or pious ascetic, who is a frequent guest at Nura's *khidma* and never says please or thank you. Across all these moments of giving and receiving, we see the material effects of thinking toward God amid the rumblings of revolution.

OF FIELDWORK AND ITS OBSTACLES

My fieldwork involved spending days at charity organizations, Sufi *khidmas,* Ramadan tables, and saint shrines, cooking and distributing, eating and talking and listening, or simply tagging along. Doing fieldwork in spaces of giving was often pleasurable and involved plenty of delicious food, most memorably at Nura's *khidma.* But doing fieldwork on charitable giving also confronted me with a range of challenges.

The openness with which people talked to me fluctuated widely. In religious terms, there is value to secrecy but, in Egypt, that ideal is disrupted by the fact that charitable giving has become a key marker of public piety. Many acts of giving are recorded, publicized, and even televised. Doing so is justified through a hadith that says, "Those who point to the good are like those who do good" (*al-dāll ʿalā al-khayr ka-fāʿilihi*). That is, advertising one's charity organization is legitimate, and so is talking to an anthropologist. Yet, more broadly, whereas in 2011, many were speaking about matters that had previously been taboo, by the summer of 2012, things had already changed. A clip broadcast on state television at the time warned the Egyptian public to be wary of spies. It showed a group of Egyptian youth sitting in a coffee shop; a foreigner enters. He joins them, and they happily share their views on Egypt's current problems: tensions between the people and the military, rising prices, transportation problems, the gas shortage. The foreigner says, in English, "Really?"—and under the table begins texting on his mobile phone. A voiceover warns:

> From the beginning, he knows his mission and target! It does not take him much effort to get to know people in a place. We're generous by default. He

will sneak into your heart, as if you were old friends . . . Don't open your heart to anyone you just met when you don't know who he is and what's behind him. Mind what you say! Every word comes at a price. A word can save a nation.

Though widely criticized and soon discontinued, the TV clips expressed, if not affected, a general wariness of foreigners. At a *mawlid,* a saint day celebration, at around the same time, a dervish asked me whether an Italian friend who had come along was a spy. In my past encounters, dervishes were the least likely to ask about one's motivations or place of origin.

A second obstacle had to do with my own entanglement with the ethos of compassion. I believe that we must look critically at a politics of pity; but no matter my belief, theoretical commitments rarely override visceral reactions. The daily confrontations with poverty took a toll on me, and, while I was intellectually intrigued by sentences such as "I don't care about the poor," or "The poor are our gate to paradise," or "God created us in classes," they also troubled me. Often I felt implicated as I, too, had to make decisions. When, to whom, and how much should I give? When distributing food in slums with the volunteers, I followed instructions, giving to some and not to others, often feeling guilty. When I sat in a charity organization's intake office, I was at times mistaken for an employee and listened to people's accounts of their hardship until a pause allowed me to interject that I could not help. At moments I interfered in minimal ways, for instance by offering my chair to an elderly woman who had come in to plead her case and was being ignored, and, like probably most anthropologists (especially those with generous research grants), I *gave* in the field. I donated clothes, medication, and money to the charity organizations where I did fieldwork, and I gave money to *khidmas.* I volunteered as a German teacher at Resala and joined in many of their activities, not always as a researcher. I tagged along with Madame Salwa to help cook meals during Ramadan, and sometimes paid for the ingredients. I offered to pay for eye surgery for Yusuf, a blind orphan who had been abandoned as a newborn in front of a police station. I had met him in a government-run orphanage one day when I was out with Madame Salwa, doing our rounds of *khayr.* I kept visiting him over the years, and things went from bad to worse. The surgery never happened for a range of bureaucratic and, later, medical reasons. It was hard to watch Yusuf and others in similar situations. I was often desperate—desperately compassionate and compassionately desperate. I was compelled to give, uneasy about giving, and always keenly aware of how insufficient my gestures were. No less discomforting were the moments when I felt myself settle into a compassion fatigue. These visceral dimensions are an integral part of fieldwork, too, and continuously reminded me that, despite my theoretical commitments, I could never simply stand back and observe—and yet, for the most part, observe is all I did.

That reality takes me to the third and final challenge: academic voyeurism. One key interlocutor who helped me understand Egypt's (un)charitable landscapes is Amal. She not only shared her own struggles with me in great detail but also introduced me to friends and neighbors in Mit Uqba, one of Cairo's slums, which are all too politely referred to as "informal areas" and are home to almost two-thirds of Cairo's population. Not everyone living in these areas is poor (Sims 2010:111), but most people in Amal's neighborhood are.[25] Walking through what she calls the "streets of the wretched" (shawārī ʿ al-ghalāba), she introduced me as a friend, or a journalist, or someone connected to businessmen who do charity work. I was never quite sure whether this was in part how she perceived me, or whether she wanted to entice people to tell me their stories. I was usually quick to add that I was doing research but, regardless of what I said, I was taken to be a useful connection, someone who could help out, or at least could put in a good word at a charity organization or with the mysterious businessmen.

Amal probed people to tell me their stories, cutting straight to the chase: "Tell her how you live," or "Tell her about your circumstances." And so they did. Stories of suffering, of husbands in prison, of charity organizations "that help only if your husband is dead"; stories of daily struggles and stories of cancer and stories of everything in between. A widow who barely gets by on her small pension took out her wallet and showed me that she only had about $2 left for the rest of the month. Unsure what I was expected to do—take out my own wallet and give her money? Present her case to one of the charity organizations I was studying? Write about her?—I said what I had heard Egyptians say in such situations: "rabbinā ysahhil" (May God make it easy).

Often my days with Amal felt like the worst kind of slum tourism. Many people were eager to introduce me to "cases" (ḥālāt) or to present their own "case" to me. They were used to such continuous self-objectification, and now they were at risk of being turned into case studies for my ethnography, filling what Joel Robbins (2013) has called anthropology's "suffering slot." Amal insisted I should document what her neighbors were telling me. "Record!" (siggilī), she would say, by which she meant that I should try to remember every word, as neither she nor her neighbors liked the idea of me turning on my digital recorder. And so I worked my memory and wrote notes for hours after getting home. As I did so, I wondered: for whom was I supposed to remember and record these stories? The desired audience most likely included local NGOs, and maybe government officials, but not the readers of a book written in English. Amal's neighbors were not interested in publicizing the extent of poverty in Egypt; they were interested in improving their circumstances. To get by, they needed to tell their story again and again, and they needed to craft the kind of story that resonates. And I became yet another person who listened and did nothing about it, other than write a book.

AN ANTHROPOLOGY OF THE OTHERWISE

And yet, occasionally I remind myself in these moments of self-recrimination: I did do something. Even if I changed nothing, I did something. Accompanying someone to an office, giving or lending money, helping out, bringing food, offering one's chair, listening, just being there, are not nothing. I, too, tend to forget this because I, too, cannot quite shake the entrenched "progressive" view that such small acts are merely Band-Aids, cosmetic covers rather than solutions. That they divert attention from the necessity of real structural change. That they undermine the demands of rights and justice.

My hope is that this account of pious givers and recipients, all within the fraught chronology of post-uprising Egypt, disrupts such certainties. While always and centrally about God, the ethics of giving I describe is also about people relating to others in moments of need, at a time when socioeconomic conditions are in decline for most. Giving to God is resolutely focused on the here and now. While Madame Salwa is concerned with an eschatological future, namely a place in paradise, she insists that we ought to act in every moment as if we were to die tomorrow. What matters is one's relationship to God in this present moment, and by extension one's relationship to others, including those in need. Recall that she distributes *food*—a gift that might go bad if saved until tomorrow, a gift that has to be given again and again. Handing out a meal is different from digging a well or building a factory, something expected to last and help future generations. Food requires continuous giving. It is a fitting gift in a pious economy in which it is the giving itself that matters because giving is a way of interacting with God. In its stubborn present-orientedness, the ethics of giving I describe has something to say to the elusive revolutionary call for social justice, and it can speak back to an authoritarian counterrevolutionary politics that combines austerity measures with investment in megaprojects. By drawing out the ethical (if not radical) implications of my interlocutors' seemingly otherworldly logics, I seek to document a world that accepts the need for sharing, distribution, and circulation, and through it all looks to a beyond.

Anthropology is about different ways of being in the world, and as such it can invite a rethinking and open up our political-ethical imagination. Tim Ingold refers to anthropology "as 'philosophy with the people in': an enterprise energized by the tension between speculative inquiry into what life could be like and a knowledge, rooted in practical experience, of what life is like for people of particular times and places" (2014:393). For me, an Otherwise—a different orientation to the world, to being-with-others, to questions of justice—can be found in Cairo's streets and alleys, in the *khidmas* and courtyards of mosques, in the endless places where giving to the poor is a way of giving to God, and where giving to God means giving to the poor. My interlocutors' ethics of giving is provocative to think with because it unsettles the ideology of development and the ethos of compassion, both at once. More fundamentally, through its very God-orientedness, it unsettles a human-centered understanding of ethics and politics. There is something profoundly disorienting and humbling, I find, about the fact that Madame Salwa cares *for* the poor without necessarily caring *about* them.

I borrow the phrase "anthropology of the Otherwise" from Elizabeth Povinelli (2011b), who envisions an anthropology that locates itself within forms of life that are at odds with dominant, and dominating, modes of being. In this spirit, my take on an Islamic ethics of giving also builds on an ethos of critique and body of scholarship, largely inspired by the work of Talal Asad (1993, 2003; Asad et al. 2013), that reads piety as depicting a challenge to secular, liberal logics (Agrama 2012; Hirschkind 2006; Mahmood 2005). But this is not a story of either/or. The divine does not erase the social; the invisible does not eclipse the visible. While taking seriously my interlocutors' orientations toward God, I agree with Dipesh Chakrabarty (2008) that we cannot simply abandon "social justice" if we want to make political claims that are recognizable in the world today. Neither my interlocutors nor I are oblivious to the world we live in. An Islamic ethics of giving is not unconcerned with "justice." Its radicalness lies precisely in its refusal to locate justice in the future.

I recognize, of course, that what is radical for me is not necessarily radical for my interlocutors. And radical might not even be the most appropriate metric of value to use here. Madame Salwa gives to God in order to give to

God, not in order to make a critical intervention against development or compassion. She is interested in paradise, not a worldly Otherwise. The people who receive her meals are interested in getting food on their table, not in undoing a secularist universalism. In this sense, I locate the disruption not in the ethnographic terrain but rather present it as my reading, inspired to a large extent by the historical uprising that formed the backdrop to my fieldwork. What I offer is not a programmatic plan for fighting poverty; I'm not sure that such a plan exists. Rather, I offer an invitation to reckon with other ways of doing good in a profoundly unequal world.

During the Revolution

ONE

—

Revolutions Don't Stop Charity

ON 25 JANUARY 2011, TENS OF THOUSANDS of Egyptians took to the
streets, beginning a movement that would alter their country and the region,
though mostly in unexpected and unintended ways. Eighteen days later,
longtime president Hosni Mubarak stepped down, and about four months
after that, I arrived in Cairo to begin my fieldwork. Between June and
December in 2011, I went back and forth between the places of ongoing
protest and the places of my research. Tahrir Square had a strong pull on me,
and so did the idea of a revolution, or what remained of it. It seemed possible,
if not urgent, to rethink and reimagine what it means to live with and among
others. This was a moment of profound and contagious hopefulness. But that
moment is over. Most of the writing of this book took place during a later
moment, when the revolution had been lost or stolen—a moment of far-
reaching oppression; a moment, as many of my activist friends would say, of
profound and contagious hopelessness.[1]

How do we inhabit this space? Between hopefulness and disillusionment,
between fieldwork and writing, between a time still infused with a revolutionary spirit, and a time when a counterrevolution has crushed this spirit? This
book combines a tense temporal arc—from uprising to disappointment—with
another arc, a spatial one: from the profoundly symbolic space of Tahrir
Square to the multiple and banal spaces of giving, including in neighborhoods
that are not even represented on the city's maps. Most of this book tells stories
of people handing out food in Cairo's alleys, slums, and Sufi *khidmas,* as well
as people at the receiving end. The people with whom I spent the other half
of my days—the activists who were fighting an increasingly losing battle—
nearly all dismiss such forms of giving as *apolitical* if not *anti-political.* At
times, it felt as though the kinds of practices I was studying were not even

translatable into a language that would make sense to secular progressives, the people with whom, I thought, I shared many values, commitments, and sensibilities. Among these people was Marwa, a somewhat marginal figure in the context of my fieldwork whose random comment nevertheless had a lasting impact on me.

I met Marwa when I was back in Egypt in June 2012, not long before Mohamed Morsi, the Muslim Brotherhood candidate, became president. At the time, protesters were once again gathering at Tahrir Square, which had also become a popular destination for sightseers. Families were strolling, taking pictures, posing. I met up with Hani, an activist friend, and two friends of his: 'Azza, who lives in Cairo, and her cousin Marwa, who lives in Paris, returns to Cairo once a year, and who introduced herself as a revolutionary. Walking past murals depicting young men who had died in the uprising, we started chatting. Mostly in Arabic, some English, and a word here and there in French. It was comfortable, smooth, and fun. We talked about politics: Did it make sense to vote for the presidential candidate Khaled Ali, the lawyer-activist fighting for labor rights, even though he did not stand a chance? How could diasporic Egyptians like Marwa support the activists in Egypt?

Later, when Hani gave me a ride home, Marwa asked from the backseat what exactly I was doing in Cairo. I gave a short answer: "studying 'amal al-khayr." The latter phrase means "doing good deeds" and is often translated as "charity." Thinking back, I suspect that the brevity of my answer was intended to cover up my own discomfort—I felt a twinge of embarrassment, as I often did, for not being engaged in a more progressive, cutting-edge, revolutionary research project. I did not want to be mistaken for an Orientalist or folklorist trying to capture quaint customs and beliefs; I tried to think of how best to explain the politics of my project. But before I could formulate my thoughts, Marwa cut me off.

"I'm against all forms of 'amal al-khayr! They keep people in a state of dependency. They don't change anything."

I felt a gulf widen between Marwa and me, and I felt defensive. What's so bad about dependency? I thought with frustration. We're all dependent; no one is autonomous.[2] And these practices don't change anything? Say that to the people who ate the meals that Madame Salwa handed out this morning. And in any case: What are *you* doing to make a difference in the lives of people struggling to get by?

I said none of these things.

Instead 'Azza, Marwa's cousin, jumped in: "Some people who do *khayr* are just after power, like the Muslim Brotherhood, but others are not." She told us that whenever the young woman who cleans their home has extra money, she gives it to the charity organization Resala. Doing good is about an attitude, an orientedness toward others, cultivated even by those who themselves have very little. "It's about everyone helping everyone else." Charity is a good thing, she seemed to be saying.

Marwa disagreed. She said it would be better to have higher taxes and to use them to fund social services. Herself a critic of neoliberal and humanitarian logics, she said that if social services are provided by NGOs, conditions are attached. If they are offered by individuals, they are unreliable. This should be the state's job. Hani joined the conversation and claimed that Egyptians already pay a minimum of 25 percent taxes on income, in addition to sales taxes.[3]

Marwa wasn't impressed.

"In France we pay over 40 percent, and if you're rich, you pay over 50 percent. *Now* we're talking! Paying taxes is an investment in the future."

We were back on familiar grounds: higher taxes. A welfare state. Investing in the future.

Was that all that remained of the revolutionary imagination that had swept us all away in 2011? Is a stronger welfare state the only viable definition of social justice? What about the stories people had been telling about Tahrir Square, tales of togetherness not contained by the framework of the state? What of other modes of being that are not contained by the state, nor dependent on it? The *khidmas*, voluntarism, Madame Salwa's meals, the sensibilities that are cultivated through seemingly mundane practices such as almsgiving. Do they not enact their own form of justice?

All this ran through my head as I sat in that car. How could I get this across to Marwa? But then again, who am I to say what a revolutionary imagination should consist of? At least Marwa is fully Egyptian, though she, too, lives elsewhere. I'm only half-Egyptian.

Hani had reached my street. It was too late to try to explain. I felt a sense of relief. I wanted to forget about this moment, the disturbing realization that my research project was utterly incomprehensible to self-declared revolutionaries like Marwa. That the gap was simply too big.

Before I got out of the car, Marwa asked for my contact information. She said we should be in touch and write an article together.

"About what?" I asked.

"About how charity is anti-social-justice."

I did not know it at the time but with this invitation, with this assertion, Marwa took part in shaping this book. This is not simply a study of Islamic charity; it is about charity at a time of revolution. My goal is not to celebrate religion's hidden revolutionary potentials; I rather hope to ethnographically open up a space in which we can think beyond the entrenched claim that "charity" inherently and necessarily stands in the way of "social justice."

In this book, the loudness of the revolution is in conversation with the quiet everyday practices of pious givers and recipients—people who tend to get far less international attention than political activists. I begin by amplifying the revolutionary moment that formed the backdrop to much of my fieldwork and to my thinking about an Islamic ethics of giving. Along with my time at Tahrir Square in the summer and fall of 2011, I draw on conversations with activists and friends over the years, and on fifteen interviews with self-declared revolutionaries.[4] Through the activists' views and recollections, impressionistic as they are, I reflect on how the uprising related to the problems of poverty and social inequality—problems that also lie at the heart of religious charity practices, yet there are differently framed, understood, and addressed.

By the end of this chapter, the revolution fades into the background only to reemerge in the form of a counterrevolution in the final chapter. Yet, voices of the revolution will echo throughout this book, inviting us to think about convergences, resonances, and frictions.

A BRIEF CHRONOLOGY

When the protests began in Egypt, I was propped up on a sofa. I had broken my ankle five days earlier, while visiting my parents in Germany. And so, we watched together: my Egyptian mother, who had moved to Germany almost fifty years earlier. My German father who, since his retirement, had been moving with my mother back and forth between the two countries. My sister and brother-in-law. And occasional visitors who were hoping to get an insider's view from my mother. The TV was on nonstop, along with two or three laptops showing Twitter feeds and Facebook posts and live streaming al-Jazeera both in English and Arabic. We called relatives and friends in Cairo.

Some were worried the city might descend into chaos; others sounded ecstatic. The streets of Egypt were filled with disbelief and excitement, but also laced with fear.

The protesters in Cairo converged at Tahrir Square, literally "Liberation Square," a large open area downtown. By nightfall, security forces had violently dispersed the crowds, but the next day, the square was again filled with people. In the days that followed, the protests continued, calling for an end to police violence; then that grew into a call for the regime's fall; and then to a full-throated demand for bread, freedom, and social justice. Despite a media blackout, everyone knew violent clashes were happening between protesters and the police, especially in Suez and Mahalla, two cities with a long history of labor organizing.[5] On 28 January, the so-called Friday of Anger, even more people joined the demonstrations after the communal Friday prayer. Police fired tear gas, rubber bullets, and water cannons into the crowds, and over a thousand protesters were injured. Later many would say that on this day they realized that something big was happening.

Withstanding the riot police's arsenal of crowd dispersal weapons, protesters began occupying Tahrir Square; others began delivering food, blankets, and medicine. Tahrir Square became an international stage and a space in which protesters were protected by their sheer numbers, even as they collectively defied the military-imposed curfew (the police had withdrawn, and the army taken over). The square became a city of sorts, replete with eight hospitals, six pharmacies, thirteen medical stations with first aid supplies for injured protesters, toilets built by volunteer plumbers, a school, barbers, security, a newspaper, a radio station, a projector and screen to watch the news and footage of clashes, exhibitions of art produced at the square, stages for musicians, memorials for the uprising's martyrs, a tent labeled "library," and a media tent.

Marked by togetherness and solidarity, the days at the square would come to fuel the utopian imagination of activists (and social scientists) for years to come.[6] The Tahrir sit-in would later also be compared to the Occupy movement, with calls such as "America needs its own Tahrir" or "Are you ready for a Tahrir moment?" and some Tahrir activists visited New York to support Occupy Wall Street. As many have noted, however, the comparison is somewhat flawed. The Tahrir occupation was far larger and far more volatile. While at times the atmosphere at the square was festive and carnivalesque, fierce battles continued to be waged against pro-Mubarak protesters trying to break in, culminating in the so-called Battle of the Camel on 2 February 2011, when pro-regime thugs descended upon the square on horses and camels, armed with sticks, clubs, whips, and swords. Using improvised shields and weapons, such as burned-out police cars and pavement tiles, the protesters defended the square as best they could. Five were killed and over eight hundred were injured, but the protesters prevailed. Over the next two days, even more Egyptians flooded the square, defying the army's calls to disperse the crowds and the anti-protest stance of the Coptic Church and of prominent Muslim scholars associated with al-Azhar, the authoritative institution of Sunni Islam.

The protesters persisted, and a newly founded federation of independent trade unions called for a general strike. Tens of thousands of workers—including those employed at large and strategic workplaces like the Cairo Public Transport Authority, Egyptian State Railways, the subsidiary companies of the Suez Canal Authority, the state electrical company, and Mahalla's textile workers—answered the call, engaging in some sixty strikes and protests (Beinin 2016). Finally, on 11 February 2011, eighteen days after the uprising had started, President Hosni Mubarak stepped down. By that time, I had returned to my teaching in Toronto, and in June 2011, having finished the semester and finally able to walk again without crutches, I headed to Cairo, a city transformed, buzzing with ideas, debates, and new initiatives. Less than a month after my arrival, protesters began another sit-in at Tahrir Square to object to the military trials and the slowness of reforms, to demand that the police officers who had been implicated in the killing of protesters be held accountable, and to once again call for bread, freedom, and social justice.

My friend 'Umar, who is an engineer and a Sufi, accompanied me on my first visit to the sit-in. As he put it, at that point the square was merely an echo of what it had been like during the eighteen decisive days, but it was nevertheless "unlike anything you've ever seen." He described feeling *sakīna* in the midst of the square, a term that refers to calm or peace but also to God's presence. To him, he said, looking at the protesters' faces was a form of worship (*'ibāda*); the faces were "God's gallery."

While the protests continued, elections were held. The Muslim Brotherhood won nearly half the seats in parliament, and Mohamed Morsi, aligned with the organization, won the presidency. Many Egyptians I know voted for Morsi but soon came to criticize him for his failure to make progress on the country's economic crisis, and they accused him of having more loyalty toward the Muslim Brotherhood than toward the nation. Capitalizing on this widespread discontent, the military ousted Morsi in July 2013 and put him into solitary confinement (where he remained five years later). Egyptian security forces subsequently raided two sit-ins of Muslim Brotherhood supporters in Cairo, killing over eight hundred people. In June 2014, Abdelfattah el-Sisi, the former minister of defense, became president. Since then, the state has been violently cracking down on the Muslim Brotherhood and numerous NGOs in the country—all in the name of stability and security. Under the same pretext, hundreds of activists have been arrested, tortured, or have disappeared.[7] At the same time, the military has expanded its business empire, while a politics of "tightened belts" has made it even more difficult for the poor to get by.

In March 2018, el-Sisi was reelected for a second term with 97 percent of the vote. His sole opponent was someone whom political scientist Mona El-Ghobashy (2018) calls "an obscure toady gleaned from the scrap heap of fourth-rate politicians," who on his Facebook page had touted his own support for el-Sisi. But, aside from the elections, across different social classes, many Egyptians continue placing hope in el-Sisi's promises of development, growth, recovery, and stability—promises to which I return in the final chapter. Most former activists I know, however, are disillusioned, skeptical, cynical, or depressed. Still, they hold on to their memories of 2011, and the things they were fighting for. It is these *things*—vague, contradictory, and elusive as they might be—that I want to put into conversation with an ethics of giving that people like Marwa are quick to dismiss as irrelevant, or even an obstacle, to the revolutionary struggle.

WHOSE REVOLUTION? WHOSE JUSTICE?

Before erupting on Cairo's streets, waves of mass protest had swept over Tunisia, where one of the key catalysts was the death of Mohammad Bouazizi.[8] A twenty-six-year-old vendor and the sole income earner for his extended family of eight, Bouazizi sold vegetables from a cart in the town of Sidi Bouzid. When a policewoman confiscated his cart and produce, he went to the local municipality officials to complain, and when his complaints were rejected, he doused himself with a flammable liquid and set himself on fire. His act of self-immolation led to mass protests. He died ten days before longtime Tunisian president Zine El Abidine Ben Ali was ousted.

The events in Tunisia inspired many in Egypt, but there, a different class dynamic was at play, centered on the figure of Khaled Said, a young man from Alexandria who had been beaten to death by the police in June 2010.

Photos of his disfigured corpse circulated widely online and inspired the prominent Facebook group "We are all Khaled Said," which is credited with having mobilized thousands of people to participate in the protests, people who came to see themselves or their children in Khaled Said's dead body. Unlike Bouazizi, Khaled Said was from a middle-class background. He reportedly loved computers and music, and policemen killed him after dragging him out of a cybercafé.

Sabri, a Microsoft employee in his early twenties, described the way the Khaled Said case affected him. While everyone knew that young people were being tortured in Egypt's police stations, he said, this case simply hit closer to home. Speaking to my research assistant Mariam, he put it bluntly:

> I'm from a middle-class background, and economically I think Mubarak was efficient. The private sector is strong and produces great products. We know that a lot of people get tortured but, really, we don't care about them. I'm being completely honest here. My problem began with Khaled Said, a guy who is connected to America, has relatives in the judiciary and doctors, has received a postgraduate education—someone like you. He was beaten to death just because he didn't want to be mistreated.

Khaled Said's death reminded Egyptians that you didn't have to be poor to be harmed. But while some, like Sabri, acknowledged their selfish concerns, others framed their activism as profoundly selfless: the well-off standing up for the downtrodden. Wael Ghoneim, one of the founders of the "We are all Khaled Said" Facebook group, and at the time a twenty-nine-year-old Google marketing executive, in an emotional TV interview in the midst of the uprising, refuted the claim that the protesters were traitors:

> If I had been a traitor, I would have stayed by the pool at my villa in the Emirates, having a good time. My salary keeps increasing and I had no problems . . . Some of us are rich, live in fancy houses, and drive the best cars. I don't need anything from anyone. I've never needed anything from anyone. Everything that was done put our lives in danger.

The moment Wael Ghoneim broke down and cried in the interview was the moment he (and the viewers on the other side of the screen) saw a succession of middle-class martyrs before his eyes, martyrs who had sacrificed their comfortable lives for the poor. The interview was a turning point for many Egyptians; the following day the square was full.

That is not to say that the uprising was exclusively a "middle-class revolution," as it was sometimes called.[9] Ultras played a central role—young disenfranchised supporters of Egypt's two largest soccer clubs, Al-Ahly and Al-Zamalek, who had extensive experience with battling Egypt's security forces.[10] And also the urban poor, street children, and working-class Egyptians participated, the latter risking their jobs by joining the protests and sit-ins. Hossam, at the time in his late thirties, heard a poem during the early days of the uprising, and one line affected him deeply; it was about "the government eating our bread." He had been working since fifth grade, often two or three jobs, but still, whenever something unexpected happened, for instance when his father got sick, or his son wanted to go to a better school, it was a disaster (*musība*). In 2011, before joining the protests, Hossam worked eighteen hours a day (twelve of them in a government job). He took to the streets in the hope for a better life, one that he did not frame in terms of autonomy and self-sufficiency—recall Wael Ghoneim's proud declaration "I don't need anything from anyone"—but one that revolves centrally around caring for his son and father.

Different circumstances, emotions, and hopes drove people into the streets, and while they united in their slogans, they did not necessarily call for the same things. One of the most pervasive slogans was *'aīsh, huriyya, 'adāla igtimā'iyya*. Bread, freedom, social justice—a call that rhymes in Arabic and that partially echoed slogans previously used in Tunisia.[11] Bread (*'aīsh*) was understood literally by some. A basic food staple, bread has long been state subsidized in Egypt. In 1977, unrest erupted in Cairo after subsidies were cut—the so-called "bread riots" in which eighty people were killed and hundreds injured, sometimes referred to as the "revolution of the thieves."[12] Affordable bread continues to be a real, literal concern. But bread is also a powerful symbol, and many used it synonymously with "social justice," a term that has become a rallying cry around the globe.[13]

What "social justice" means is wide open, and some were dismissive of other people's definitions. Sara, a sixty-year-old self-declared socialist and feminist, criticized dominant liberal understandings: "I don't even understand what liberals mean by social justice. Probably they talk about slightly better work laws and collective means of bargaining." To her, social justice means something different: the redistribution of wealth. She and many others were also suspicious of the Muslim Brotherhood's appropriation of the term, claiming that for this organization there are "degrees of justice," and that they think "Copts were created to serve them." Others criticized the

"Social justice is an essential demand for protecting my family's and my people's dignity," Tahrir Square, July 2011. Photograph by the author.

Muslim Brotherhood for limiting social justice to the redistribution of alms (*zakāt*) or said that the group is fatalistic and believes that "God provides for whom He wills without account."[14] One woman offered this caricature: "If you're poor, what can we do? It's from God!"

Muslim Brotherhood supporters, in turn, emphasized the organization's long history of social service provision. They conceded that complete equality is not their goal but in this, notably, they were no different from liberal activists, who similarly insisted that the goal is not equality but reducing the gap between rich and poor. To quote an upper-class activist in her fifties: "Justice is not telling the rich not to be rich. Life is this way. God created us in classes. But the gap shouldn't be this horrendous." When "social justice" is about reducing the gap, it easily becomes associated with the idea of a welfare state, characterized by high taxes, and exemplified, in activists' accounts, by countries such as France, Sweden, or Canada; by Gamal Abdel Nasser's socialist experiment in the 1960s; or, for Muslim Brotherhood supporters, by Islamic state models with a centralized alms collection and distribution system.

Others underlined the limitations of the call for "social justice." 'Ali, a middle-class engineer, argued that the very emphasis on social justice is tied to privilege. The poor might not use the language of social justice but they, too, have legitimate demands:

> The people who came out of the slums [during the uprising] or the people we describe as thugs, they're people we can't simply distance ourselves from. You might describe them as something alien, but they still have their demands. You have your demands, you want social justice for example; and he wants to threaten someone with a knife and steal from him. This is what he learned. You're saying what you were taught. And he is doing what he thinks is best for his life.

While playing on the common stereotype of the ignorant and violent poor, 'Ali reminds us that not all languages resonate equally across communities. As Lila Abu-Lughod (2012) notes as well, reflecting on how the uprising was lived in a village in Upper Egypt, the language that was most easily picked up by the media and international observers did not necessarily resonate the most locally. For some, social justice was just an empty slogan.

Shaykh Salah, who gives out food every day at a mosque not far from Tahrir Square, offered a related critique: the young activists, he said, have good intentions but they have their heads in the clouds. They know nothing about what life actually looks like for the poor, and they far too quickly became distracted by the game of politics: who should take on leadership, who one should vote for, and so on. Some activists would agree that the priorities shifted in the wrong direction, and that economic demands were too quickly pushed into the background. Out of this concern grew the campaign "the poor first."

THE POOR FIRST

In July 2011, a poster caught my eye. It had been taped to an electric box on a street close to Tahrir Square. It read "The Poor First" and showed the image of an old bald man with sunken cheeks, presumably hungry—the kind of image commonly found in ads televised by charity organizations, in Egypt and elsewhere. The poster, however, did not call for donations; it called for a march in the name of the poor.

As I learned later, the phrase "the poor first" had been adopted from an angry blog post titled "The Poor First, You Sons of Dogs" (al-fuqarā' awwalan yā awlād al-kalb), which had been written by Mohamed Abu El-Gheit, a medical student and blogger from Upper Egypt who criticized the class bias prevalent in the public commemoration of revolutionary martyrs.[15] He pointed out that many unemployed youth and young people from poor neighborhoods had participated in the protests. Many of them died, as well; but they were not publicly remembered and celebrated. Echoing the title of a poem by the late Egyptian vernacular poet Ahmed Fouad Negm, Abu El-Gheit asked: were these young martyrs not part of the "flowers that blossomed in the gardens of Egypt"? And he went further, suggesting that the image of flowers was not enough: "These people never really cared about flowers because they had something more important to worry about: bread." He quoted the Palestinian poet Mahmoud Darwish: "We love flowers / but we love bread more / And we love the fragrance of flowers / but we find wheat spikes much purer." For people from low-income neighborhoods, he insisted, the uprising was about material, real-life concerns:

> These people didn't take to the streets to demand a constitution or elections or because they wanted a secular or religious state. They took to the streets for reasons affecting their daily life: the price of food, clothing, and housing that has been rising madly; the policeman who stops his brother's microbus to exhort a fifty-pound bribe [about $8.50]; the officer who investigates and tortures him despite his innocence; his sister whose wedding he cannot afford; his uncle whose pension is cut after the factory is privatized; his aunt who died of cancer because no bed was available in a public hospital.

Abu El-Gheit went on to note that 40 percent of Egyptians live under the poverty line; 12 million (out of total of about 80 million at the time) live in slums (*'ashwā'iyāt*); 1.5 million live in cemeteries.[16] For him, not only did the poor participate in the uprising; the uprising had also been *about* them. But the solidarity across class was short-lived. A few months after Mubarak's ouster, the poor were again forgotten.

The widely circulating blog post prompted the administrators of the We Are All Khaled Said Facebook page to adopt "The Poor First" as its new slogan and to implore its readers to strive "if not to end poverty altogether, then at least to ease the pain of the poor."[17] Youth groups called for a million-man march on 8 July 2011 under the banner "The Poor First." The black-and-white poster on the electric box, drowning in a sea of slogans, signs, and graffiti, was leftover from that campaign.

In the end, the march never took place. Clashes between the military and protesters had reshuffled the uprising's priorities once more. But even earlier, the campaign had been met with criticism. Ibrahim Eissa, a well-known Egyptian journalist and TV personality, wrote a response to the campaign titled "Freedom Is More Important than the Poor."[18] In it he asked:

> Who said that the people were angry, went out, and revolted . . . for a bite of bread? . . . People didn't go out because they're poor. They came out because they felt humiliated, degraded, and abused by despotism, injustice, and hereditary rule [i.e., Hosni Mubarak passing on the presidency to his son]. This was not a revolution of the poor and hungry . . . The revolution was about freedom—and freedom comes before eating bread and before bread itself— dignity, pride, and self-respect . . . There is no point to minimum wages if our heads remain low. What we need now is democracy, a constitution, and free elections. Without them you will never get just wages and respectable health care.

Amr Ezzat, a blogger, activist, and self-proclaimed "member of the elite," was equally critical of the label "the poor." In his weekly column for the daily *al-Masry al-Yawm,* he wrote, "When oppressed groups take action to defend their rights, they don't use labels like 'the poor' unless they're asking for pity. They organize as workers, farmers or members of communities demanding their rights. The slogan 'The Poor First' reeks of elitism."[19]

Ezzat argued that the slogan "The Poor First" risked transforming the revolution "from a political act into a charity walk." Bringing to mind Hannah Arendt's account of the failure of the French Revolution—at the moment "when the poor, driven by the needs of their bodies, burst on to the scene," the moment when "freedom [had] to be surrendered to necessity, to the urgency of the life process itself" (1965:54–55)—Ezzat insisted that political rights have to come first. In his view, framing people as "the poor" and ascribing to them an exclusive concern with survival is infantilizing, instrumentalizing, and elitist.

Critiques of this kind overlook the varied social lives of the category "the poor"—including the ways it is actively put to work by those struggling to get by, demanding their rights, and fighting for social change. When stenciled graffiti in downtown Cairo demanded, "Stand up, Egypt! The poor are hungry" (*qūmī ya masr, al-faqīr gaʿān*), everyone knew who the graffiti was referring to. Images and stories of "the poor" had been proliferating, and they had real effects. A businessman reported that Egyptians like him joined the protests because they were outraged by "photographs of children looking for food in rubbish dumps and stories of families who only have a meal

Martyr mural of a street child, Mohamed Mahmoud Street, August 2014. Photograph by the author.

every other day [that] were filling the papers" (Rushdy 2011:43). Popular Egyptian literary works such as *The Yaqoubian Building* and *Taxi* had been confronting readers with tales about impoverished peasants who had moved to the city and were living in shacks on Cairo's roofs, and overworked taxi drivers. Since 2009, the weekly TV program *Wāhid min al-Nās* (One of the People) had been taking viewers into slum neighborhoods, underlined with melodramatic music, the camera searching for dirt, decay, garbage, flies, and rodents. Driven by hunger, the host explains, people in the slums eat from garbage. Or, in a different episode: "In this neighborhood, children don't watch cat and mouse on television; they watch rats and mice in real life!" A friend of mine, who herself barely manages to scrape together the money needed for her children's clothes and school expenses, told me she likes to watch the program because "it makes [her] cry."

As a category, "the poor" are alive and well in Egypt. For this reason, I am wary of the claim that no one would have taken to the streets under the label of "the poor," and I find the claim that "The Poor First" reeks of elitism, well, elitist. It is easy to prioritize freedom over eating bread if you have enough food to eat. Nevertheless, a critique directed at a "politics of pity" offers a provocative place from which to think about Islamic charity. It also offers a place from which to think about Tahrir Square, a space that, according to many, was not organized around class lines and in which sharing and giving were driven by something other than pity.

TAHRIR UTOPIA

Built in the nineteenth century as a symbol of modernity, Tahrir Square had long been an important location for popular gatherings and protests, and in 2011, the square became a key site and protagonist of the uprising.[20] Countless stories about the square at that time foreground the erasure of class differences. This is a central element of what made it utopian for many, and troubling to others. The one time I managed to convince Madame Salwa to accompany me to a sit-in at the square, she complained afterward about a shabby-looking young man who had rudely searched a wealthy-looking older man at one of the square's entry points. To Madame Salwa, this breakdown of hierarchies was upsetting. To others, especially a younger crowd, it was exhilarating. For many activists, the square became a space in which people were able to live, however temporarily, what they were fighting for—something quite elusive, a different way of being with, and caring for, others beyond all differences.

Cairo is a city increasingly divided, marked by "emergent hierarchies of exclusion and reordered patterns of structural violence" (Singerman and Amar 2006:16); a city in which the mushrooming of gated communities and satellite cities has put large distances between the well-off and the poor (Denis 2006). In this city, Tahrir Square was an exceptional space that enabled encounters among people from a vast range of social backgrounds (Hafez 2012). Activists described the Tahrir experience as an exceptional "state" (*ḥāla*) in which people stood side by side without judging each other, a state in which class and ideological divisions fell away. Muslims, Christians, and atheists came together, and people watched out for one another. An upper-middle-class activist recalled fighting against regime supporters; fighting alongside him were a poor orphan, a working-class Ahly soccer fan, and a man who looked like a thug but later turned out to be a surgeon. This togetherness was remarkable (and such stories worth telling) precisely because of the strong class divisions that normally mark Egyptian society.

Many activists described the Tahrir experience not only as exceptional but also as *ideal,* as "the best-case scenario ever" of a large number of people coming together. They emphasized that during the eighteen days there was no harassment; not a single cell phone was stolen, no one touched you. Everything was shared. An Egyptian lawyer recalled how "a cup of tea would be passed around between maybe seven or eight people before it was finished" (Abdel Ghaffar 2011:64). Shirin, an upper-class activist in her fifties, similarly underlined an ethos of selflessness:

> Look, we were in charge of delivering supplies. One thing I remember is that people used to fast on Mondays and Thursdays, so we brought them food [*ifṭār*] to break their fast. These people were fasting, and they were extremely poor [*aghlab min al-ghulb*] . . . I was in charge of the area from Abdel Munim Riyad Square to Tahrir Square, and Doctor [A.] was in charge of the field hospital. When you see what they looked like and then you give them food and they tell you, "No, I've already eaten, thanks-be-to-God." Of course he only ate a small piece of bread or something! Then he would tell you, "Go check behind the tank." I go check behind the tank, and [the person there] tells me, "No, thanks-be-to-God, we already broke our fast, keep going because no one passes by those over there." No one wants to take a sandwich before making sure the others have eaten. Never before in my life have I seen this spirit! For example, someone passes by, distributing kebab. You find one person taking just a small piece from the plate and passing it on to the person next to him. It was automatic. Everyone taking a piece and passing on the plate to the next person. No one ever kept something just for himself or herself.

Such accounts resonate with the pious economies we will encounter shortly—ones profoundly committed to circulation and to never keeping something just for yourself—but they also have a worldly utopian resonance, one that many non-Egyptian leftist thinkers picked up on as well. Slavoj Žižek (2011) commented on the "totally new" political happenings, without hegemonic organization, charismatic leadership, or party apparatuses, that created the "miracle of Tahrir." Alain Badiou (2012) praised Tahrir Square and all the activities that took place in it—fighting, barricading, camping, debating, cooking, and caring for the wounded—as a new way of doing politics. Judith Butler (2015) commented on how the congregation of bodies, their assembly in a crowd, laid claim to space in ways that effectively contested the line between public and private. Solidarity, she said, originated in the shared vulnerability to police violence and the practices of care that were necessary to sustain bodies in the square. For Hardt and Negri, the Arab

Spring, Europe's Indignados movement, and Occupy Wall Street expressed the longing of the multitude for a different kind of polity that might supplant the hopeless liberal renderings of corporate capitalism.[21]

To many Egyptian activists, the days at the square were indeed transformative, pointing to a different future through the experience of being differently in the present. They were, in the words of Egyptian anthropologist Hanan Sabea (2013), "a time out of time, excised from the everyday, yet simultaneously constituting the ordinariness of another world that was imagined as possible."

Rifat was one of the many Egyptians who spent day and night at the square during the eighteen days. A thirty-year-old Copt, he was raised in England and moved back to Egypt in 2008. Speaking to Mariam (in English), he described the uprising as a political awakening.

> Those eighteen days were a particular time. People saw how good things could be, how we could be without the police and the state. It was just people feeding each other, taking care of each other. When you see that, you want to fight for it. Was it a utopia? Yes in a way. OK, people still littered. There was almost no sexual harassment but probably some. And people died, like at the Battle of the Camel. But it was just beautiful how good people were with each other. It sounds cheesy because we've heard it so much but it didn't matter if you're a man, woman, Christian, Muslim, and that's so rare. You're lucky if it happens in your lifetime. And if it happens for eighteen days in your lifetime, you're pretty happy!

Like many others, Rifat saw Tahrir Square as a model for how people could live together outside of the machinations of the state. As long as we live within a state, he said, it is the government's responsibility to redistribute resources. "Some say this is like the rich giving handouts to the poor but actually they made all their money through the poor. They owe them that; they've used their labor." But Rifat's ideal society points beyond the framework of the state; it would involve "people living in communes in the countryside." Decisions would be consensus based; if there were leaders, they would be people one knows personally; the community would be small and close-knit. Maybe it sounds nostalgic, he conceded, "but there would also be solar panels and maybe Internet!" In imagining this ideal society, Rifat draws direct inspiration from his days at the square: "If you took ten thousand people off Tahrir during those eighteen days and put them on small farms, you'd be halfway there!"

Rifat's vision sounds hopelessly naïve. Cairo alone is vastly larger, and it is not clear how a population of close to 100 million people in a country mostly composed of desert could be redistributed to small farms. Yet Rifat's naïveté is evidence of how inspiring the days at the square were. They made people hope for a simple, kind version of life that goes against all of our ingrained cynicism and pessimism.

Like Rifat, many found value in a Tahrir utopia (and later, a Tahrir nostalgia). Others emphasized those things that were not perfect. Mona, a sixty-year-old human rights activist, challenged the idea that people overcame their differences: "The unity they say existed during the eighteen days is a myth (*ustūra*), or at best it only consisted of one thing: to defend the square." In her view, activists started idealizing the eighteen days at the square, seeing them as days "in paradise" (*fil-ganna*). They erased the fact that torture and harassment were happening, that "Tahrir wasn't paradise!" According to her and other critics, the square itself became a space of exclusions and hierarchies that often followed familiar class lines. Street vendors were asked to leave at night because, says Mona, they "allegedly corrupted the spirit of the square," and protesters took it upon themselves to punish those who they perceived as violating the ethos of the square. Consider the familiar class hierarchy underpinning this striking description of the "ideal protester" by a middle-class Egyptian activist: "someone that is dressed nicely and goes on the street to chant without the usage of swear words while focusing on his freedom ... Someone who saw people abroad and understands things. Someone who understands basic human rights" (cited in Mellor 2014:82). Maybe it wasn't all equality, peace, and happiness.

Another activist offered a critique of a different kind. He noted that idealizing the Tahrir experience is dangerous because it narrows our understanding of resistance:

> Look, no one can deny that things were different. That life in the square was different in its essence, people's participation, love, and altruism. People's values and morals changed drastically during those eighteen days ... But I feel that creating a stereotypical image of Tahrir and the eighteen days as a utopia is an idea pushed by the system ... to say that these are the only forms of resistance available and this is what everyone should follow— a sit-in, a nice sit-in, in the middle of a square in Cairo—as if this were the best and only way. Even though there are so many others. What the media promoted was the nice, cute 25 January youth who cleaned the square [on the day following Mubarak's resignation] but no one spoke of the battles that

took place on 28 January even though they were the reason for the sit-in at Tahrir afterward. No one spoke of the battles that took place in the different administrative districts and no one spoke of the workers' strikes and the fact that they stopped production completely, which was one of the main reasons that forced the regime to push Mubarak to resign.

For this activist, romanticizing Tahrir diverts attention from more violent aspects of the uprising and from the struggles that happened in other places and that took other forms. Tahrir, especially what he calls its "cute" and "nice" image, was easily digestible but, as a result, was also easily cleansed of its political urgency. In a similar effort to decenter Tahrir Square, other activists spoke about the neighborhood groups (*ligan sh'abiyya*) that formed during the early days of the uprising after the police had withdrawn from the streets, when men (and some women) of various ages got together to guard their neighborhoods, armed with sticks, baseball bats, and knives, huddling around makeshift campfires and discovering a new solidarity and togetherness. Particularly in poorer neighborhoods, these groups did not dissolve after Mubarak's fall. Forming "alternative movements for local self-rule" (Amar 2013), they continued meeting and organizing and took neighborhood matters into their own hands.

Others conceded that the eighteen days at Tahrir Square had indeed been special but insisted that the experience was limited in space and time. People spent huge amounts of money to support the protesters, more than they could afford; others lost their jobs because they went to protests instead of going to work. This could not go on forever. At the same time, Tahrir was exceptional precisely because of its liminality, and, even during the sit-in, people behaved differently inside and outside of the square. Shirin recalled the unique solidarity that existed inside,

> but once I left the square, I would find thugs. Upon leaving, I would get harassed. "*Ya muzza!*" [Hey, babe!] ... Even during the eighteen days, as soon as I left the square, I felt I'm back in normal Egypt. I never felt at the square that I'm a woman. I'm a creature. I'm a human being. No one ever tried to touch or harass me.

Tahrir was exceptional. But part of its uniqueness stemmed from the fact that it wasn't replicable. Maybe it was possible to organize a few square blocks of eager humans democratically (or even anarchically); but not a country of 80 or 90 million people. And so, as critics see it, it is wrong to look to Tahrir as a goal; instead, we should see it as a means.

To Shirin, Rifat, and many others, by contrast, goal and means were one. Tahrir Square opened up a space for experimenting with, and thinking about, different forms of being-with-others, including people who have far more, or far less. Central to this *being differently* was the act of giving, an act that figured in many stories about the square. Giving more than you could afford; making sacrifices in order to contribute to the community; passing on the sandwich to others after only having taken a bite; and for a few people, giving their lives for the cause. After the sit-ins were dissolved, many activists held firm to their memories, eagerly trading their stories, collecting glimpses of an Otherwise, of a what-could-be. I take these stories as an invitation to shift our attention to what already is—to existing practices of giving and sharing embedded in Egyptian life, practices far removed from the spotlight of the revolution. As we already know, not all activists would agree with this move.

FINDING THE JUSTICE IN CHARITY

Most Egyptian activists I know want to keep religion out of politics, a concern that was only heightened after the Muslim Brotherhood's temporary rise to power (and, shortly thereafter, the specter of the so-called Islamic State, or Daesh).[22] They worried about Islamists imposing their worldview and told me that they did not want "to be told what to wear" or that the "hands of thieves would be cut off." They did not want to be arrested for "holding a beer bottle"—they wanted to "have the right to do stupid things." Often, they dismissed not only political Islam but, along with it, the possibility of drawing political inspiration from everyday religious practices. In their view, the revolution would be aided by reading Che Guevara or Gandhi. And by studying the history of revolutions. But not, they said, by wasting time with traditions that refuse to acknowledge the great changes that our moment demands, with traditions that stand in the way of progress and social justice. The uprising must come from fighting today's institutions, not conforming to their calcified habits.

For many self-declared revolutionaries, then, practices like food distribution and almsgiving have nothing to offer to the revolutionary struggle. Worse, they can hinder this struggle. As one activist put it, "If you're stuck in a room and you can't breathe, you'll break the door. But if someone shows up every couple of days to open the door and let in some fresh air, he imprisons you even more." The idea that charity offers just enough to prevent the poor from dying—or from revolting—resonates with longstanding leftist critiques. Slavoj Žižek (2009), for instance, reads charity as integral to a feel-good capitalism, but nothing else. He draws on Oscar Wilde (1891), who argued in the late nineteenth century that "the worst slave owners were those who were kind to their slaves, and so prevented the horror of the system being realised by those who suffered from it ... Charity degrades and demoralises." Comparing charity recipients to "petted animals," Wilde asked: "Why should [the poor] be grateful for the crumbs that fall from the rich man's table?"[23]

Many Egyptian activists would agree. One problem with Islamic charity, they say, is that it is a *moral* practice and not tied to *rights*. Sara, the self-declared socialist, emphasized the difference between charity and rights-based claims:

> One needs to understand that when you help a [poor] boy through school, you're doing something charitable [*'amal khayrī*]. If there were true justice, then this would be his right [*haqq*]. He wouldn't have to wait for someone to be charitable toward him ... Social justice can't be just whenever I feel like it! ... You cannot build a just society that relies on the readiness and desire of individuals. It has to be about the *rights* of the other.

The irony in Sara's position is that the same people who criticize Islamic charity for being "only a moral practice" tend to also be skeptical of a political Islam that foregrounds a Quranic logic of rights and obligations. In secularist circles, religious possibilities for social justice are often dismissed by default. Another irony is that many activists themselves drop the language of rights when speaking about those at the receiving end. Instead they shift into an idiom of deservingness, and often they express a profound disdain for beggars, those who, by simply extending their hand, demand a share without offering anything in return. At best, Sabri, the Microsoft employee, explained, one should give to people who provide a service, such as cleaning a car:

> I can give to him more easily and feel better about it ... I feel that one shouldn't humiliate oneself under any circumstances. [Beggars] present themselves as weak and humiliate themselves. Others try to make you feel guilty; it's a form of robbery ... I feel more comfortable giving to those who don't ask, but rather try to offer a service in return for the money, for example, who clean my car well, don't just pretend to clean it. Or remove a rock from in front of my car. I mean in general those who give me some added value so I can give them money while feeling satisfied and comfortable.

People like Sabri prefer an exchange—your labor for my money—and find the thought of giving to a beggar troubling. This unease toward beggars is not unique to Egypt. In her study of humanitarianism in New Delhi, anthropologist Erica Bornstein reflects on a related question: why does it make her feel better to give to someone selling balloons on the street than to someone merely extending his or her hand?

> The illusion of supporting a business instead of a human being begging makes the giver feel better because an object is exchanged for the money (in this case, the balloons). It is a form of commodity fetishism, in which the thing given (in this case, balloons) takes up and absorbs the emotion of the moment; it neutralizes social relations and makes disparity easier to comprehend and make sense of. (2012:127)

An entrenched belief connects Erica Bornstein's insight and Sabri's rationale: that earning one's living is somehow better than merely extending one's hand. The beggar (or, in the words of an Egyptian activist, someone "sitting down at a different Ramadan table each day, waiting for people's mercy and compassion") is the counterimage to the productive and hard-working citizen, or those who at least *try* to work or, if nothing else, *pretend* to work. Despite their experiences at Tahrir Square, many Egyptian activists place faith in the hard daily work of individuals and the broader development work of organizations and the state. In line with this logic, the poor who are trying to stand on their own feet are better than beggars, and charitable giving is damaging because it encourages laziness and affirms the status quo. We are by now familiar with this logic, the idea, to quote one activist, that charity is "a form of narcotics [*musakkināt*] that lessens oppression, death, and poverty just enough that people get by and don't revolt."

Such arguments, needless to say, typically come from a privileged position. Those living precarious lives would likely not argue against their subsistence and would probably be dismayed by the idea that they should be pushed over the edge for the sake of the "revolution."[24] A similar privilege, I find, is often at work in the leftist opposition to charitable giving. It is easy to be smug about charity if you're not at the receiving end.

In Egypt, a counterview to this widespread suspicion toward "charity" is found among followers of the Muslim Brotherhood. Among them is Ashraf, in his twenties. He insists that divine revelation is in fact key for achieving social justice. Refusing the distinction between "morality" and "law," or "charity" and "rights," he explains,

God gave us laws [*qawānīn*] because He wants for us what is good [*khayr*]. He wants for us rewards in this world and the next. So anything that God has instructed us to do will lead to social justice ... God can best tell us what is right and what is wrong. He created us.

Part of Ashraf's vision of social justice is an Islamic ethics of giving in which one ought to share whatever one is blessed with. If you are healthy, he explains, you have to make sure others have good health too. If you have money, you have to help the poor. Every blessing comes from God, and one is obliged to thank God through the same blessing. But for Ashraf, charitable giving is only one aspect of a larger Islamic vision of justice. Even rituals that are seemingly about self-cultivation are closely tied to the principle of social justice:

The communal prayer—it's a complicated philosophical topic. I don't know if people will believe this but I do. The Prophet started communal prayers after the *hijra* [the migration from Mecca to Medina in 622 CE]. Nothing he did was mere coincidence. I don't remember the actual [Quranic] verse but it says that if you want to be close to the Prophet and enter paradise, stay close to the Prophet. So the Prophet in Medina founded a mosque. It's a psychological idea. If people meet five times a day in the mosque, they will put aside their social differences. The servant [*farrāsh*] is the same as a company director who is the same as a garbage collector. There's no difference between them. What matters is who knows more Quran. The world [*al-dunyā*] is removed; people return to God. That's the first point. The second is the orderliness. People stand in rows. And there's something else that's even more important: mutual love and respect [*tarāhum*]; there is no difference between people. We're all the same in front of God [*uddām rabbinā*]. And you see each other five times a day. You know who has problems, is unable to marry, can't afford to buy food.

Ashraf's account of the way to paradise—performing the required rituals, staying close to the Prophet Muhammad—echoes descriptions of Tahrir Square as a paradise-like space in which class differences were blurred. The servant prays next to the company director and the garbage collector, and they are the same. The orphan, the working-class soccer fan, and the surgeon fight next to each other, and they are the same. Both kinds of stories foreground equality and togetherness. Like Tahrir Square for others, for Ashraf the Islamic tradition offers resources for (re)imagining what it is to be in this world and to be with others. Ashraf would likely not approve of all the forms of Islamic religiosity that we are about to encounter; he would probably be suspicious of Sufi *khidmas,* and he would most certainly be skeptical of dervishes. There are as many tensions between different articulations of Islam as there are between self-proclaimed secularists and pious believers. But Ashraf's linking of collective prayer and social justice points to openings beyond such frictions.

TURNING ELSEWHERE

When protesters on Cairo's streets called for "social justice," the term was open-ended and ripe with potential. Only a few months later, that call had been narrowed and emptied of its promises. Whenever I think about this process, my mind goes back to a two-day event held at the Sawi Cultural Center in September 2011, where about a dozen political parties presented their platforms. I collected flyers, chatted with party representatives at their booths, and listened to speeches—ranging from a highly choreographed presentation by a Muslim Brotherhood member, to a mumbled speech by a shy young representative of a newly founded party, to a speech yelled in Classical Arabic by a man defending his party against the charge that it had ties to the old regime. One representative of a socialist party offered a passionate critique of neoliberalism; all others defended a free-market economy or promoted a "capitalism committed to social justice." Most argued for some version of a welfare state. All appropriated the uprising. A particularly surreal video showed slow-motion images of the Battle of the Camel set against Cirque de Soleil music while a party representative was speaking on the stage. The images and echoes of the uprising did little to diffuse a pervasive sense of emptiness, predictability, and commodification, at least for me.

Similar feelings stuck with me when, a few months later, in the weeks leading up to the parliamentary elections, Cairo's streets became cluttered with banners featuring election slogans: "Deeds, not Words," "Together for a Better Life," "Justice is Hope," "A New Generation for New Responsibilities," "From Tahrir to Change," "Together We Build a New Homeland," "Come on, Let's Transform Egypt," "Together We Change the Injustices of the Past with the Light of the Future," "We'll Bring Back Security," and the Muslim Brotherhood slogan, "We Bring Goodness [*al-khayr*] to Egypt."

Against such co-opted and eroded articulations of what a more just society might look like stands a different vision, an embodied and visceral one that is kept alive in stories people tell about Tahrir Square, particularly stories about giving. Many hold on to their stories about the eighteen days at the square, a time when people shared generously, watched out for one another, and felt social differences fall away. Paradise-like, some say. God's gallery. An experience unlike anything you've ever seen. Utopian. Too cute, say others. Too limited in space and time, by definition liminal, an anti-structure that inevitably would fall back into structure, worse and more repressive than the one preceding the uprising.

Tahrir Square couldn't last. After each major sit-in, the tents were dismantled, traffic resumed, graffiti was painted over, and people returned to their lives. By the time Abdelfattah el-Sisi became president, most of the activists I know were disillusioned. Some conceded that revolutions take a long time; that they move through different phases, or they spoke of a counterrevolution (*thawra mudādda*) that needed to be overcome.[25] All agreed that the Sisi era was no time for political activism. It was a time for keeping one's head down.

In this bleak present, we return to the year of the uprising but shift the focus to other spaces in Cairo—to practices that existed long before, during, and after the uprising. Because while Tahrir Square became a household name, it is of course just a tiny fraction of the city—and the country—as a whole. The vast majority of life happens elsewhere, and the vast majority of social justice, or the lack thereof, happens elsewhere. The ethics of giving I describe eschews a revolutionary jargon about building a better Egypt and instead seeks to address the immediate needs of the Egypt outside your front door. It runs counter to an emancipatory liberal politics but it resonates with stories told about Tahrir Square. Within this ethics, all humans are fundamentally dependent, not only the poor. At the same time, a continuous orientation toward God repositions the poor by reframing them, or putting them *off-frame,* in insisting that all gifts come from, and are directed at, God. This reframing evades a politics driven by pity, but also one organized around social justice. In a pious economy, the poor rely neither on compassion nor on solidarity. They come first by coming last.

Giving

TWO

———

Divine Minimum Wage

THE RAISED FIST IS AN INTERNATIONAL SYMBOL of resistance. First used as a logo by the Industrial Workers of the World in 1917, the image eventually also came to be adopted by the Egyptian Revolutionary Socialists: a red fist, on top of a yellow star, enclosed by a black circle. During the uprising, the red fist appeared on posters, in pamphlets, and on banners. Its omnipresence was not surprising since the uprising had sprung, at least in part, from workers' longstanding struggles. Though the mass protests in January 2011 are what began the deluge of international media attention, many strikes had erupted in the months and years prior. The most significant one, at Egypt's largest textile company in Mahalla, had grown into the call for a general strike on 6 April 2008. The April 6 Youth Movement, named after the strike, later became one of the most active Facebook platforms coordinating the protests in January 2011.

After Hosni Mubarak's fall, the strikes continued. Throughout, one of the workers' central demands was the call for a minimum wage, echoed by stenciled graffiti in downtown Cairo: "a maximum wage for those living in palaces, a minimum wage for those living in graveyards." In January 2012, the interim government raised the monthly minimum wage for public-sector workers to 700 pounds ($116); two years later, after further protests, that figure was increased to 1,200 pounds ($167).[1] Both moves were widely dismissed as insufficient since the minimum wage only applied to about 5 million workers out of a total workforce of over 27 million, and the amount did not refer to a starting wage but included bonuses and pay raises. An outraged friend told me that after acceding to the new minimum wage, government offices began reclaiming a portion of their employees' salaries "for national recovery." She shrugged her shoulders, looking defeated: "They give to you with one hand and take with the other!"

Regardless of such setbacks—and there were many—the struggle for social justice continued. And for workers and other activists alike, the raised fist was a symbol of that struggle.

Yet the closed fist is only one of many forms that the hand can take.

At sit-ins at Tahrir Square, I was always moved by the moments when protesting hands turned into praying hands. When raised arms lowered; when fists loosened. In these moments, five times a day, activity at the square came to a pause, and a number of protesters fell into the same movements. Hands spread toward ears with the palms facing forward; palms gently folded onto one another; then palms came to rest on the floor as praying bodies bowed down; then, finally, right index fingers were lifted while the *tashahhud* was recited: "There is no god but God . . ." In these moments, the state no longer was the addressee, or the source of justice and of minimum wages; believers turned to God.

From protest to prayer, from raised fists to raised index fingers, and back again. These momentous days seemed able to encapsulate both. The jump from politics to piety did not seem like a jump at all; rather, it seemed at the square that they were intertwined. To some, prayer might have offered a break from protesting, but, I am told, for others prayer was not a break but a way to reenergize—a reminder of something bigger than the state, even bigger than life.

The person who taught me most about the convergences (and occasional tensions) between a this-worldly fight for justice and an otherworldly spiritual realm is Shaykh Salah. A retired army engineer, he now spends most of his time at the Sayyida Zaynab mosque. The mosque is not far from Tahrir Square, but Shaykh Salah went to none of the protests. Instead, he spent his days as he always does, buying vegetables at the local market, washing lentils, peeling potatoes, stirring huge pots of food, scooping the food into bowls, and handing the bowls to whoever is waiting. Shaykh Salah's hands—or rather, his right hand, the right being preferred over the left in the Islamic tradition—continuously crafts itself into something akin to God's hand. The way he sees it, divine agency works through him. It is his hand that gives, not he as a person. A prophetic hadith promises that one of the "seven whom God will shade on Judgment Day" is the person who "gives in charity and hides it, such that the left hand does not know what the right hand is giving."

Shaykh Salah on his way to the Sayyida Zaynab mosque. Photograph by Inger Marie Vennize.

This ethics of secrecy and concealment is echoed in charitable contexts throughout Cairo. Yet, for Shaykh Salah the issue goes beyond secrecy. For him, the emphasis on the giving hand—and not the giving person—is connected to the goal of *fanā'*, of self-erasure, a merging with God's will. Shaykh Salah is a Sufi, and it is because of his devotion to giving and because he is widely read in the Sufi tradition that many, myself included, call him a "shaykh," a title of respect. He is not the kind of Sufi that is affiliated with one of Egypt's over seventy officially recognized Sufi orders, which since the early twentieth century have been overseen by the government-sponsored Higher Council of Sufi Affairs. His Sufism is of the informal kind—the kind that pervades the everyday lives of many Egyptian Muslims yet that people like Shaykh Salah take to a different level. Central to this kind of religiosity is devotion to the Prophet Muhammad and his saintly descendants (*ahl al-bayt*) (Hoffman-Ladd 1992), as well as an openness to being-acted-upon by the Divine (Mittermaier 2012).[2] This openness—and undoing of the self—is actively cultivated by people like Shaykh Salah through practices such as serving food, day after day.

Food distribution (*it'ām al-t'ām*) in Sufi communities was first documented in the mid-twelfth century, and by the mid-sixteenth century had become the sine qua non for Sufi seekers who understood service as a spiritual practice

(Rodriguez-Mañas 2000).[3] Called *zāwiyah, khanqah,* or *takiyah* depending on the geographical context, communal kitchens and Sufi lodges offered poor relief, handed out stocks of food, and provided temporary accommodation to travelers, pilgrims, and beggars. They also provided refuge during times of political turmoil; in Morocco, they were sanctuaries to outlaws and to opponents of the ruling dynasty (60). In Egypt, Sufi spaces of food distribution are called *khidmas,* short for *khidma li-llāh,* literally "service for God." Unlike other elements of Sufi belief and practice that are firmly embedded in Egyptian life, many Egyptians barely know what *khidmas* are, let alone where to find them. As dervishes and pilgrims know, however, *khidmas* are a constant and ubiquitous feature around saint shrines. During saint day celebrations (*mawlids*), a temporary *khidma* might consist of a tent, carpet, or reed mat put out on the sidewalk, or an apartment that is rented for the duration of the celebration where food or tea are served, and sometimes a place to sleep is offered. Other *khidmas*—apartments, whole houses, or just a corner in a mosque's courtyard—are open all year round. For Shaykh Salah, the term *khidma* refers not only to the space but also to the act of distribution—"feeding those who ask, regardless of who they are."[4] Even though Shaykh Salah's devotion might seem extraordinary and exceptional, I read his *khidma* as the epitome of a broader Islamic, and more particularly Sufi, ethics of giving.

Shaykh Salah's *khidma* is attached to the mosque that houses the shrine of Sayyida Zaynab, the Prophet Muhammad's granddaughter. Like other Sufis, Shaykh Salah sees the Prophet Muhammad as a manifestation of God's light, and members of the Prophet's family as carriers of the Muhammadan light. As he explains, all saints have a particular concern (*himma*), which stays with them when they are in the *barzakh,* the realm in which the spirits dwell until Judgment Day. Besides being the Prophet's granddaughter, Sayyida Zaynab was also the sister of Imam Hussain, who, along with his companions, was killed at the Battle of Karbala in 680 CE. As a woman who suffered much during her life, Sayyida Zaynab is said to understand the problems of women (particularly regarding health and infertility) and to be able to intercede for them.[5] Shaykh Salah tells me that when Sayyida Zaynab's brother was killed, she prayed the prayer of gratitude (*salāt al-shukr*). That is, amid the greatest misery, she was able to say *al-hamdu-li-llāh* (thanks and praise be to God)—a sign of her submission to God's will, or what is called *ridā* (pious contentment). She was also very generous.[6] This explains, according to Shaykh Salah, why so many people distribute food around her mosque, many of them not as systematically as Shaykh Salah, but no less devotedly.

Shaykh Salah's giving is directed by God and orchestrated by Sayyida Zaynab. He aspires to the Sufi goal of spiritual annihilation of the self (*fanā*'), or at least he hopes that his left hand will not know what his right hand is giving. But he is only human. He is attached to his hand, and so are his wishes, thoughts, hopes, and opinions. He is charismatic, laughs loudly, and is a great storyteller. He is outspoken about his views on politics and the shortcomings of the revolutionary youth. Not infrequently we would fall into a familiar gender dynamic: an old knowledgeable man lecturing the younger female anthropologist. He gave long and unprompted lectures about how I should approach my work or why I was doing it all wrong—that I should be mapping out all major *khidmas* "from Alexandria to Aswan" instead of only focusing on a handful; or at least I should do my research in Upper Egypt, where people are more devoted to giving. That I should be getting my hands dirty, cooking and serving food, instead of asking so many questions. I like Shaykh Salah, but spending time with him also often reminded me that the spiritual aspiration to dissolve your self does not mean that you can't have a big ego at the same time. The path toward *fanā*' is always a journey, and like everyone else, Shaykh Salah is not free of contradictions.

At times I found him self-involved; other times I was awed by him. He could sound terribly condescending when speaking about the poor: he enumerated endless reasons why they are to be blamed for their poverty and lamented their limited ability to plan ahead. But he is also an astute critic of the structural conditions that create and perpetuate poverty. He could talk for hours about the Prophet Muhammad's spiritual presence, and then, with equal passion, about the daily struggles of Cairo's street children. Shaykh Salah belies the common stereotype of a Sufi: as otherworldly, out of touch with reality, seeking refuge with the saints, and clouding their minds through ecstatic forms of entertainment such as daylong celebrations of saints' birthdays. He is a Sufi but also deeply interested in, and opinionated about, Egypt's political situation.

Other Sufis, to be sure, actively participated in the uprising, and some Sufi orders founded political parties afterward.[7] But most men and women who run *khidmas* described them to me as first and foremost spiritual—*not* political. This political quietism might partially have to do with the close association some Sufi circles have historically had with the Egyptian regime, and their corresponding distrust of the revolutionary activism in 2011.[8] Yet, in the case of Shaykh Salah, the distinction between spiritual and political becomes unstable. For him, giving is a spiritual practice but also one that responds to worldly material conditions. In 2011, he explained to me why he cooks day after day, echoing but also appropriating a central demand of the uprising: "It's not a personal choice," he said. "We have to give food to those who are hungry because food is the divine minimum wage [*al-hadd al-adnā al-ilāhī*]." Shaykh Salah's notion of a divine minimum wage picks up on the revolution's insistence on social justice, but offers a radical alternative: provisions that are offered not by a more just state, but by God.

24/7

My first evening with Shaykh Salah remains a vivid memory: it was July 2011, a time when Tahrir Square had been reoccupied by protesters. We were sitting in the small ground-floor apartment that Shaykh Salah rents close to the Sayyida Zaynab mosque, drinking hot hibiscus tea. Next to me were Mariam, Hassan, and a journalist-friend of Hassan's who was struggling with his atheist leanings and had come along, curious to meet the shaykh we had been talking so much about.

Shaykh Salah had taken off the tracksuit that he usually wears while cooking and had put on a white *gallābiyya* and prayer cap. Quranic recitations were blasting from a small tape player; he turned it off so we could talk. Without much prompting, he began to lecture me on the spiritual underpinnings of the *khidma*. I tried to pay close attention but was only half listening. Most of my attention was directed toward the half-closed wooden door that leads to the bathroom, a small stall with a squat toilet. I tried to focus but was too distracted by a rat's tail that, through the gap underneath the door, I saw moving around the bathroom. Then a moment later I saw the rat in its full splendor, sitting on top of the door.

I stared at the rat, and then tried not to stare; no one else seemed to notice, or maybe everyone else was more used to rats or too polite to give it much attention. I felt like a lousy anthropologist, unfit for doing research in the real, messy world. But what I also felt was respect and admiration for Shaykh Salah and what he was doing on a daily basis. I already had an inkling at that point, having caught a glimpse of the large heavy pots earlier that evening, pots in which he cooks two meals a day, each feeding more than a hundred people.

And so, despite the rat, I came back, day after day, to learn more. Shaykh Salah gets up every morning at around 4 A.M. and, after the morning prayer, leaves the spacious suburban apartment in which he lives with his wife and travels on the metro for an hour to come to this cramped apartment, located in the midst of a crowded neighborhood, with a bathroom occasionally shared by rodents. The apartment's narrow entrance area and a second room in the back function as the kitchen. In them are a fridge and a portable gas stove (*butaghāz*) with three grates. When I took pictures in the kitchen once, one of the men who help Shaykh Salah placed the larger pots on a grate, one by one, as if the pots were posing. They are, after all, what the *khidma* is about. It is about the food that God provides, not the people who make it.

The apartment's front room has been turned into a sitting area. Its walls are decorated with old prayer rugs from the mosque that provide warmth in the colder winter months. The floor is covered with two carpets, reed mats, and a few pillows. Everything in the room has been donated to the *khidma*. One day, as he was telling me the story of each object and how it was given to him for free, Shaykh Salah paused to comment: "This is how society should work."

Though only occasionally articulating such utopian visions, Shaykh Salah arguably *lives* them through his daily work. When he arrives in the morning, he first goes to the mosque to spend about an hour in prayer before buying groceries in the local market. Then he prepares the first meal. When the meal is ready, he or one of his helpers takes it over to the mosque, to the men's entrance for the noon prayer and the women's side in the afternoon.[9] These are his spots in a busy charitable landscape. Once, he drew a map for me, marking all the locations around the mosque where people give: a woman who lives close by and distributes cheese, jam, and bread every morning; a man who used to distribute falafels inside the mosque after the sunset prayer until the mosque's hours were shortened due to "security reasons"; a man who hands metal cups filled with water to passersby in the courtyard; a man in his sixties who feeds the feral cats around the mosque, day after day, because of a dream in which a cat spoke to him; and Shaykh Salah's own *khidma*. In his words, "The courtyard of Sayyida Zaynab has food 24/7. Its divine characteristic is that there is always food."

To get from the apartment to the mosque, Shaykh Salah uses a wheelbarrow or a small metal cart to transport the large pots, metal plates and spoons, a bag with loaves of flatbread, a plastic stool, a bucket with water for the dirty dishes, coolers with drinking water, and metal cups. Someone keeps an eye on the cart while Shaykh Salah enters the mosque to pray the noon prayer. A crowd starts forming, and one of his helpers begins handing out plates, spoons, and bread. Back from his prayer, Shaykh Salah takes a seat behind the pot. People approach one at a time; he scoops food onto each plate. The people spill out onto the sidewalk or find a spot in the shade alongside the mosque's wall. Most people eat quickly. Some ask for a second serving. A helper rinses each plate and then Shaykh Salah refills it for another guest. Usually after ten or fifteen minutes, the pots are empty. Back in the apartment, Shaykh Salah does the dishes and prepares the second meal before returning to the mosque to distribute it. He cleans the kitchen, and after the sunset prayer or nighttime prayer, he heads home, going to sleep about two hours later only to start the same routine again the following morning. He cooks and distributes food seven days a week. He takes no holidays. He goes through all this trouble for people who otherwise would have no food to eat. And he goes through all this trouble for God, *li-llāh.*

Shaykh Salah is particularly busy during the *mawlid,* the celebration of Sayyida Zaynab's birthday, which officially lasts one week but, according to him, goes on for an entire month "because our lady [Sayyida Zaynab] deserves that much." During this festive season, a large number of visitors come to the shrine from outside of Cairo, and Shaykh Salah cooks four meals a day for about three hundred people each. During Ramadan, too, he is especially busy, distributing large amounts of food inside the mosque after sunset. But he is critical of people who give out food only during Ramadan: "It's wrong for people to only give during Ramadan. What should happen is that Ramadan becomes like a study period for examining the needs of society. But then once you've seen it, you should give during the other months too. Did the hungry die? Did they leave town?"

Shaykh Salah cooks persistently, and over time he has developed a schedule: on Sundays, Tuesdays, and Thursdays, he makes pasta for the first meal (after the noon prayer) and *malūkhiyya,* a spinach-like vegetable, for the second meal (after the afternoon prayer). On Saturdays, Mondays, and Wednesdays, he first serves lentil soup and later potatoes in tomato sauce. On Fridays, he distributes breakfast in the morning and one meal after the communal prayer around noon; then he goes home to rest.

He explains why he prepares different kinds of food: "I cannot serve pasta every day even though they really like it. But if I served it every day, I would be harming them, because it is made of dough and doesn't contain any vegetables." And even if he could afford it, he would not serve meat every day because he finds that when you serve meat, people leave whatever it is served with—rice or bread—which is wasteful.

Though on a divine mission, Shaykh Salah cares about worldly details, from nutritional values to wasted food. The season matters too: he finds that

Shaykh Salah cooking. Photograph by Inger Marie Vennize.

pasta makes for a good summer dish; lentils are good in the winter. But he also offers spiritual explanations. Lentils, he says, make tender (*yuraqqiq*) the heart; they make it compassionate and kind (*shafūq*). "They create tears. Lentils make you softer, more human." Seen this way, the food that is served is not only an effect of God's generosity; it can also *create* kindness by softening the hearts of those who eat it.

THE *KHIDMA* AS NEXUS

The *khidma* connects believer and God, but it also brings together a wide range of people—those who give, those who receive, those who cook or wash dishes or donate or simply hang around. What is cultivated here are not just pious selves but also relationships.

Among the many people who are connected to the *khidma* are the donors. To keep things running, Shaykh Salah needs money: around $55 for the monthly rent; a new gas canister every three days (about $3 each); electricity; sometimes a helper, who might receive $3 a day; and money for the ingredients. Most of Shaykh Salah's monthly pension is spent on his own family's needs. The *khidma* relies on donations (*nafahāt*). One donor (whom I never met) pays the monthly rent. Others drop off donations on a semi-regular basis. Occasionally Shaykh Salah also receives money from people who come to the mosque to visit Sayyida Zaynab and want to repay the saint for a favor she has done or as a way to ask for her help. Visitors to Sayyida Zaynab's shrine—which is off on the side of the mosque, with separate sections for men and women—touch the metal enclosure surrounding the tomb, or sprinkle cologne onto it. Some bring flowers for the saint, "even expensive flowers from Italy," Shaykh Salah reports. Sayyida Zaynab accepts their gifts, but what she really wants, he says, is for people to take an interest in the poor who visit her. Some visitors drop bills into the donations box (*sundūq al-nudhūr*) but many distrust the mosque administration and instead give money to Shaykh Salah after seeing him distribute food. They walk up to him and slip a rolled-up bill into his hand, which he then discretely moves into his shirt pocket.

The way Shaykh Salah sees it, people give money to him for different reasons. Some face a problem and hope that God will help them if they give to Sayyida Zaynab. Others simply like good deeds (*khayr*), or they know they have a responsibility toward the poor. Some have committed sins and want to make up for them. Shaykh Salah remembers a university professor whose father cheated the other family members out of their rightful share of inheritance and left all his wealth to her. She now donates a large amount every Ramadan to make up for this injustice. A pious man (*min ahl Allāh*) whom Shaykh Salah consulted about the professor's money told him that all her good deeds count as divine rewards (*thawāb*) for the people who were deprived of their rightful share. He offered this analogy: "Imagine I stole a tree from your garden and planted it in mine. To whom would the tree's *thawāb* go? It would go to *you,* the tree's rightful owner."

Shaykh Salah appreciates the bind that the professor feels and is happy to take her money, but there is another category of people from whom he does not like accepting donations—people who are hoping to make up for their own bad deeds by donating. As he put it, "Bad money can't do good works" (*al-māl al-sayyi' la ya'mal khayr*) because "God is good [*tayyib*] and only accepts what is good." He says he can feel it if money comes from an unclean source, and his guests only like the food if the money is permissible according to Islamic law (*halāl*). This means that it is important that the donors "pay their taxes and treat their workers well . . . We don't want the money of big businessmen. Their money is dirty. Better a pound here and a pound there, but clean."

Along with donors, local vendors contribute to the *khidma* by selling their goods to Shaykh Salah at discounted prices. Female vendors help by cutting potatoes or pulling *malūkhiyya* leaves off the stems. Shaykh Salah drops off the vegetables in the morning and picks them up a few hours later, making sure the women receive a warm meal in return.

On and off, Shaykh Salah has also employed helpers, especially after economic conditions worsened in the months following the uprising: "People are coming so fast, the pot burns my hands!" One of these helpers is Hamza, whom Shaykh Salah calls a dervish or his cook, but who prefers to call himself a servant (*khaddām*). Hamza was in his mid-forties when I met him. He had grown up as an orphan after losing both parents when he was four years old, and he spent thirty years "at the door of Sayyida Zaynab." In material terms, Hamza gets nothing out of helping at the *khidma* except for some tea and food, plus a few pounds each day for cigarettes. Nevertheless he is very devoted to his work. Twice, however, he caused a fire in the kitchen. According to Shaykh Salah, he has a "problem in the brain" that occasionally makes him lose focus. After the second fire, Shaykh Salah kicked him out, but when he saw Hamza sitting a few meters away from the *khidma* and watching it "as if the pots were his children," he took him back.

Behind this division of labor lies a practical concern. Shaykh Salah explains: "It makes the job faster. I don't want the food to get cold, because it becomes tasteless. For example, spinach is very healthy and people love it, but it has to be eaten hot." But just as important, the *khidma* helps to incite mercy (*rahma*) in those who help out. As Shaykh Salah puts it, "We move that part in them and we build it." Creating more merciful selves, he says, is critical for creating a better, more merciful society.

The people who eat at the *khidma* are an eclectic group. Among them is a man who is raising his three children on the street. He takes them inside the mosque to sleep whenever it is open; Shaykh Salah wakes them up when it is time to eat. One teenage homeless girl shows up almost daily, as does a man without legs, in an old, heavy wheelchair. A young policeman from the police station next to the mosque occasionally stops by for a free lunch. Some come with plastic bags that they ask Shaykh Salah to fill so they can take food home for their children. According to him, about half of the people that show up are regulars, among them, "maybe an employee with a low salary or a worker who doesn't work every day; widows and divorcees, homeless people, people who were displaced from their homes, street children." In general, those who eat at the *khidma,* he says, roughly fall into three categories: the poor (*fuqarā'*), those in need (*masākīn*), and travelers (*'ābir al-sabīl*), all of them listed in the Quran as deserving of alms. Shaykh Salah defines the poor as those who have no money at all. Those in need have some income (*rizq*), but not enough. The last category, he explains, includes people running errands in the city who stop at the mosque to pray.

Ultimately, however, Shaykh Salah is not guided by abstract categories but by what he sees on the streets. After the uprising, he noticed that more and more well-dressed people were going hungry. Those who used to be well off but lost their jobs had no choice but to "go from *khidma* to *khidma,* asking for food for themselves and their children. They don't know how to be thugs or thieves." Often they were embarrassed, but Shaykh Salah reminded them that the food is "something from God" (*hāga min rabbinā*).

In line with North American self-help discourses about how helping others is a way of maximizing one's well-being, even of combating depression, Shaykh Salah emphasizes that giving makes him happy. He takes visible pleasure in giving. At the mosque, the pot in front of him, a scoop in his hand, he joyfully calls out to people walking by: "Come and eat" (*ta'āla kul*), "Come on, have lunch" (*yalla itghadda*), "Eat, my father" (*kul yā bābā*), "Take, dear lady" (*khudi yā hāgga*). As he cajoles his fellow believers, he instructs us helpers with equal vigor: "Hand a plate to that good man over there" (*hāti lil-rāgil al-tayyib da*), he tells me. At these moments the people who receive the food are not homeless or poor; they are his guests, or more precisely the guests of God. Other times Shaykh Salah praises the food ("this is beautiful *malūkhiyya*") or tells passersby that the food has a healing power and comes directly from Sayyida Zaynab (*di shifā; di nafha min sittinā*).

Over the years, Shaykh Salah has come to know the people who eat his food. He emphasizes his care for, and even friendship with, them. If one of his regulars misses a day, the next time he sees them he asks why they didn't show up (*ghibt 'annī leeh?*). If someone declines a plate, he jokingly says, "Don't make me mad!" (*haz'al minnak*). He explained to me that kindness and patience are central to his work and that he cares about how his guests see him:

> I'm their friend. If one of them doesn't come one day, I ask about him; and when I see him, I tell him, "It's been a while since you last came!" They ask me what I'm going to cook for them, and I tell them. There is a relationship between them and me; it's not simply that I feed them and then I leave . . . I even ask for their opinion. Sometimes they comment on the quality or quantity of the food, and I make the changes they ask for . . . A good relationship is a must.

This emphasis on kindness and humility is not merely a rhetorical claim. One hot August afternoon, Shaykh Salah was distributing potatoes in tomato sauce, and people started complaining that the food needed more salt. Instead of being offended by their seeming ingratitude, Shaykh Salah apologized to every single complainant (and there were many) and sent someone running to a store to buy a bag of salt. He added a pinch of salt to each plate while continuing to apologize. Through such gestures, Shaykh Salah prevents his self (*nafs*) from taking pride in his giving, and he reminds himself (and his guests) that he is merely a channel for God's gifts. His hand gives what God provides.

GOD'S ARMIES

Shaykh Salah's full name (which he asked me to use) is Salah al-Din Nafari Muhammad, but most people simply call him Shaykh Salah or Hagg Salah, both references to his spiritual authority, or more informally 'Am Salah (Uncle Salah). When he first gave me his phone number, he asked me to record it on my cell phone under Salah al-Sayyida (the Sayyida's Salah), underscoring not only the location of his *khidma* but also his spiritual connection to Sayyida Zaynab, and ultimately to the Prophet Muhammad.

Shaykh Salah was born in 1944, the seventh of nine children. In the early 1960s, he started working for the Egyptian army as a technician (*fannī*), and he participated in the War of Attrition (1967–70), the October War (1973), and the First Gulf War (1990–91). From working for the military, he slowly drifted toward working for what he calls "God's armies." It all began in a rather nonspiritual way, with him looking for ways to make a difference. In the mid-eighties, he began going to the annual book fair in Medinat Nasr to buy stacks of books at discounted prices and resell them at the same price in low-income neighborhoods with the goal of "culturing" (*tathqīf*) people. At around the same time he became interested in questions of development and sustainability and started writing proposals on how to reduce water consumption in households. He suggested incentives that could help turn people into "good citizens" (*muwātin sālih*) by making monthly assistance contingent upon their reduced electricity and water consumption, and he proposed having competitions between schools around who saves the most water, and to raise awareness at mosques, which, in his view, use far too much water for the ablutions before prayer.

Having sent proposal after proposal to different ministries without ever receiving a response, he realized that the government officials were not interested in his ideas, and so he decided to address the problems in more direct ways. Ideas of "civil society" and "good citizens" receded into the background, and, instead of teaching others how to use water more responsibly, he began fixing dripping faucets and water pipes in mosques. Increasingly he turned his attention to "serving Sayyida Zaynab," helping out at a Ramadan table at her mosque, distributing homemade jam in its vicinity, and cleaning the mosque's bathrooms.[10] In 2009, when he was sixty-five years old, he opened the *khidma*.

I never received clear answers to my questions about why Shaykh Salah chose Sayyida Zaynab's shrine and why he made the shift from fixing faucets to serving food. Others spoke of dreams or other divine signs to explain why they opened their *khidmas*. Shaykh Salah spoke more vaguely (though in line with his military background) of having been enlisted (*tagnīd*) by an invisible spiritual government that directs humans:

> Whoever helps with cooking or distributing food becomes part of God's armies [*gunūd Allāh*]. In Sufism it is understood that every place has its armies. You're directed to a place by a dream order [*ashāra manāmiyya*] or a feeling [*khātir*]. I couldn't do what I'm doing at Zin al-'Abidin [a different saint shrine] because I didn't get that order.

The *khidma*, then, is a spiritual task, tied to a particular place, and assigned to a particular person. Another time Shaykh Salah explained that although he feels spiritually closest to Hasan, the Prophet Muhammad's grandson, Sayyida Zaynab attracted him "the way a wife attracts a husband." Whenever Shaykh Salah needs something for the *khidma*, he says, Sayyida Zaynab delivers it right away. (If he needs something for himself, he adds with a smile, he might have to wait a bit.)

Despite Sayyida Zaynab's continuous support, Shaykh Salah has run into problems with mosque officials, who have asked him to relocate, who keep reducing the mosque's hours, and who "kick [street children] out of the mosque, even with a stick. They have no heart."[11] He emphasizes that the mosque administration, including its imam, are appointed by the state and not the saint. His own connection to Sayyida Zaynab, by contrast, has been confirmed through other people's dreams and visions. Entering the apartment where he cooks, visitors have reportedly seen the Prophet Muhammad and Sayyida Zaynab—generally in the form of light. According to Shaykh Salah, this is not unusual because the dead are around us. The Prophet, and to a lesser extent Sayyida Zaynab, guide us at every moment, even though not everyone can see them: "The Prophet is light, and he is always around us whether we see him or not. He's sitting here with us right now. It's like TV rays. They're here whether you have a TV to receive them or not."

A particular dream Shaykh Salah likes to retell was reported by a poor woman (*sitt ghalbāna*) who sits by the mosque and receives food from him every day. In the dream she saw him at Imam Hussain's mosque, next to a horseman (*fāris*) on a horse. Shaykh Salah and the horseman greeted each other. The horseman said: "If you are hospitable [*tukrim*] toward those whom you know, you are giving to me. If you are hospitable toward those whom you don't know, you are giving to God." Shaykh Salah was deeply moved by this dream. The horseman, he explained to me, is either the Prophet Muhammad or Imam Hussain. In another dream, reported by a friend of his, Shaykh Salah was going on the pilgrimage (*biyihigg*) once a week. Shaykh Salah interpreted the dream for me: "This means that one week of giving food equals one pilgrimage, and doing the pilgrimage cleans you and rids you of your sins."

These dream-stories take us back to the thin line between self-erasure and self-aggrandizement. The first story presents Shaykh Salah as someone who is spiritually advanced and exceptionally close to God. The dream's retelling stands in tension with the goal of humility and self-erasure. Equally, the idea of exchange—giving food to erase one's sins—stands in tension with the idea that God gives *through* Shaykh Salah, that he is merely a channel (*magra*) for God's generosity, as he often explained to me. In one model, the individual's intentions and deeds matter; in the other, one's will is erased. Both ideas coexist, though somewhat uneasily, in Shaykh Salah's account of what the *khidma* is all about. He speaks of giving as a technique of self-erasure but also as a pious obligation, if not a personal accomplishment. Ultimately, however, he insists that it is all up to God: "If God likes my work, He makes sure someone gives me money, gives me a place, gives me people who work with me, and brings me people who will eat the food. This is a divine matter [*qadiyya ilāhiyya*]."

And Shaykh Salah takes divine matters seriously. I never saw him turn away a guest. He says it is not up to him to decide who eats the food he provides. This points to a central difference between his idea of giving and the kind orchestrated by a welfare state or by charity organizations, which seek to identify those who are truly deserving of help. Giving at the *khidma* is free of conditions and expectations precisely because it is God who gives, not Shaykh Salah. In one of his longer monologues, directed at me and my recorder, he explained:

> Look, Shaykh El-Shaarawi [a popular cleric who died in 1998] said, "The stomach does not lie." If [someone] is hungry, give to him. Sometimes I also see that someone isn't hungry and it might bother me, but I don't have the right *not* to give to him. He takes the food, and eats as much as he wants. If he comes and asks, I can't tell him no . . . The guest is God's guest [*dayf Allāh*]. If someone enters the *khidma,* he is not *my* guest. He is God's guest. Didn't you hear that the alms donation falls in God's hand first, before it falls into someone's hand? That is why 'Aysha [the Prophet's wife] used to bless the dirham. Because it falls into God's hand. The true Muslim doesn't see anything in the universe but God. All the rest are appearances [*ashbāh*]. This is true. When one reaches a certain level of spirituality, one doesn't see anybody in the universe but God. All other things are just appearances placed there for a certain purpose. The Sufi knows that . . . God wants to liberate me from myself; He doesn't want me to have a will. My will disappears in God's will. In the Sufi path [*tarīq*], what do they say? "We want what you want, God." This is a high level of spirituality but most people want things for themselves. I'm only a server. It's God's *khidma.* We can't tell someone yes or no. God does everything.

The idea that the *khidma*'s guests are "God's guests" has important implications, among them that Shaykh Salah's mood and feelings toward them do not matter, and that not even hunger is a prerequisite for receiving a free meal. In turn, for Shaykh Salah, foregrounding God also means that he should never ask anyone for help (*mayinf 'ash utlub*). Indeed, though asking for donations is central to our notions of charity, it is antithetical to the *khidma.* Because the *khidma* is built upon a continuous orientation toward God, it is built upon an orientation *away* from the humans who do the actual giving and receiving. Shaykh Salah explains that God constantly reminds those running *khidmas* not to rely on particular donors:

God gives to me sometimes, and other times He gives to other people. God doesn't want me to get attached to a specific person. He tells me to pray to Him, and He will give me whatever He wants. For example, sometimes I wait for a specific person to give me money and that person never shows up. Then the money comes from a completely different direction. This is God's way of telling me: "Address your needs to me. Forget about people." God is the only one there. You should forget about everyone but God.

God's lesson, paraphrased by Shaykh Salah, is: "Ask me for help. It's none of your business where the help comes from." Shaykh Salah's only job is to show up in the morning and open the door. The rest is up to God.

Whenever Shaykh Salah receives donations—from donors, but ultimately from God—he tries to keep them in circulation. When someone gives him money, he spends it the same day, and when he has food, he distributes it right away.[12] He says that according to divine planning (*tartīb ilāhi*), it is wrong to let food sit in the *khidma* overnight. Trusting that God will provide, then, also runs counter to typical ideas of how we should plan ahead, save for the future, guard against uncertainty, and prepare for the unexpected.

DEBTS AND DUTIES

For Shaykh Salah, being a medium for God does not imply passivity or sitting back. In fact, he insists that we all carry a debt toward society. And the Egyptians' debt is particularly grave because "they fail to understand the sanctity of work." Here "work" (*'amal*) figures in a narrow sense, as commodified labor tied to an income. Shaykh Salah seems to evoke a familiar stereotype, that of the "lazy Arab," though he might also be referring to Egypt's inflated civil sector, a result of Gamal Abdel Nasser's declaration, made in the 1960s, that every college graduate was entitled to a government job. Ultimately, he makes a more general point, beyond the historical particularities of Egypt. The ideal he seems to imply is a robot-like worker who never wastes a single second. Precisely because we are not robots, we all carry a debt. Reflecting on his own past, Shaykh Salah explained that when he was working, he tried to be careful to work as much as possible, and he always asked for extra work. But surely there were times when he had nothing to do at work and still got paid. As such, he, too, carries a debt. He offered another example: that of a friend who is a tax collector but goes to work only twice a week because there is no work on the other days. Shaykh Salah told him that the salary he receives for the other days is forbidden by God (*harām*) and that he should make up for it by helping at the *khidma* or volunteering at a charity organization.

At times, Shaykh Salah seems to imply that the Quran is more concerned with worker efficiency than with caring for one's neighbor. That if a person were perfectly efficient at their job, then they would not have any responsibility to the poor. His emphasis on wasting time sounds almost Calvinist. But his logic of debt is not only about wasted time. It also contains a profound social critique. People, he says, mistreat each other, and they are overly invested in social hierarchies. Civil servants disrespect farmers and workers while failing to recognize that "the civil servant's salary comes from the work of the farmer and the worker." In Shaykh Salah's view, we owe something to the people we have mistreated or exploited, even inadvertently. And even if we have never done anything wrong, we would still owe something simply because we live in a society full of injustices. He explains:

> I'll give you another example. The vendor sitting outside, he had a child in primary school. Ignorant as he is, he decided to take him out of school. The Ministry of Education was going to spend 1 pound on me and 1 pound on the vendor's kid. Now that he is no longer in school, I ended up taking his pound as well and I kept on taking until I finished my education and started working for a salary. [The vendor's child] didn't take anything. I took what belongs to him. Because his family is ignorant, they took him out of school. And I enjoyed the resources that he was supposed to have. Therefore I am in debt to him. So when I give him food, I'm not giving him charity. I'm giving him his right.

In this example, the boy's father is to blame, and so is the Ministry of Education, which should work harder to make sure resources are distributed justly. But it is Shaykh Salah who is in debt to the boy, and it is God who judges the transaction. As Shaykh Salah puts it, "I'm in debt to God and to the people" (*anā madīn li-llāh wa lil-sh'ab*). By giving to the poor, one pays off a debt but one also gives to them what rightfully belongs to them and what they were deprived of through structural inequalities and their personal circumstances. One gives them their rightful share.

For this reason, even though he himself occasionally uses the word, in Shaykh Salah's view, people are mistaken when they call food distribution a form of good deeds (*khayr*). The *khidma* is a way of making up for wasted hours at work and an attempt to right things in a society of many wrongs.

Only once all one's debts are paid can it become possible to say one is doing *khayr.* "At least that's how I see it," Shaykh Salah concluded. "Other people see it very differently; they don't realize they're falling short, and they say they're doing something good. They think they're doing something amazing when really they're just doing their duty!"

While making up for debts accumulated in the past, the *khidma* also functions as a school—for those who help out, for street children, but also for activists, anthropologists, and politicians, a point Shaykh Salah often made in conversations with my research assistant, Mariam. Her father is a historian who was temporarily appointed minister of culture in 2011. On several occasions, Shaykh Salah would stop talking to us and instead directed his words to Mariam's father, asking her to pass on the message. "I have something I want to say to your father!"[13] Once, during Mohamed Morsi's presidency, he instructed Mariam to ask her father and other liberal politicians to consider why the Muslim Brotherhood had been so successful. In his view, their success was due to them having "penetrated all classes and sectors of society . . . They offered something, they opened clinics, mosques, orphanages." Liberal politicians, he insisted, are too far removed from ordinary people.

> Today, for example, if [Mohamed] ElBaradei [a prominent Egyptian liberal] or your father went to a village and got invited to someone's place, and had to sit on the floor and eat with them, would they even know how to? No, they wouldn't know! It's just for the media and for taking pictures. Amr Moussa [former minister of foreign affairs and, in 2011, a presidential candidate] went and ate with a peasant and left. Did he learn anything? No. He needs to come live this life, the life we're living. When he comes to live our life, he will understand. Through books and lectures he will not understand.

Most liberal politicians, in Shaykh Salah's view, are elitist.[14] If they go to a slum or a village, it is only for publicity and photo ops. And so, repeatedly, he issued an invitation to Mariam's father. He offered to leave him his keys and all the supplies, and even to teach him how to cook. At the *khidma,* he would come to meet "the common people" and he would learn more than from reading one hundred books.

In Shaykh Salah's view, politicians ought to be interested in real-life struggles because ultimately it is the state's job to take care of the poor. He believes in the idea of a welfare state and insists that taxes and state revenues should go to the poor—again, not as charity but as their rightful share.[15] But that does not mean that the rest of us are off the hook. A welfare state can only be brought into existence and sustained through the efforts of ordinary people. According to Shaykh Salah's maybe-nostalgic account, people used to do more, which made the rulers feel guilty; they felt watched, "and so they started doing things too, like building mosques and schools." In particular, in many Sufi communities "the kitchen would always be active," putting pressure on the government to become active as well.

Against this historical backdrop, Shaykh Salah often highlighted the shortcomings of both state and society in present-day Egypt:

> I'm going to tell you a story: ten years ago, I was standing by the mosque's backdoor, on a cold winter day, distributing food. I would sit at times near that door, reading the *Ibrīz* [his favorite Sufi text]. Once, when I was about to sit down, I found four straw sacks by the door. Three were knotted, and one was open, so I got closer to the open one and found a boy inside. I opened the other three sacks, and each had a child in it. One of them had knotted the other three and then climbed into the last sack. They did this to stay warm! Need is the mother of invention. But where did our humanity go? How can I be in my safe room, on my bed, with a blanket and a heater and a shut window, while they had to do this? What does such a child get out of the national revenue of our economy? Where is his share from the revenue of the Suez Canal? Where is his share from the revenue of the oil industry? Where is his share from the revenue of taxes?

In this account it is almost as if the state blocked the rightful distribution of goods, which is God's will. But equally those are to blame who sleep in their warm rooms under their blankets while street children have to make it through the night. In the absence of a welfare state, and at a time when most people are "disconnected from the state" (*munfasilīn ʿan al-dawla*)—when they no longer trust that the state will do something for them—the well-off should take it upon themselves to address the poor's most pressing needs.[16] When the state is weak, our responsibility increases—a philosophy that Shaykh Salah *lives,* particularly in the aftermath of the uprising. To him, the *khidma* is a space that provides a divine minimum wage instead of waiting for the state to do something. This is not to say that Shaykh Salah is against political participation or against protests. But protesting—fighting for a better future—should never take away from attending to the needs of this current moment. Equally, calling for a more just state should not obscure one's own responsibilities within a divine economy of rights and obligations.

Ultimately, for Shaykh Salah, the state itself is never situated *outside* a divine order. Unassuming government officials, too, can become tools of

God's will or unknowingly act by Sayyida Zaynab's orders. In October 2011, the Ministry of Interior Affairs temporarily interdicted "food gatherings" (*tagammuʿāt al-akl*) around the mosque in an effort to drive away the "thugs" (*al-baltagiyya*), a term that here implies disorderly and violent behavior but ultimately encompasses all the people Shaykh Salah gives food to. Shaykh Salah offered an explanation that at first sight seems apolitical but that also radically reframes the question of government. He explained that the ministry's order "was only appearance." In reality, he said, Sayyida Zaynab was upset because the hygienic conditions in the neighborhood's mosques had been neglected. She wanted Shaykh Salah to go back to fixing the plumbing at the mosques. At around the same time he dreamed of a pot of lentils falling over, which he interpreted to mean that he should stop distributing food for a while. He followed Sayyida Zaynab's orders and found that many faucets were broken and pipes blocked. He worked for days fixing them. Then, likely following another sign, he returned to the *khidma*. Bureaucratic actors and devoted Sufis alike are entangled in a divine order *and* in concrete material contexts.

VISIONS OF POVERTY

An avid reader, Shaykh Salah has recommended various books to me: about the Mamluk era, the saints of Morocco, and the history of bread in Egypt; biographies of the nineteenth-century ruler Muhammad ʿAli and the twentieth-century president Gamal Abdel Nasser; the medieval travelogue of Ibn Battuta; and the Arabic translation of a book by the German sociologist Horst Afheldt on welfare and the decline of social solidarity.[17] He often cites from the Quran (a favorite verse of his, no surprise: "[The truly virtuous are those who] give food—however great be their own want of it—unto the needy, and the orphan, and the captive") and from the sayings of the Prophet Muhammad ("O people, spread the greeting of peace, feed the hungry, and pray at night").[18] His favorite book is *Kitāb al-Ibrīz* (literally, the Book of Pure Gold), a text popular in Sufi circles, which contains the teachings of the Sufi master al-Dabbagh, recorded by a religious scholar in Fez around 1720.[19]

Drawing on these varied sources and his own quasi-ethnographic observations, Shaykh Salah has developed different theories about poverty and what we ought to do about it, theories that do not always match up with his concepts of debt and duty. Some of these theories burst with stereotypes about the "East" and the "West." He claims that the West suffers from individualism but that Egyptians, too, today often live in isolation:

The problem in the modern age is that people have less time. This started when cinema came. Before that, people had time which went into doing good deeds [khayr]. Today they don't think about others [al-ākhar]. Today you have television, and people live more separately. Recently someone died in Zamalek [an upper-class neighborhood], and no one even noticed. This is like the West. In poorer areas this couldn't happen. There people are well aware of their neighbors' circumstances.

In Shaykh Salah's view, Cairo's upper-class neighborhoods are "like the West," where only the "I" counts and people forget about the "we." This is the reason, he says, why people from those neighborhoods flock to the poorer neighborhood of Sayyida Zaynab when they want to "feel the spirit of Ramadan." Wealth doesn't make us happy; togetherness does. Shaykh Salah cites a line from a poem: "If paradise were only for me, I would not want it!"

Being part of a "we" means taking care of others' basic needs, but charitable actions alone are not enough. They have to be accompanied by the right intentions and maybe also the right politics. Shaykh Salah is critical of those who give because they are after fame (Bill Gates is his favorite example), and he is equally critical of those who act piously only when it is convenient for them:

I know a businessman who works in the building industry. My son used to work for him, and the man was very unjust with his employees. But he sends poor people to Mecca for the pilgrimage! This is wrong because the first thing should be to treat one's employees well; you shouldn't exhaust them. Exhausting one's employees is against our religion. He shouldn't ask them to do something beyond their capacities or take away their rights.

When ranting against exploitative and unjust businessmen who "suck the blood of their employees, make big fortunes, and then pray to God," Shaykh Salah seems to gesture toward something we might call "social justice." He is clear on his dislike for the selfish rich. He is less clear on his views on the poor, and on why they are poor.

At times he describes poverty as a symptom of the state's failure, as a breakdown of social relations, or as the result of an unjust system of distribution. Or he describes poverty as God-given and inevitable: "Every country must have poor people. This is God's wisdom so the rich give to the poor. Poverty is a human thing [al-faqr hāga insāniyya]." Other times he says that

God made some people poor to lift them up spiritually. But also, a less common view, that God punishes the poor with poverty because they fall short in their religious and ethical obligations:

> [The poor] steal, they fight, they don't say *al-hamdu-li-llāh* [all praise and thanks be to God]. They don't let others have their share, they don't pray or fast. In Ramadan most of the people who come to the *mā'ida* [where they receive a free *iftār*, the evening meal to break their fast] aren't even fasting! They're not practicing their religion. Not all are like that, but many of them are. So God gives them what they deserve.

Here poverty is a divine punishment inflicted on nonpracticing Muslims, maybe to protect them from more severe punishments in the afterlife. Regardless of what lies at the root of poverty, the poor, according to Shaykh Salah, are "ignorant, rowdy, and uncivilized." Echoing popular theories from the 1960s that attributed poverty to a "lack of impulse control, a strong present-time orientation and relatively little ability to defer gratification" (Nagi 2001:16), he insists that the poor are incapable of thinking about the future. In his own case, not saving for and not worrying about the future is a pious stance—one of *tawakkul;* in the poor, it is a moral shortcoming. The problems of the poor, Shaykh Salah says, have to be addressed practically. He tries to help street children by teaching them how to be "useful." He says, "With pleasant treatment you can turn these people into human beings." To emphasize the importance of teaching the poor, Shaykh Salah draws on a story about the Prophet Muhammad's life:

> A poor man came to the Prophet Muhammad to ask for help. The Prophet asked him what he had at home. The man said he had some fabric that he sometimes wore and sometimes used to sit on. The Prophet told him to sell the fabric, and the man sold it for two dirhams. Then the Prophet Muhammad told him to buy food for his children with one dirham, and to buy an axehead with the other dirham. He asked the man to cut wood and sell it. The man collected ten dirhams, which he used for food and clothes.

Shaykh Salah explained: "Instead of giving material aid to the poor man, the Prophet—peace and prayers be upon him—helped him think differently about his life." Turning the poor into entrepreneurs, helping them think for themselves, according to Shaykh Salah, is the biggest gift one can give to them—a widespread logic in present-day Egypt and beyond. He sometimes describes food distribution as only a part of what he would like to be doing; other times he describes it as absolutely essential: a social, human, and divine duty.

During my fieldwork I often found Shaykh Salah's apparent vacillation between contradictory positions maddening. With some distance, I can appreciate more fully the ways in which he holds together all these different strands, and the ways in which his vision refuses to be neatly translated into a language of "social justice." It seems odd that someone so deeply invested in the idea of "civilizing" the poor, of turning them into responsible, entrepreneurial subjects, would work so tirelessly for these very same people, devoting all his energy and resources to—as the proverb says—"giving a man a fish" instead of "teaching him how to fish." The seeming contradiction is telling. Shaykh Salah gives *despite* himself. His right hand gives without his left hand knowing. He serves food even if his convictions would seem to point him in nearly the opposite direction. He gives because God asks him to give. He gives because food is a divine minimum wage.

RETURNS

During one of my return visits to Egypt, in August 2014, I stopped by the Sayyida Zaynab mosque to see whether Shaykh Salah was around. The noon prayer had just ended, and there he was, cheerful as ever, an enormous pot in front of him. I waited until he was done. He seemed happy to see me, and we chatted briefly. Would he have time later in the afternoon to catch up? He said a different day would be better; he had to rush home to shower and change before joining his son's wedding celebration in the evening. Once again, I was reminded of Shaykh Salah's unshakeable commitment to making and distributing food. A commitment to God but also to the people who have come to expect that daily meal from him. Even his son's wedding could not justify a day off.

I never had a chance to ask Shaykh Salah's son how he felt about that day. Presumably, by dedicating his life to God and to feeding the poor seven days a week, Shaykh Salah at times falls short as a father and husband. Serving God can come at costs, and giving to random strangers means *not* prioritizing relations of proximity. This is just one of the tensions that run through Shaykh Salah's life. Another exists between his faith in development and his daily practice of giving. Even though he is one of the strongest believers in development I know, in his daily work he gives in the here and now, feeling compelled to do so by his understanding of Islam.

Shaykh Salah's giving is not affected by his mood, his personal views on the poor, his concern with "educating" or "civilizing" the poor, his empathy or lack thereof, or his own son's wedding. He does not even ask whether his guests work—and this, notably, despite his disdain for those who lack a proper work ethic and waste time at work. In the end, the food his guests eat is not really a wage or compensation; it is their right.[20] Sidestepping the wage relation that lies at the heart of capitalism, a "divine minimum wage" links a worldly, pragmatic demand of the revolution to the otherworldly and divine. Shaykh Salah shifts effortlessly between spiritual and political matters. He speaks of debts, responsibilities, rights, and duties, but all these terms are inflected by a divine economy. He speaks of the Sufi goal of becoming liberated from oneself, but embodying God's will for him does not mean withdrawing from the world; it means providing for the homeless, street children, and the unemployed and underemployed. It is Shaykh Salah's take on divine justice—and not simply "social justice"—that drives his daily ethics of giving and grounds his critique of big businesses, the exploitation of workers, the shortcomings of Egypt's revolutionary youth, and the government. At the *khidma,* the material and the spiritual, the visible and the invisible, are always already entangled. What Shaykh Salah calls his "philosophy of giving" is always about both: this world and the next, the poor and God, a spiritual economy and the political economy.

In February 2018, last time I saw Shaykh Salah, the *khidma* was still going strong, and he told me that he dreams of buying the entire building in which he cooks. He wants to expand the kitchen so he can feed an even larger number of people, and to use one or two floors for creating a safe space for homeless girls where they can shower and sleep. He tells me how much it would cost to buy the building—the equivalent of about $200,000—and notes: "To some this is nothing!"

Seemingly contradicting his belief that he is not supposed to place hope in other people, he tells me that maybe someone will come forward with a donation that will enable him to buy the building.

"Maybe after reading your book."

THREE

Caravan to Paradise

"WHERE ARE THE SEVENTY VIRGINS?"

"They're with the Charlie team."

This exchange featured in a cartoon in the so-called "survivors' issue" of *Charlie Hebdo,* the French satire magazine. One week prior, on 7 January 2015, two French Muslim brothers of Algerian descent had forced their way into the magazine's headquarters and killed nearly half the staff. The cartoon depicts one of the brothers arriving in paradise, assuming he will be welcomed as a martyr and rewarded. He is quickly disillusioned; the virgins prefer to party with the killed cartoonists. The cartoon is meant to be funny on multiple levels. Some might feel Schadenfreude at the foolish Islamist who is cheated out of his desired reward. Others might laugh at the absurdity of the cartoonists having ended up in a Muslim paradise of all places. And finally, the cartoon recycles the supposed belief that seventy virgins (or houris) will be given to those who enter paradise, an idea that has long amused secular critics.[1]

But I am haunted by this cartoon. I don't find it funny. It reminds me of a longstanding Orientalist fascination with Muslim eschatology, pitting a sensual East against a rational West. And it reminds me of a more recent proliferation of media stories about suicide bombers dying to make it to paradise. It is impossible to shake these images and polemics as I am trying to write about the volunteers at Resala, one of the fastest-growing charity organizations in Egypt. Would it be better if I left out paradise altogether? If I emphasized the volunteers' role in Egypt's civil society? If I noted that some Egyptian activists praise Resala despite their general distrust of "charity"? If I said that, like volunteers elsewhere, the young men and women at Resala want to help the poor, counteract social inequalities, and at the same time feel good about themselves? That their volunteering is very much about *this* world? It is. And yet such a framing would miss something essential. Almost all the Resala volunteers I know cannot speak about volunteering without also speaking about God and the afterlife.[2]

My thoughts go back to a gathering with the volunteers. "*Fil-ganna liyya makān*," they sing. In paradise I have a place. Again and again. Louder and louder. Sameh plays the drum. The other young men have interlinked their arms and jump up and down. Higher and higher. Young women clap their hands; some take out their cell phones to film this celebratory moment. I do the same, in part to cover my discomfort for not singing along. Later on, as I watch the video clip on my phone, I will once again be reminded of paradise's role at Resala—its centrality but also the striking certitude of the volunteers' assertion: "In paradise I have a place." As if Judgment Day had already happened. As if paradise were now. As if you could ever be certain. You can't, no one can, and the volunteers know that. Their proclamation of certitude is a technique of piety that goes hand in hand with an active and continuous striving toward a place in paradise. In the volunteers' eyes and in their songs, their place in paradise is fundamentally connected to being a *Risālāwī*—belonging to, and volunteering for, Resala.

Paradise is omnipresent at Resala. No virgins are involved, however. No rivers of milk, honey, and wine, either. In fact, hardly any concrete images at all. Although there are countless historical depictions of Muslim paradise—think of paintings of the Prophet Muhammad's Night Journey, or Dante's *Divine Comedy,* which is said to have been inspired by Arabic sources—at Resala, paradise is a rather abstract but powerful promise.[3] The volunteers are guided by paradise—not as a home to seventy virgins but as a constant reminder of all that exceeds the visible world and human life, and that at the same time compels them to respond to the needs all around them.

While paradise as a destination remains abstract, the path to paradise does not. Many of the volunteers' conversations revolve around the process of collecting rewards (*thawāb* or *hasanāt*). "The poor are our gate to paradise," they say frequently, explicitly, and almost proudly. For the outside observer, the apparent contradiction between the volunteers' selflessness and their simultaneous selfishness can easily raise suspicions. But let us recall here, once again, Marcel Mauss's *The Gift,* which effectively deconstructs this supposed contradiction by arguing that each gift, even an ostensibly charitable one, brings with it the expectation of a countergift.[4] Unlike Shaykh Salah's Sufi vision, in which all things belonging to God might point to things that belong to all, Resala volunteers stick more closely to a framework of gift exchange. For them, the countergift comes from God in line with an eschatological logic that urges believers to "sell" their life on earth for life in the afterlife.[5]

The idea of accruing rewards by performing good deeds is not new, but the pervasive emphasis on rewards might have become more prominent since the Islamic Revival in the 1970s. Samuli Schielke (2012a) suggests that the "concern for the fine details of maximizing reward" among young Egyptian Muslims is characteristic of a particular moment of capitalism. Egyptians of an older generation tend to be dismissive of the idea of "trading with God" (*tagāra maʿa rabbinā*) and often told me that in the good old days, people helped their neighbors and gave to the poor simply out of goodness (*khayr*), not with an eye to hoped-for rewards.[6] Such nostalgic memories of a pious indifference to otherworldly rewards resonate with a common Sufi attitude, most famously articulated by Rabʿia al-ʿAdawiyya (d. 801 CE), a Sufi mystic and saint who is said to have prayed to God to burn her in hell if she worshipped Him for the fear of hell, and to exclude her from paradise if she worshipped Him in the hope of paradise. Worship should not be about fears or hoped-for rewards: "But if I worship You for Your Own sake / grudge me not Your everlasting Beauty." Or take these words, quoted in an early collection of pious sayings: "I would be ashamed before God if I served Him in the hope of paradise, for then I'd be like a worker who only works for a wage and does not work when he does not receive it."[7] For Sufis and Egyptians of an older generation, true piety means doing good for its own sake, and worshipping God without expecting any rewards.

Sometimes Resala volunteers, too, sound like Sufis even though they are generally critical of "Sufism." In those moments, they speak of trying to shape their bodies, actions, and words in accordance with what they think God asks of them. There is an irony, in fact, in using the word "volunteering" to describe their efforts—a word that etymologically foregrounds one's will (*voluntas*). The Arabic word for "volunteering," *tatawwuʿ*, etymologically comes closer to "rendering oneself obedient." At Resala, giving means imagining oneself to be giving to and for God, both at once. These two orientations—trading with God and becoming a medium for God's gifts—are both articulations of *li-llāh* and sometimes the two logics converge. The emphasis among the volunteers, however, is on gained points and expected rewards.[8]

They unapologetically worry about paradise and hell. In their view, doing so is integral to piety. This does not mean that the volunteers are *weltfremd*, as one would say in German, "strangers to the world." Their concern with the afterlife animates their concern with this world.

LATE MORNING

Today, in the kitchen on the second floor of Resala's eight-floor building, a couple of the volunteers have arrived early, at around 8:30 or 9 A.M. Others were up late last night, studying for exams or lingering on Facebook. They show up later, with glassy eyes. The boys wear sweatpants. The young women wear jeans, long sleeves, and hijab; some high school students are unveiled. Mona wears a *niqāb,* a veil that covers the full face except for the eyes. A secretary, one of the few employees at the organization, makes her rounds with a form, asking each volunteer for their name and phone number, and noting their time of arrival, before disappearing into her office. The kitchen quickly becomes too small for all who want to cook. Most end up standing around in the hallway, chatting. I'm about to join a conversation when Tante Layla, a volunteer in her early fifties, directs me to the balcony where I am to clean rice with Halimah, a twenty-three-year-old volunteer from Imbaba.

The balcony functions as a storage space; there is barely enough room for the two of us. We clear a corner and start working, picking pebbles and tiny ants out of a huge pile of grain on a tray. Halimah tells me she has been volunteering with Resala for two months. She had long been wanting to do *khayr,* and then she saw Dr. Sherif Abdelazeem, the organization's founder, on the satellite television channel Iqra and liked what he had to say. Although Halimah has enjoyed her time at Resala, she has not invited any of her friends or relatives to come along; she believes that it is best to do good deeds in secret. She tells me that she would never clean the rice this carefully at home, but "you have to give your best when it's for others." Another young woman, sticking her head out onto the balcony, nods emphatically: "Here we get divine rewards [*thawāb*] for what we do, but not at home!"

Back in the kitchen, we hand the cleaned rice to Mona, who has flipped back her *niqāb*. Mona is a dedicated volunteer, an experienced cook, and sometimes a bit pushy. With the help of two other young women, she begins boiling the rice and cooking hamburgers. Suddenly high flames spring up

Volunteers in Resala's kitchen. Photograph by the author.

from the gas stove; someone has spilled oil. Mona quickly pulls down her *niqāb* to cover her face and calls out to the hallway for help. Muhammad, a shy young volunteer, runs in and tries to take care of the fire but only makes things worse. Eventually Tante Layla takes charge and extinguishes the fire. A young woman asks with concern whether the fire happened because we did not pray when we heard the call to prayer from the prayer room down the hall. Tante Layla reassures her that unexpected difficulties only mean we will receive extra *thawāb*.

Resala has over sixty branches throughout Egypt. This one is located in an upper-middle-class neighborhood in Cairo and attracts a large number of volunteers who describe themselves as Salafi.[9] Here the kitchen is a women-only space (except for emergency situations or when heavy items need to be lifted), and music is forbidden (*harām*). In other branches, young men and women cook together, and volunteers plug their iPods into loudspeakers, filling the kitchen with pop music and echoes of the uprising, such as Hamza Namira singing about Tahrir Square and reminding Egyptians to raise their heads up high. At the more religiously conservative branches, the kitchen is filled with the sounds of sizzling burgers, evocations of God, and conversations that revolve around Islamic texts, religious TV programs, and preachers, but often, inevitably, more mundane matters as well.

This day, once everybody has settled back into their tasks—cleaning rice, cooking burgers, washing dishes—Mona comes over and asks whether I've had a chance to read the book she lent me the previous week: *How to Love God* (*kayf nuhibb rabbinā*).

I say I started.

"And? Did it change you? You *want* to change, right?"

Trying to think of an adequate answer, my gaze falls on the sign above the stove listing the rules that the volunteers in this branch have agreed on. Among them: (1) stop working and go pray as soon as you hear the call to prayer; (2) girls work in the kitchen, and boys in the hallway; and (3) on the bus leave a row of seats empty between girls and boys.

I say something vague, something about all of us wanting to change to become better human beings.

Mona, frowning, opts for a more direct approach: "Have you thought about wearing the hijab?"

I say that veiling is not one of my priorities. Mona looks unconvinced.

I escape to the hallway as Mona calls after me, asking me to promise to think about the hijab. "We want to see you in paradise!"

THE VOLUNTEERS

Resala attracts a wide range of young Egyptians. Some see its commercials on television; others learn about Resala by word of mouth. Though familiar with the idea that good deeds should be done in secret, many of the volunteers tell others about the organization and its activities, inviting them to come along. Resala's TV ads and the habit of bringing along friends are equally justified through the prophetic saying, "pointing to *khayr* is as good as doing it." Similarly, my presence was welcomed; volunteers applauded me for wanting to write about *'amal al-khayr,* the doing of good deeds, in Islam and reminded me that the line between doing *khayr* and studying it is blurry. By studying these things, I was told, I was accruing divine rewards too.

The majority of volunteers are in their late teens or early twenties. Younger (and somewhat involuntary) volunteers are the orphans who live in Resala orphanages and occasionally are taken along on trips to the slums. Often the volunteers are also joined by a "tante" ("aunt" in French), an older woman who informally supervises them. Some of these older women are welcomed warmly; others, it is whispered, "have their nose in everything." One tante was praised as a matchmaker; rumor has it that she has enabled four successful marriages among volunteers already.

Most volunteers I know come from working-class backgrounds and live in low-income neighborhoods that are often quite far from the Resala branches. Among them are high school and university students, or recent graduates, with degrees in fields ranging from archaeology and tourism to accounting and business administration. The lucky few who have jobs juggle work and volunteering, sometimes spending up to twelve hours at Resala on their one day off. Their jobs range from informal to high paying. Halimah makes some money by translating soccer news, largely relying on Google Translate. At the other end of the spectrum, and more exceptional, was a volunteer in her late twenties who had previously worked for the Egyptian stock exchange and at the time was trying to start an independent business. Most of the recent graduates, however, are unemployed and report feeling bored at home; they speak of an overwhelming amount of "empty time" (*waqt farāgh*).[10]

Yet, Resala is more than a place where young people kill time. As many of the volunteers would say, doing *khayr* is first and foremost about drawing closer to God. Officially Resala is not an Islamic organization and it welcomes non-Muslims, but especially the self-declared Salafi volunteers praise it as a space of collective self-cultivation and moral education. In Egypt, skeptics view Salafism as an import from Saudi Arabia and associate it with an overly detail-oriented orthopraxy and with distinct dress codes (full face veils for women; beards and ankle-length pants for men). Historically largely quietist, after the uprising, Salafis entered the political scene through the newly founded Nour Party. When Resala volunteers call themselves "Salafi," they do not necessarily align themselves with this party, nor do all the women wear face veils, or the men grow beards. Rather, the volunteers imply that they seek to align all their actions, thoughts, and feelings with God's commands. Some of the self-proclaimed Salafi volunteers were brought up in religiously conservative households; others describe how their pious strivings have caused frictions with family members. Resala, at least this branch, offers a substitute family of sorts, and for many it is a religious boot camp.[11]

Achieving piety is a collective effort, and friendship both among the men and among the women is valued and encouraged. In lessons for newcomers, more experienced volunteers emphasize the role of love. Consider this lesson, offered during a bus ride to a slum. Backgrounding those to whom the charitable activity is ostensibly directed—the people living in the slum—one volunteer tells us:

> We're doing all this out of love for God but also the love between us is important. We should all get to know each other better on this trip. I've made amazing friendships through Resala. I used to think very religious people don't have fun but now I know better.

Love and friendship here do not imply uncritical acceptance but include the willingness to point out shortcomings in others. One volunteer gave me two choices: she could be a regular friend (*sāhiba*) who says hello and "how are you," or she could be a true friend (*sadīqa*) with whom I could talk about problems, who would correct me if I spoke badly about others, and who would call me every day to make sure I was awake for the early morning prayer. Finding polite ways to decline such offers was one of the ongoing challenges of my fieldwork. Volunteers often assured me that they, too, had struggled at some point and wanted to help me on my presumed path to a more pious lifestyle.

EARLY AFTERNOON

Mona and the other two women are still cooking. Three high school students are washing pots. Halimah scoops the cooked rice onto Styrofoam plates. Tante Layla plans the meals for the following week: beef, green beans, and rice one day; pasta and kufta the other. Like most branches, this one dedicates two days per week to food distribution (*it ʿām*), preparing two hundred to three hundred meals each time, to be delivered to about ten different slum neighborhoods on a rotating basis.[12]

The secretary returns to record the names of latecomers. I join Halimah and a group of young women who have been chatting about their respective fields of study; they quickly turn to ask me questions about Germany. Halimah wants to know whether there are slums in Germany. Someone asks me to explain "why Europeans are so against the veil." One young woman pulls me aside to ask whether I think it's wrong to have a boyfriend. A bit later, another woman asks me half-jokingly whether I have a brother or male cousin she could meet. She has been looking for a potential marriage partner for two years.

Heba, in her mid-twenties, joins us. She is asking for advice, and all listen attentively. She tells us she is engaged to her neighbor. He works in Saudi

Arabia and will be there for another year. In the meantime she is living with his family but doesn't get along with them. She is thinking of breaking the engagement. Rasha, a student of Islamic architecture, about the same age as Heba, advises her against doing so. "It's not easy to find a good man," she says, and all agree. "Think about it carefully, and pray *istikhāra*." Heba tells us she has already used this prayer, through which one asks God for guidance. The response often comes in the form of a dream. Heba prayed and did have a dream (she doesn't share details) but is still confused. A general discussion ensues about *istikhāra*. One woman argues that you can't rely on dreams, even ones experienced after this prayer, because your unconscious interferes and "you see what you want to see." Rasha disagrees: "You're supposed to use the prayer only if you're completely undecided." A young woman asks what happens if you already know what you want. Rasha explains that in this case you simply ask God whether there is *khayr* in your decision or not. Another woman asks whether you *have* to follow what you see in a dream after using the prayer. All agree that you do. Rasha says: "Look, you might pray *istikhāra* and see a dream that tells you to marry a man, and later you get divorced. But then that was your fate. It's written the moment you're born."

The *istikhāra* prayer is a technique through which believers seek to directly engage with God, one that circumvents conventional structures of authority.[13] Yet in Resala's kitchen, the prayer not only connects believer and God. It also connects the volunteers who advise and guide each other in matters of everyday life.

The conversation topic moves from marriage to preachers. Done with the dishes and now joining our circle, the high school students tell us about Moez Masoud, and why they're "head over heels for him" (*bamūt fīh bi-sarāha*). Masoud grew up not speaking Arabic. He used to drink and party. He went to the American University in Cairo. He was completely transformed when close friends of his died in an accident, and then he, too, had an accident in which he nearly died. He realized that life is short and it is not enough to merely enjoy it. He memorized the Quran and became a preacher. Conversion stories of this kind—from fun-loving to deeply devoted—are inspirational for the volunteers, who generally do not have a past of drinking and partying but are still concerned with continuously improving and changing themselves.

Halimah tells me she is particularly fond of Mustafa Hosni, a charismatic preacher famous for his TV and radio programs. She invites me to an upcoming event at the Sawi Cultural Center, where he will lecture about how we can speak to God directly in our prayers. Preachers like Mustafa Hosni have a large fan base among Egypt's youth, including among Resala volunteers. Echoing Sufi registers, but also discourses common among evangelical Christians (Luhrmann 2012), they speak of God as a friend, a companion, someone close by. At the same time they promote an ethos of pious activism, optimism, and entrepreneurialism.[14] The volunteers cobble together their Islam, drawing on these preachers' lectures, books, and sermons, as well as formal lessons and informal advice offered by other volunteers. Far away from mosques and other institutions of learning, Resala is a place where young Egyptians teach each other religious knowledge and talk about how to love God and how to make sure that one is loved by God, how to orient oneself toward God, day after day, minute after minute.

RESALA AND ITS POLITICS

Since the 1970s, the Islamic Revival and a parallel Coptic Revival have transformed Egyptian society. Since roughly the same time, the state has increasingly cut back on its social services. As a result of these two coinciding developments, hundreds of charity organizations have been founded in Egypt. Resala is among the biggest and fastest-growing of these organizations. Literally, *risāla* means "message," which can easily be misunderstood to refer to the idea of *da'wa,* helping fellow Muslims become more devoted in their religious practice. The first generation of Resala volunteers, however, chose the name to evoke not the message of Islam but the message of volunteering. The founder of Resala, and now its chairman, is Dr. Sherif Abdelazeem, a professor of engineering at the American University in Cairo (and previously at Cairo University). Dr. Sherif is a pious Muslim, prays regularly, and has memorized the Quran, yet he understands volunteering not as particularly Islamic but as a global phenomenon grounded in universal values.[15] In fact, it was during his studies in Kingston, Canada, that he first came to appreciate the idea of volunteering. Counter to Shaykh Salah's account of a quintessentially individualistic "West," Dr. Sherif recalls how deeply impressed he was by Canada's strong "civil spirit." Upon his return to Egypt after eight years abroad, he spoke to his students about what he calls the "not my problem" syndrome (*wa anā māliyya*), meaning that Egyptians care only about what affects them personally. A group of students approached him after a lecture to ask what they could do and together they decided to form a student group.

This was in 1999. In a meeting of sixty students, the name Resala was chosen out of twenty-five proposed names. The goal, the group declared, was to spread the "culture of voluntarism" (*thaqāfat al-tatawwu'*).

The group began with activities at Cairo University, such as blood donation campaigns and a "beautification of campus" initiative, and then expanded their work to visit senior homes. In June 2000, the relative of one of the volunteers offered the group a building in Faisal, a neighborhood in Gizeh. He reportedly had long wanted to use the building for a charitable purpose. The volunteers did most of the renovation work themselves, convinced salespeople to donate tiles and cement, and completed the project in only one year. Recalling these beginnings, Dr. Sherif would later explain to new volunteers: "What's important to volunteering, or really anything you want to get done, even a job? Two things: dedication [*hamās*] and sincerity [*ikhlās*]. The former means putting all your energy into the project. The latter means having faith in God, getting closer to God [*na'arrib min rabbinā*]." This dual approach continues to shape Resala's ethos. It is the volunteers' activism that makes things happen. But it is always also God.

Over the years Resala has grown rapidly. Every year a total of about 250,000 young Egyptians volunteer in one of its branches, and, according to Dr. Sherif, a million people each year profit from their activities. When new volunteers sign up, they tick off on an intake sheet which activities they are most interested in. Taking them into Cairo's slums, to villages in the Nile Delta, Upper Egypt, or the Western Desert, the options include the following: deliver appliances to families in need, work with street children, assist disabled children, donate blood, renovate mosques and schools, offer free language or computer classes, promote environmental activities such as recycling, sort through donated clothes and redistribute them or sell them at symbolic prices, visit orphanages and senior homes, prepare and distribute meals, assist the vision impaired and hearing impaired, provide medical services, teach literacy classes, offer professionalization workshops, tutor school children, help the poor set up small businesses, mentor orphans, sell small Resala items to spread the word about the organization, support children with cancer, help Muslims memorize the Quran, beautify villages, promote health education such as anti-smoking campaigns, assist with medical caravans, and help run a "bank for the poor."

The list of activities is eclectic, ranging between an ethos of development and more traditional forms of charity, or between what Mona Atia (2013) calls the three clusters that characterize Egypt's Islamic NGOs: (1) "good deeds and that's it," (2) a fish and a fishnet, and (3) Islamic development. Some Resala activities aim to turn the poor into productive citizens. Others are about giving in the here and now. Still others are about promoting Resala and bringing more volunteers into the organization. Many are about nonmaterial gifts: visits, mentoring, tutoring. *It ʿām,* literally "food distribution," is one of the most popular activities, and it is the one in which I participated most regularly. It started with volunteers collecting leftovers from restaurants and hotels to distribute them to the poor, but often the volunteers ended up with not enough food or received only sweets. And so, eventually, they started preparing meals themselves.

Resala keeps growing but has also faced setbacks. In 2007, all branches at public universities were closed for fear of "Islamist organizing" (Sparre 2013:61). The year 2011 was also critical, marked by debates over whether Resala should formally become involved in the uprising. Resala branches were closed for two months, but privately many volunteers participated in protests and later claimed the images of young people sweeping Cairo's streets and squares as an unofficial Resala legacy.[16] In February 2011, volunteers wearing Resala T-shirts reportedly provided blood bags and medicine to injured protesters (165). Others told me that when volunteers wanted to distribute meals at field hospitals at Tahrir Square, the NGO's administration insisted that "Resala should not take a side in the conflict." The extent and nature of Resala's political involvement had to be renegotiated day by day.

When the branches officially reopened, a number of young women signed up as volunteers because, they told me, their families had not allowed them to go to protests but they, too, wanted "to do something." Some saw volunteering as directly related to the revolutionary fight for social justice; others became concerned with social justice as a result of volunteering. One woman in her early twenties told me that her parents insisted that "the revolution was wrong" but she disagreed: "I wasn't sure but then I went to all these slums with Resala and I saw the poverty and I knew [that Mubarak had to go]!"

When election time came around about a year after the uprising, most of the volunteers I know voted for the Muslim Brotherhood's Freedom and Justice Party or the Salafi Nour Party, sometimes debating which one was "more Islamic." Just as often, volunteers would disrupt political discussions at Resala: "Let's not talk politics here!"

In the meantime, volunteers at a different branch created a new activity called *tawʿiyya siyāsiyya* (political consciousness-raising), later renamed *taw ͑iyya insāniyya* (literally, "human consciousness-raising"). Piggybacking on the food distribution trips, the group organized mock elections in schools in slum neighborhoods where children could run as candidates and present an election platform, and their classmates voted. The group also invited Amr Hamzawy, a political scientist and human rights activist, and Ahmed Harara, a revolutionary icon who had lost his eyes during two different clashes with the security forces, to speak at Resala. Later, the group toned down its political language and instead began talking to people on the street about environmental issues, littering, and sexual harassment. Dr. Sherif, too, was increasingly careful to emphasize (as he had in the Mubarak era) that Resala did not engage in politics in any way.

When I last spoke to him, in August 2014, at a time of renewed and brutal oppression of the Muslim Brotherhood, the situation had become precarious. It now was crucial for the volunteers' safety to emphasize that they were not associated with any political group. The funds of Islamic NGOs such as al-Gam ͑iyya al-Shar ͑iyya had temporarily been frozen. Many claimed that Resala was secretly a Muslim Brotherhood organization, a dangerous accusation in the Sisi era. Donations had declined by a third, and rumors were going wild. A friend of mine claimed she had seen Dr. Sherif at the Muslim Brotherhood sit-in at Rabaa Square. Dr. Sherif knew of the rumor; someone had even shown him a photo, supposedly of him at the sit-in, but it was, he insisted, a different person. Other rumors held that weapons were being stored at Resala.

While Resala was battling these rumors, ironically Dr. Sherif also received pushback from the other side. Neighbors living next to the less conservative branches started complaining that "girls and boys work together in Resala kitchens," that it was an immoral organization. Dr. Sherif conceded that these were difficult times. He looked tired. But, he told me, he knows why he keeps going even though he could be arrested any day. "I do all this for God. This is my belief. I'm in this world only temporarily and I want to do something. God will protect us."

In a hostile political environment, his understanding of Islam lifts Dr. Sherif out of the murky terrain of worldly affairs. At first sight, the otherworldly renders Resala apolitical. The volunteers are not out to stage a revolution; they are collecting points for paradise. But the otherworldly is also empowering. Despite the state's threats and oppression, the worldly does not confine Dr. Sherif and the volunteers. They put this world in its place by evoking something that exceeds it.

We are behind schedule. We ran out of rice about an hour ago, and Muhammad had to hurry to a nearby store to buy two more bags. Now, finally, the cooking is done. We scoop the remaining rice onto the plates, add burgers, and pass the plates to Karim, who is handy with the plastic wrap machine. He deftly cajoles the old and moody machine, sealing each plate in plastic wrap and handing them to Yusuf, who divides them into piles of ten and counts them repeatedly. Heba joins them in the hallway and puts each pile into a black plastic bag. By now, more volunteers have arrived. The secretary shows up with a new sheet to take down the information of those who have come for "distribution" (*tawzī'a*). At around 4:30 P.M., we're told it is time to go. We carry the bags down to the street, where a bus is waiting.

The bus, which can seat around fifty people, belongs to Resala; the organization's name is written on both sides, as well as its slogan: "The joy of giving" (*mut'a al-'atā'*). The driver is an elderly man who is employed by the organization. He is remarkably patient. He will have to put up with the noise of adolescent exuberance—shouting, lecturing, laughing—while navigating the bus through overcrowded streets and later through narrow, unpaved alleys. He will wait on the bus while the volunteers distribute the meals. A young woman who is worried about her curfew asks him what time we will be back. He says, "Only God knows. It depends on whether God opens the way for us."

The volunteers rarely manage to stick to the official schedule. Sometimes, like this afternoon, they run out of food while cooking. Or, just as we are about to take off, the afternoon call to prayer is heard, and volunteers insist they need to pray first. Or volunteers who have been fasting run out to buy bean sandwiches or bags of chips so they can break their fast on the bus after sunset. (They would never eat the food they cook for the poor, not because they think they are better than the poor, but because, they insist, the food "does not belong to [them].")

Eventually we get going. A young man recites the travel prayer (*du'ā' al-safr*); everyone repeats after him. Usamah, in his mid-twenties, soft-spoken, with a round, boyish face, gets up to invite newcomers to "like" the Facebook page and upload pictures, and to ask them to bring along friends next time ("Resala doesn't need donations; it needs people."). Then follows a religious lesson (*dars*), just like every time.

Today's is given by Ahmed, who is playfully but also respectfully addressed as "shaykh" despite his young age. He stands in the front of the bus. His voice is warm but loud and clear. Many of the volunteers admire his learning and religious commitment. When others present a lesson on the bus, some of the volunteers prefer to chat, nap, or slip on their headphones and listen to music. But Ahmed is skilled at capturing everyone's attention. At times he interrupts his sermon-like speech to ask questions. When a male volunteer answers, he smiles at him warmly. When a woman puts up her hand, he calls on "our sister" while ostensibly averting his gaze.

His lesson begins with a popular topic: gossip. Ahmed explains the difference between talking about someone who is absent (*ghība*) and hearing something about someone and repeating it (*namīma*). Both are bad. Then he discusses what to do when one overhears someone else gossiping. You can walk away, or you can tell them that what they are doing is wrong.

There is nervous laughter on the bus. Volunteers sometimes chide each other for gossiping, but they find it difficult to break the habit. The topic is a perennial favorite for these bus lessons because it offers an example of how the most mundane social interaction can weigh heavily in one's otherworldly account. Listening to Ahmed, I wonder how many of the nodding volunteers will apply the lesson and try to alter their behavior. Piety is difficult, and it is a full-time job.

Traffic is slow, and it will be a while before we reach our destination. Ahmed turns to a different topic. He asks: Why are we going to the slums to distribute food? "To make the poor smile," says one volunteer. "To do good" (*khayr*), says another. "Because these are difficult times," says a third. Yes, answers Ahmed, "all that is true, but what is the most important intention [*niyya*]? It's not doing good, and it's not helping the poor. The most important intention is doing all this for God." He reminds the volunteers that Christians do charity too; he says authoritatively that nearly all Christians volunteer and donate 10 percent of their income to charitable causes. Buddhists, too, help those in need. So how is what we are doing any different? He doesn't wait for an answer: "It's human nature [*fitra*] to help. So how is what we [Muslims] do any different from what Christians do? We don't do *khayr* just because it's good. We do it for God [*li-llāh*]. We do it because God wants us to do this."

Ahmed concludes that we should dedicate the trip entirely to God. We should say, "I do this for You and because of You" (*līk wa ʿashānak*). The volunteers' labor is a gift to God, but they also should remember that they are on that Resala bus only because God put them there; it is always already written (*maktūb*) who will join these trips. The volunteers can't take credit but they can still hope for a divine reward. Doing so is only human.

In the volunteers' transactions with God, the poor are the medium, somewhat akin to their role as a "visa into eternity" in Catholic economies of salvation (Scherz 2014:78). And precisely because we need the poor, says Ahmed, we ought to treat them well.

> The poor don't need us. God deprived them of things on earth so they will get [these things] in paradise. The poor will all be in paradise. So if you help someone today, an old woman or man, someone hungry, when the time comes, you'll find them taking you by the hand and leading you into paradise. They don't need us but we need them.

Hadiths promise that the poor will enter paradise forty (or five hundred) years ahead of the rich. Another well-known hadith reports that the Prophet Muhammad said, "I looked into paradise and I saw that the majority of its people were poor." (Notably, the thousands of young women who volunteer at Resala, partially driven by the hope for a place in paradise, seem to ignore how the hadith continues: "And I looked into Hell and I saw that the majority of its people were women.") For people like myself, shaped by a profound attachment to *this* world, the emphasis on the poor's place in paradise is difficult to swallow. It seems to rationalize poverty, almost rendering it into something enviable, and as Egypt's socialist president Gamal Abdel Nasser suggested in the 1960s, it seemingly undermines the poor's right for a share in *this* life.[17] But as I look around me on the bus, I remember that despite *and* because of their attachment to paradise, these young men and women are spending hours every week cooking and distributing meals to those in need. They insist that the poor don't need us, and at the same time—and for the same reason—are deeply invested in meeting the needs of the poor.

By now, we have entered the slum. The bus slows, navigating a maze of alleys crowded with pedestrians, mopeds, and potholes. Eventually the bus stops. It is getting dark. Ahmed ends his lesson, and we get off the bus, huddling together until we are told what to do next.

HIERARCHY OF INTENTIONS

Volunteering is on the rise around the globe.[18] And that, says Dr. Sherif, is a good thing.

It is the summer of 2014, and we are at a so-called Mini-Camp, a daylong event for new volunteers, where Dr. Sherif explains Resala's history and mission. He is full of energy, has a contagious smile, wears jeans and a Resala T-shirt, and, after his lecture, patiently poses with volunteers for countless shots that will later appear on Facebook. His lectures are funny, entertaining, and motivational.

Resala volunteers accomplish amazing things, says Dr. Sherif, telling a number of stories that are received with enthusiastic applause. One is the story of a blind man from Alexandria who contacted Dr. Sherif to thank him because "[he] couldn't have finished [his] PhD without Resala." He needed books that were only available at Cairo University. None of his relatives was able to take him, and so he called one of Resala's offices in Cairo. Volunteers picked him up at the train station, and fifteen different volunteers spent three days with him at the library. They finished what would have normally taken him a year. Similar stories of gratitude abound. Another story makes the volunteers laugh: a man phoned Resala and said that he was lonely, that no one ever visited him. "Can't you send someone?" Two weeks later he called again and said that's enough: "I can't cope with that many visits anymore!"

Dr. Sherif knows how to keep his audience engaged. Some stories make the volunteers feel good about themselves; others remind them that they should try even harder. Like this one: a volunteer used to take care of a blind man who was suffering from kidney failure. Three times a week, he picked him up, drove him to the hospital, stayed with him for six hours of dialysis, and took him back home. One day the old man slipped, broke a bone, and had to be put in a cast. The hospital staff asked the volunteer for the man's full name. He said he only knows him as Shaykh so-and-so. The hospital staff, who had seen the volunteer come in day after day, couldn't believe it. "You're not his son? Not a relative?" In the end they called him "an angel from heaven" (*malak min al-samā'*). From that day on, whenever the volunteer and the old man came to the hospital, they let them sit in the director's air-conditioned office, and they treated the volunteer like a king.

Dr. Sherif emphasizes that everyone has the ability to do something; everyone can be an angel from heaven. "You like cooking? Join the *it'ām* team. You know English? Teach free English classes. You have blood? [*'andak damm*, which also means "Are you a decent person?"] Donate some!"

Walking the volunteers through a PowerPoint presentation, Dr. Sherif explains that voluntarism is "true religiosity" (*tadayyun sahīh*), "true nationalism" (*wataniyya sahīha*), and "true humanism" (*insāniyya sahīha*). The effects of volunteering are equally multilayered. The point of Resala's Big Brothers Big Sisters program (inspired by the U.S. program of the same name) is to help orphans feel that they belong to a family. But often what is good for those in need, he explains, turns out to be good for society too: "Someone might be poor and live under the stairs, but if they have a family, they won't turn into bad people." So, helping an orphan brings with it multiple benefits: "You assure yourself a place in paradise; you protect the orphan from becoming a criminal; and you protect Egypt from thugs." In Dr. Sherif's stories, the volunteers benefit, and so do the recipients. You reduce crime while at the same time helping the poor. You make this world a better place while simultaneously building your house in paradise. In conversations among the volunteers, these multilayered benefits are echoed but also become hierarchized, adding an extra layer of piety.

Newcomers might join Resala for all kinds of reasons—wanting to help the poor, to make friends, or even to find a marriage partner—but over time they are taught how to align, redirect, and prioritize their intentions. They learn how to put God first. Of course, regardless of how much you focus on God and the afterlife, the poor do not become invisible. There are times when volunteers go into a slum with the intention of collecting divine rewards and end up breaking down in tears when confronted with the material realities of poverty.

LATE AFTERNOON

We are standing next to the bus. Usamah reminds us of some of the rules: Don't wear sunglasses or headsets. Don't talk politics. Never comment in front of people on how they live. If you smell something bad, or a dog comes close to you, don't say anything; don't scream. Don't take pictures. No joking between girls and boys. And don't give away meals randomly.

The number of meals has carefully been calculated and counted (ten meals per each plastic bag), and the total number of meals matches the number of families that have been chosen as recipients, one meal per each family member. Often people who are not on the official list ask for food, or a family will ask for extra meals. Going against his own instructions, Usamah will later hand one meal to an old man sitting on the ground in an alley, and he will give two extra meals to a woman who says she has four children to feed and no income. As it turns out, we will still have enough meals. As volunteers often told me, despite being carefully calculated and counted, the number of meals can miraculously increase thanks to divine *baraka*.

At Resala, the miraculous coexists with the bureaucratic. Whereas the volunteers on the "distribution team" generally do not worry about who is at the receiving end, the question of which families should receive meals, and how many, was answered earlier by an "exploration" (*istikshāf*) team of volunteers that visited homes in the neighborhood. They ask questions, take detailed notes, count how many appliances families have, and keep an eye on whether they seem to spend money on what Resala sees as useless things, such as cigarettes. These volunteers usually collaborate with someone from a smaller Islamic charity organization, typically in the neighborhood or nearby, which has a better sense of the area. Today that same local organization has sent two guides: a woman who wears *niqāb* and seems to have intimate knowledge of the entire neighborhood; and Shaykh Hamid, a short man in *gallābiyya,* whom the volunteers know from previous trips and do not seem particularly fond of.

I am in Shaykh Hamid's group. He leads us through the neighborhood, pointing to homes, instructing us how many meals to drop off. Because about thirty volunteers have come along, more than are needed, each volunteer gets to carry and distribute only one bag with ten meals. The rest of the trip the volunteers simply walk along. Four young women congregate around me and practice their German ("Gute Nacht," "Ich liebe dich"). Later, when I fall behind, they make sure to bring me back into their midst. It's safer, they say.

We pass a ping-pong table in an alley. A dozen kids run circles around it, swatting the ball back and forth with their hands. More kids, playing soccer. Young men riding motorbikes through the narrow alleys. Two teenagers painting a familiar slogan on a wall with red paint: "Raise your head up high, you're Egyptian." Women selling bags of chips from makeshift stands and overturned crates.

"Third floor, to the left," says Shaykh Hamid, pointing to a building's low entrance, "two meals." We keep moving, knocking on doors, entering homes, always in groups of two, cell phones lighting the way on dark staircases. The visits are brief. A damp room with an old woman lying on a mattress. A room with a woman sitting on the floor, two children sleeping on a bed. A communal squat toilet in a tiny bathroom just outside her door. An elderly woman sitting in the dark; a cell phone flashlight briefly illuminates the room; someone gives her a meal. Next room. Again a woman on the floor, three children next to her. The room is empty except for a half-broken wheelchair and a few blankets. On to the next place, a blind man's home. Then a paralyzed woman, maybe in her early twenties. Glimpses of poverty. Stills.

Resala volunteers distributing meals. Photograph by Yomna Magdi.

No story, no narrative, other than someone whispering, "No one asks about her!"

As they hand over the meals, some volunteers say, "May each year be good for you" (*kull sana w-inti tayyiba*), a saying exchanged on joyous occasions of all kinds. Most people accept the meals without saying a word. No one asks who we are except for one deaf woman who gestures: "Where is this from?" In response, Ahmed points to heaven. In line with the idea that what they receive is really their God-given right, few recipients thank the volunteers. Some ask for more food, and occasionally people complain about our system of distribution. As we turn away from the entrance to one building, a woman leans out from a window across the narrow alley and yells at us that the people who just received meals from us are in fact well off (*nās nās*, literally "people of people").

We keep walking until at some point Shaykh Hamid overlooks a hole in the ground, falls, and injures his leg. A young woman next to me mumbles that this happened because he is unkind. He had been telling the volunteers to move more quickly, and he was impolite with the recipients. He fails to understand, she says, that "what we're giving to these people is actually their right" and that "it's not enough to give to them; *how* we give matters too." A woman from the area who must have overheard us comes closer and agrees that the accident was a form of divine punishment. She whispers that Shaykh Hamid always gives to the same people; he is unjust. Later I hear the rumor that he guides volunteers to families who previously paid him. We finish our rounds without Shaykh Hamid as best as we can.

Although (or because) trips into the slums can be difficult, some volunteers see them as a form of entertainment. Stepping over large rocks and heaps of garbage, Yasmin, a young unemployed graduate from a tourism institute, jokes to me, "Here you have your safari!" Others struggle. Aya, a first-year college student, is new to Resala. We are in middle of the slum, facing a half-collapsed house, next to it a mountain of garbage, covered with cats looking for food. A dog with a missing leg walks by. Suddenly Aya bursts into tears. She joined Resala because she liked their TV ads. She was not prepared for this. She cries into her friend's shoulder and is told to pull herself together. "Don't cry in front of the people here!" Someone instructs her to go back to the bus but she insists on finishing the rounds. Later, on the bus, she starts crying again, and another volunteer confirms that it is hard to go into the slums, especially the first time: "There's a difference between knowing slums exist and seeing them!" During the bus ride back, Aya's roommate probes her: "What about the rice in the student dorm?"

"*Tuhfa!*" (Amazing!), exclaims Aya.

"What about the rooms in the dorm?"

"*Tuhfa!* I'll never complain again!"

Face-to-face encounters with the urban poor leave emotional traces but these traces, too, can be folded back into a divine economy. The lesson then becomes one of gratitude. The volunteers remind each other of how much they have. They remind each other to stop complaining and to thank God for His blessings (*ni 'ma*). Each blessing, in turn, is an obligation: to share what one has with those in need, to give back to God by way of giving to the poor. And maybe, just maybe, the volunteers will be rewarded in turn.

TRADING WITH GOD

When Dr. Sherif speaks of divine rewards, he tends to emphasize rewards in *this* world (*thawāb fil-dunyā*). "You only need to take one step, and God will help you," he says. At the Mini-Camp he cites a Quranic verse that promises that God will pay back ten times what you have given.[19] Then he recalls how a young man told him once that after donating to Resala, he received a

100-pound bonus at work. Dr. Sherif asked him how much he had donated. The man said, 20 pounds. Playing with the idea of a tenfold reward (and seemingly binding God to a contract with predictable revenues), Dr. Sherif joked: "They cheated him! He should have received 200 pounds as a bonus!"

Another story Dr. Sherif likes to tell is about a woman struggling with infertility for ten years, who one day decides to go to Resala to help distribute food in a slum, with the intention of doing so purely for God. On the way home she receives a phone call and learns she is pregnant. The point of this story is not only that God rewards believers already in this world. It is also that one is rewarded precisely when expecting no reward. Dr. Sherif notes that he has told this story many times already but that by now, two more women have reported equally miraculous pregnancies. He says he used to joke: "If you want to get pregnant, do something good [khayr]. If you want to pass an exam, do something good. But it turns out, it's not a joke! We should begin charging. Exam: this-and-that much; pregnancy: this-and-that much."

In these stories, divine rewards seem predictable. God appears rather close; someone you can trade with, someone you can rely on. If volunteers do this-and-that, they will be rewarded by this-and-that. The volunteers' laughter at these stories seems to combine the joy at God's closeness with the implicit acknowledgment that in the end, despite the Quran's own commercial language, God's rewards remain unpredictable.

When it comes to paradise, time is less linear. The volunteers hope to eventually end up in paradise but they are also already on their way to paradise. Posters at Resala call distribution trips to villages "caravans to paradise," and they invite future volunteers with the promise that in exchange for volunteering, they "receive the keys to [their] house in paradise" (istaslam muftāh baytak fi al-ganna) and "become one of the Prophet's neighbors in paradise."

Ahmed, in one of his lessons, reminds the volunteers,

> There is a hadith that says that someone went to paradise for having given water to a dog. Someone else went to hell for not having fed a cat. And those are a cat and a dog! Now imagine us, giving food to people. This is our gate to paradise!

While engaged in the worldly, social, and material act of giving food to the poor, the volunteers learn how to continuously redirect their attention to God and to the afterlife. They learn that the more they tire themselves out, the more divine rewards they gain. Labor is exchanged for points. One

"Caravans to Paradise," poster at Resala. Photograph by the author.

afternoon a volunteer invites me to scoop rice onto plates: "Take some points!" (*khudi thawāb*), she says, handing me the spoon. A young man is instructed to move a big pot from the stove: "Lift it, and God will lift your sins" (*shil wa rabbinā hayshīl zunūbak*). A woman burns her hand on the stove and is assured that she will receive extra rewards; she answers *yā rabb!* (I wish!; literally, "Oh God!"). When, during a prayer break in one of the slums, I tell a volunteer that I don't want to enter the mosque because I forgot to bring a scarf, she tells me that for that intention alone I will receive the same rewards that I would have received for having worn a scarf.

The math can be dizzying. Keeping track of one's points often involves addition. Handing out ten meals is presumably twice as good as handing out five. But God can also multiply rewards. A young woman skips the prayer one day in order to lend her wide blouse to a woman who is dressed in only a T-shirt but wants to pray. She is told that she will receive the same rewards she would have received if she herself had prayed. I can get points for something someone else does if I enabled her to do it. My effort does not take away from her points; God simply doubles the rewards. Other times, it seems to be a zero-sum game. There is the sense, at such moments, that the total supply of points—unlike God himself—is limited, rather than limitless. For this reason, more experienced volunteers keep a close eye on how many meals each volunteer distributes in the slums. Sometimes the concern with paradise leads to cooperation. Other times it leads to competition.

The logic of *thawāb* implies that it is somewhat unimportant *what* you do as long as your deeds lead to divine rewards. You can pray extra prayers or you can distribute meals in a slum. The needs of the poor are not the primary focus of, or rationale for, volunteering. There are times when the volunteers are so focused on God—or so focused on their own version of trying to be pious— that they don't see what is in front of them. Shaykh Salah tells a story about a group of several dozen Resala volunteers that once arrived at the Sayyida Zaynab mosque, each carrying a broom. He asked what they were doing. They said they wanted to clean the mosque. He told them that the mosque owns vacuum cleaners, but the volunteers went ahead anyway. Preoccupied with paradise, they forgot to ask what kind of help was needed in this world.

EVENING

We are on the bus again, heading back to Resala. The woman sitting next to me asks for my phone number; another asks if I'm on Facebook. We're inter-rupted by Usamah, who calls for everyone's attention. He asks what the vol-unteers liked about the trip and what could be improved. A young woman complains that the distribution was unfair. She saw people who looked much poorer and did not receive any food. "We didn't bring enough food; there was far more need." Someone notes that on the way into the slum, we passed by a group of construction workers who asked what we were doing; to be polite, we should have given them food. "But they work," another volunteer responds. "It's better to give to those who have nothing." A high school stu-dent who received a concerned call from her mother says we should try harder to stick to the schedule.

Usamah responds: "We tried our best. It will never be 100 percent right." Then, as the bus enters heavy traffic, and as if to shift our attention from human shortcomings to divine provisions, he tells a story: One time he went to a poor neighborhood to help assess the needs of local families. They met an old man with a disabled child. The man made and sold falafels but was very poor. His wife complained to the volunteers that when he makes a few pounds, he gives them to his widowed neighbor for her children. The volunteers were so impressed that they collected money among themselves and gave it to the man, but he passed the donation on to his neighbor. "My provision [*rizqī*] is not in your hands," he said. "I ask only God for help." The story moved everyone on the bus. One of the women who had previously complained looked at me with tears in her eyes.

The man in this story orients himself solely toward God, and so, the story implies, should the volunteers. This orientation can mean caring for others or turning away from others, or both at once. The story made me wonder about the pious man's wife and disabled child. The volunteers, too, are sometimes uncertain about what their piety means for their kin relations. Joining Usamah in the front of the bus, Ahmed now tells a story that speaks to the question of competing moral obligations:

> One month ago, a young man joined us for the first time. He was so impressed by the "charitable caravan" that he said from now on he'd join us every week. But he didn't come the following Friday. Why not? Because seeing old people in the slum whom he didn't know reminded him that despite all his respect and love for them, he ought to visit his parents the following week. They live in the countryside. And he said he wouldn't go the way he usually does, asking them to make food, bring him tea, and so on, but he'd see them with new eyes. Usually he's too embarrassed to kiss his mother's hand, but this time he'd kiss her feet, and he'd kiss his father's feet too.

The story addresses an issue many volunteers struggle with: do they owe special deference to their parents, or should they devote all their energy to volunteering? The consensus seems to be that those close by, and one's parents in particular, are more important than the remote poor. But such hierarchies of concern are rarely stable. What, for instance, if one's family happens to be uninterested in piety? On a different occasion, Ahmed explained that while one should always be polite and respectful, it is crucial to surround oneself with people who continuously orient themselves toward God. He presented a hypothetical dilemma: what if you're invited to a wedding at which pop music will be played, women and men will dance together, and women will be dressed in provocative clothes? His solution: you offer your congratulations by phone but don't go. If it is the wedding of a close relative, you go briefly and then excuse yourself. In order to live piously, you need to surround yourself with the right people and engage in the right activities. The volunteers' piety, then, can direct them away from their nuclear families. It might even make them feel superior. Ultimately, what matters most, in Ahmed's view, is our duty to God.

As we get closer to the Resala branch, Ahmed reminds us once again that continuously orienting our lives toward God is absolutely essential. After all, we do not know how long we will live. He recently saw a microbus that had gotten into an accident. All the passengers died. "Young people like us, twenty to twenty-five years old." As often happened in Ahmed's lessons, stories of sudden, unexpected death serve as a reminder that we ought to commit to pious practice right now, this very second.

> It's not OK to say I'll study, then find a job, get married, settle down, and when I'm sixty years old, I'll get to know God. It might be too late! We should live as if we'll live forever—we should all have ambitions, that's a good thing—but we should work for the afterlife as if we'll die tomorrow—and that is what we usually neglect.[20]

Ahmed concludes with an image of hell. "Look, it's hard to fast for a day during Ramadan, right? Now imagine spending fifty thousand years standing up, and it's hot. Can you do that?" The image is tame compared to some of the more graphic images of hell the tradition offers up: sinners clothed in rags of fire or boiling copper, forced to eat bricks of fire, or suffering from massively swollen bellies; rich people who have shown off their generosity punished by being dragged over the ground on their faces. But the thought of standing for fifty thousand years seems to do the trick.[21]

With images of road accidents and hell on our mind, we get off the bus, the men first, then the women. The good-byes are quick. It's late, and to get home, the volunteers will need to take multiple microbuses, a cheap means of transportation that traverses all of Cairo.

"See you next week," says Aya.

"God willing," I answer.

Mona says, "May God bless you" (*rabbinā yakrimik*).

Ahmed politely waits until everyone is off the bus but he does not address the volunteers. Instead he addresses God, asking Him to accept what we have done (*taqabbal*).

THE AFTERLIFE IS NOW

"Start with yourself" (*ibda bi-nafsik*) was a widely resounding slogan after the Egyptian uprising. Don't look to the government. Start with the little things. Don't throw garbage in the streets, don't gossip, be polite, help others. Resala rhetoric emphasizes this too: you can make a change and put a smile on some-one's face. Just as important, you are responsible for your fate in the afterlife. Ultimately, you will face God alone. Keenly aware of the responsibility this entails, Resala volunteers are pious entrepreneurs. They take their other-worldly fate into their hands and keep close count of their good deeds.

Young men and women join Resala for all kinds of reasons but, in some branches at least, they learn over time that the purest, most pious intention is to dedicate all one's volunteering efforts, and in fact, one's entire life, to God. It is to let *li-llāh* override all other intentions. A bit less pure but maybe more human is to direct all one's worldly actions toward a place in paradise. Many of the volunteers hope for a divine countergift—secretly or explicitly, humbly or with exigency. The constant evocation of paradise marks volun-teers as pious, as striving.

By joining Resala, the volunteers enter a dense web of temporalities, one in which they might gain some sense of control over their future (by passing a difficult exam, or finding a marriage partner), and in which they infuse the present moment with meaning by connecting it to the afterlife. Paradise is all at once: located in the future, outside of time, and intertwined with the cur-rent moment. In many texts of the Islamic tradition, the boundary between this world and the otherworld is described as thin, if not permeable. Stories report how people (including the Prophet Muhammad) have traveled to the otherworld and back, and how certain objects, liquids, sounds, and smells move between the two worlds. Pomegranates contain at least one seed from paradise; snakes and scorpions shuttle back and forth between earth and hell. In this sense, paradise is not only what happened a long time ago during the lifetime of Adam and Eve, and what will happen in a world to come. It is always already present (Lange 2016).[22]

Paradise's nonlinear temporality—suspended between the here and now and the afterlife—runs counter to revolutionary and counterrevolutionary ideas of improvement that rely on a linear this-worldly sense of tomorrow. This results in a different way to act in the present. In reaching to overturn the world, revolutionaries sometimes end up ignoring the world right before their eyes. In contrast, the work of the pious volunteers is repetitive and monotonous. It has no grand political scaffolding, no desire to overturn the world. Indeed, it is not even all that concerned with this world. And yet, ironically, in their orientation toward God, the volunteers address pressing needs in the here and now, day after day. They do so not always successfully (recall the army of volunteers arriving with brooms at a mosque that owns vacuum cleaners), but they do so very persistently. The almost-purposeful overlooking of the recipients can be painful to watch; it instrumentalizes the poor. But it also frees the recipients from the burdens of charity.

When they give, Resala volunteers are driven by duty and calculation. But while refusing an ethos of compassion (compassion is for Christians!), they are no heartless robots. Their relationships to the slum residents are shot through with emotions even though emotions are not what initiates or organizes these relationships. While looking toward a beyond, the volunteers inhabit a material world. Sizzling cooking oil burns their hands; they breathe the stuffy air in the kitchen; they stumble over the uneven ground in the slums; their eyes scan the cramped rooms and the squat toilets shared by dozens of people; their ears hear barking dogs, the recipients' silence, and their occasional, though rare, outbursts of gratitude. While looking to God, praying to God, and dedicating all their actions to God, the volunteers still live on what Mike Davis (2007) calls the "planet of slums." It is through and because of their God-orientedness that they come face to face with the material reality of poverty, a reality that many middle- and upper-class Egyptians try to escape by moving to gated communities and satellite cities (Sims 2015).

The Egyptian philosopher Hassan Hanafi once wrote that the kind of thought that could help Islam overcome its modern predicament would be "concerned with life rather than with death, with living people in urban areas in big cities, such as Cairo, and not with those in the grave."[23] The volunteers might respond that being concerned with death *is* being concerned with life. Thinking about the grave means dealing with, and giving to, the poor. The way up to paradise leads down into the slums.

Receiving

FOUR

———————

Performances of Poverty

DURING RAMADAN, STREET CLEANERS MULTIPLY MIRACULOUSLY.
At least that is what Madame Salwa tells me. Or, I should say, she didn't
really *tell* me, not the way you tell an anthropologist-friend about the facts of
social life, in a reporting-kind-of-way. Rather, she yelled it at me, her voice
raised to a pitch usually reserved for expressions of moral outrage, like the
time she complained about the disorderly tent city at Tahrir Square ("You
know what happens in those tents at night!"), or, later, about the Muslim
Brotherhood camp at Rabaa Square, which she was able to observe from her
sister's balcony ("They shit anywhere, like animals!"). The miraculously mul-
tiplying street cleaners were equally upsetting. Because really it isn't a miracle.
It is the pragmatic exploitation of those with soft hearts, a show put on by
people too lazy to work.

In a taxi, crossing one of the main bridges that go over the Nile, Madame
Salwa pointed to a skinny elderly man in an orange uniform. For about thirty
seconds, he would sweep the street halfheartedly; then he would stop, still holding the broom in his left hand, and extend his right hand to cars passing by.
Traffic was slow but hardly anyone stopped. I could feel Madame Salwa shift
into agitation: every Ramadan there are thousands of street cleaners. Most of
them merely pretend. You can buy a street cleaner's uniform cheaply in the
bustling downtown markets of ʿAttaba; some beggars rent the uniform for the
month. Fake street cleaners try to take advantage of a seasonally enhanced
charitable spirit. They extend their hands on every bridge and every street.

Madame Salwa paused, her breathing heavy with frustration.

The taxi driver agreed: "They come out by the thousands!"

Long after we had passed the bridge, far down the Corniche, Madame
Salwa was still complaining that many people merely pretend to be poor, that

fake beggars often hide their wealth at home, and that "in Islam, if you have money, you ought to spend it and dress well; it's wrong to be rich and wear rags."[1] Madame Salwa was aggravated, and the taxi driver kept nodding.

The taxi driver did not know that Madame Salwa and I were ourselves on a charitable mission. We were heading to Islamic Cairo, where we were to cook about one hundred meals, using alms and Ramadan-specific donations that Madame Salwa had collected from relatives and friends. Every Ramadan, Madame Salwa spends days cooking and distributing meals to all who extend their hand. Her goal, just like that of Shaykh Salah and the Resala volunteers, is to give *li-llāh,* to God and for God. When distributing meals, she gives generously and for the most part indiscriminately. But that does not mean that she has no judgment about those at the receiving end. She feels bad for some (especially older men who have to stand in line and beg for food—men, notably, who do not look all that different from the street cleaner on the Nile bridge). Others she finds ungrateful, pushy, demanding. A couple of times each Ramadan, she loses her patience and tells the crowd that they do not deserve her gifts, or she warns them that she will take her charitable activities to a different neighborhood the following year.

Judging neighborhoods and individuals alike, that day Madame Salwa chose not to give to the man on the bridge, instead going into a rant about his undeservingness. What had gone wrong? In line with the Quranic logic of almsgiving, Madame Salwa says that she primarily gives to the poor (*al-fuqarā'*) and those in need (*al-masākīn*), along with orphans and sick children. She also likes to use the word *al-ghalāba,* which roughly translates into "downtrodden." The street cleaner simply wasn't downtrodden enough. He was deceitful rather than authentically poor. Or he wasn't the right kind of poor.

How, then, does one successfully perform one's poverty? When does suffering matter in an Islamic economy of giving that is organized around concepts of duty and rightful shares? What kind of labor is involved in crafting oneself into a worthy recipient? And what does it mean to have to rely on people like Madame Salwa, who seek to give "to God," an act for which they *need* the poor without necessarily feeling compassionate toward them? In short, what do Egypt's charitable economies look like from the receiving end?

As I sat in the taxi, listening to Madame Salwa berate the imposter street cleaner, I became acutely aware of the gulf between us and that man. Madame Salwa, like most of the givers I came to know, was remarkably, even shockingly, generous, giving a great deal of time and money and effort to the poor.

And yet, she remained at a distance from those she gave to. She already assumed that she knew everything she needed to know about their lives. She wanted to *give to* them, not *engage with* them. Sitting in the taxi, watching this man "clean," I realized that I had no idea what his life actually consisted of. And it would be difficult, if not impossible, to find out. I never saw that man again, and I never had a conversation with a beggar in Egypt that went beyond mumbled and formulaic exchanges. Speaking to those at the receiving end never got easier, no matter how often I tried.[2]

Which is why I felt so lucky, a few weeks later, when I met Amal. Not destitute and not a beggar, Amal nevertheless situates herself within the broad category of "the poor." Raising five children on her own, she lives in one of Cairo's slums. She relies on different forms of aid, ranging from microloans to tokens of support provided by charity organizations to gifts given by people who know her, including me. Amal knows that the poor are needed as part of a social and religious division of labor, but she also knows how easily they can be ignored. Herself a pious Muslim (though often too busy to keep up with the five daily prayers and the religious lessons she would like to attend), she knows about the different and sometimes seemingly contradictory ways in which the poor figure in the Quran, hadith, and sermons of Muslim preachers. On the one hand, Imam Ali is reported to have said, "If poverty were a man, I would kill him"; the Quran says it is Satan who threatens you with poverty, and a hadith says that *giving* is better than *receiving*.[3] Seemingly, then, poverty is bad. On the other hand, the poor are assured a place in paradise, and hadiths predict severe punishments in the hereafter for those who hoard. So maybe wealth is bad; poverty is good?

While their spiritual status is ambiguous, the poor are indispensable to Egypt's charitable economies. Amal's story draws this dynamic into view. She is frank, outspoken, critical, and cynical, and tells her story to anyone who cares to listen. Her inexhaustible narrativizing never quite works, or works a little bit sometimes but not other times, and often falls short. But her ability to narrate (and to draw others into her narrations) is one of the only resources she has available to her. She puts these skills to work to support herself and her five children. Because she depends on NGOs and the goodwill of individual donors, Amal is a "case," or tries to be one.

In retelling her story, I run the risk of turning Amal into a case yet again, or, to be more precise, a case study—the example of a recipient. I recognize the dangers of voyeurism and sentimentalism, of reducing people to their suffering (Robbins 2013), but I also believe that painting Amal's portrait in brighter colors would constitute its own form of violence. In the context of this study, more significantly, it would mean going along with a pious economy that gives to the poor while intently looking away from them. Subject to "humanitarian reason" as I am, I do not want to be complicit in the sweeping erasure of "the poor" that comes with a foregrounding of God. Instead, I try to hold God and the poor in the same frame.

Sometimes Amal herself foregrounds God and decenters the agency of her fellow humans, instead defaulting to a complete reliance on God's all-consuming goodness. Instead of simply blaming the government, she calls upon God to "help the government help those in need." After having been turned away by an NGO one too many times, she says that from now on she will only ask God for help (*batlub min rabbinā bass*). She calls upon God to "destroy her husband's house" (*rabbinā yikhbrib baytu*), and she says that when people are unjust, they don't know God (*da mish ʿārif rabbinā*). In all these expressions, God is the ultimate arbitrator and source of justice. Amal knows that in the Islamic tradition, helping those in need is a divinely pre-scribed duty. She knows that the well-off *need* the poor as their "gate to para-dise," and she knows that the Quran imposes upon them the duty to dedicate part of their wealth to the poor. But she also knows that in order to receive her divinely ordained share, she needs to show that she is the right kind of poor. She knows that while relying on God, she inevitably relies on people.

THE ART OF GETTING BY

I first met Amal on a Saturday afternoon in October 2011. I was in the kitchen at Resala, where cooks more experienced than I am were busy cooking. I was standing around, trying to look busy, and answering volunteers' questions: "Do you live by yourself? Do you cook? What is typical German food like? Which is better: Germany or Egypt?" I don't know if it was the all-too-familiar questions, the oil-heavy air, or general fieldwork fatigue, but I was in a bad mood that day. I thought of leaving early, but then Amal walked in, dressed in a black ʿabāya, a traditional long overcoat worn by women from low-income backgrounds. She was accompanied by her ten-year-old son Shihab. Making eye contact with me, she seemed to understand immediately that I didn't quite belong. She began talking to me, and quickly drew me into her story. She was older than the other volunteers, closer to my age, and she was very blunt. Talking to her was a refreshing change from the usual chitchat at Resala.

A few minutes later, while scooping rice onto Styrofoam plates, Amal was telling me she has five children and is raising them on her own. She worries every day about how to get food on the table. Besides volunteering, she is also a registered "case" (*ḥāla*) at Resala, and even though she likes cooking with the volunteers, she hardly ever finds the time. That day she was planning to stay for only one hour, but when she learned where we were going to distribute the meals, she changed her mind: we were heading to Mit Uqba, her own neighborhood! And so, about two hours later, sitting next to Amal on the Resala bus, I went to Mit Uqba for the first time, a neighborhood less than a fifteen-minute walk from my apartment yet one I had barely known existed.

Mit Uqba is a poor area in the middle of Mohandeseen. The latter (literally, "engineers") is a neighborhood that was built on agricultural lands in the 1950s to offer cheap housing to engineers. Today real estate prices in Mohandeseen are among the highest in Cairo, and Arab League Boulevard, which runs through the neighborhood, is lined with expensive stores, supermarkets, and fast-food franchises. In the midst of Mohandeseen, but hidden from the visitor's view, lies Mit Uqba. It is commonly thought to have grown in defiance to the modern, organized neighborhood around it, but in reality, Mit Uqba is older. It grew out of a village that was surrounded by farmland until it was engulfed by the spread of tenements. From the roof of her building, Amal can see the wide streets of Mohandeseen; she can also see the 26th of July Corridor, the road that was built in 1999 to connect downtown Cairo with two of its satellite cities. The highway project resulted in the demolition of a large area with over four hundred apartments, and in the process, cut Mit Uqba into two halves.[4]

Having reached Mit Uqba, the Resala bus came to a halt, and we were received as usual by a guide from a local charity organization. We stopped at a neighborhood mosque, where about half the volunteers prayed while the rest of us, including Amal and me, lingered in the back. The guide then led us through the narrow alleys, directing us to the families to whom we were to deliver meals. I soon lost all sense of orientation. We knocked on door after door, never staying long. Aside from a group of children throwing rocks at us until they were shooed away, all seemed to be going smoothly. But then Amal started insisting that the people we were helping were not the ones most in need. She said she knows "cases" far worse off on the other side of the market. The local guide seemed uncertain, but Amal was very certain, so we ended up following her for a while. Eventually, the volunteers were grumbling that Amal's plan seemed random, but she was content. At least some of the people she knew had received a meal that day. To me, these people on the other side of the market did not look any worse off than the ones we had visited earlier. I could not help but wonder if Amal simply wanted to be seen doing *khayr* and giving favors to people on her street. It was not until later that I came to understand that this, too, is a survival strategy: to be seen as generous, a good person, by one's neighbors. This was less about giving to and receiving from God and more about the very human side of things. Amal knows all too well that if you give to others, you are more likely to receive help from them when you have no one else to lean on. At the same time, she actively inhabits an ethics that disrupts straightforward reciprocity; she is not troubled by being a recipient in relation to Resala, and an occasional donor in relation to her neighbors.[5]

We finished our rounds, the volunteers dissatisfied by how the trip had unfolded but, I think, glad to be done and to be heading home soon. It was getting late. Amal and I exchanged phone numbers. She and her son stayed behind; the rest of us got back onto the bus.

After that day, Amal and I talked a few times on the phone, and in the weeks and months that followed we met often in the evenings to stroll together. I became someone for Amal who listened to her seemingly endless stories of suffering with interest and patience. She, in turn, became my most knowledgeable and outspoken guide to Egypt's charitable economies as seen from the receiving end. Besides being a recipient, she is also an occasional giver, but she does not have the privilege of devoting herself fully to giving. She identifies with Egypt's poor, and, appreciative of the idea of fieldwork, she wanted me to grasp their world. "Each place has a story to tell," she used to say, taking me by the hand while leading me through Mit Uqba. She used the common term for slums (*'ashwā'iyāt*) to point to her neighborhood's many problems: collapsing houses, an insufficient garbage collection system, ground water and sewage accumulating in many older buildings that had sunk below street level. Amal describes the people in her neighborhood as poor, downtrodden, and forgotten. Like her, many of them spend much of their time in government offices and at NGOs, pleading their case again and again, performing their suffering, telling their stories, insisting they are poor—not any kind of poor but the kind that deserves to be helped.[6]

Amal's own story is one of social descent. She calls herself *bint nās* (the daughter of people); she comes from a well-to-do family, which, she says, makes her current life even more difficult to bear. She was born in Mit Uqba in 1973. She has a brother and two sisters. Her father was what she calls "financially able" (*muqtadir*). He worked as an employee in the Ministry of Local Development and also made money on the side. Amal describes him as a hardworking entrepreneur, someone very different from the beggars in Cairo's streets. Echoing a familiar work ethic, she recalls her father's restlessness:

> Nothing stood in our way. Things were very good, thank God. My father was an employee and he would take on additional jobs. Like, for example, when there was a house for sale, he would go and get information about it and try to sell it and get the commission. Or a car. He wasn't one of those people who just sit around and do nothing. As long as someone is walking in the path of God, God will help him. He didn't like to sit still. He always would say, why don't I go look for something to do?

Amal's father did not expect her to work but nevertheless encouraged her to learn a skill. After finishing high school, she studied weaving and fabric printing at the Technical Industrial Institute in Cairo. She graduated in 1992; that same year her father died. At first she did not look for work because she was certain that her father had provided for everything. He had been hard working but also generous, and by helping others, he had put the family under God's protection:

> We had everything, thank God. When my father was alive, I wasn't missing anything. My father used to help and support people . . . So thank God, maybe his good deeds are what supported us. Whoever does *khayr* gets what they deserve, and the same goes for people who do bad things. My father used to give and do good deeds. A lot of people have been behind me and supported me. All the good my father did stayed.

Gradually, however, things became difficult. Maybe, after all, Amal once mused, when her father died, the *khayr* went with him. Shortly after his death, Amal's mother claimed that the father had spent all their money. Amal had no choice but to believe her since her father had disliked banks and kept all his money at home. Amal started working and a few months later got married to a cab driver, with whom she had had a lengthy courtship. They lived happily for five years but then he began to disappear for days and nights. At first she thought he was cheating on her; then she realized he was spending all his income on gambling. By then they had three children. She began selling her jewelry to provide for them.

The husband stayed away for longer and longer periods. One time he was gone for eight months and returned for only one week before leaving again. During that week she got pregnant, and over the course of the next three years she had two more children. She kept on living off her savings and jewelry until she had nothing left. At that point she separated from her husband and went to live with her mother, planning to get a divorce. But even divorce was difficult; seeing a lawyer would have cost the equivalent of about $25. "Wouldn't I rather use that money to buy food for my kids?" she asked me wryly. At around the same time she realized that her mother had stolen her father's inheritance and given all the money (about $10,000) to her brother. She discovered her brother's name on a new building, which, she later learned, was one of many buildings he owned. She confronted him and demanded her share but he refused and began making her life unbearable.

It was her brother's avarice that led Amal to experience poverty, but she quickly came to identify with the poor at large. She insists that poverty is a structural problem, linked to corruption, unjust distribution, widespread unemployment, and rising food prices. Poverty, she says, means "feeling like you really need something and are unable to get it." It means "being unable to properly raise and educate one's children, to buy clothes and food for them, to make them happy." Amal says that poverty is nothing to be ashamed of. And there is one upside in her vision: her poverty is (only) a material condition; it does not signal spiritual poverty or what she calls "poverty of the self." At times Amal even claims that the rich envy the poor for their simple food—their bean sandwiches—presumably because simple food has *baraka* (blessings), but maybe also because wealth can be a burden and a trial (*ibtilā'*). And yet, behind Amal's expressions of pious content lies a keen sense of injustice. Like Shaykh Salah, who critiqued the state's unjust system of distribution, she criticizes the government's lack of commitment to sharing the country's revenues with its citizens: "In Egypt, one-fourth lives a good life and has fancy cars; the other 75 percent struggle. Egypt is not a poor country. It's a very rich country. We have oil. We have the Suez Canal. But the money never makes it to the people."

According to Amal, even the 2011 uprising, in which she participated, has not brought any improvement. About a year after Mubarak's ouster, she commented: "No one is eating. Most people can't find food. Children sleep in tears because of hunger. I see them in my street. There is no justice, no justice whatsoever." She reports that since 2011, even more Egyptians have fallen into poverty. More and more people are unemployed or are unable to make ends meet despite having a job, "depending on every piastre they make when they have work: bread crumbs."

Against this bleak backdrop, Amal continues looking for ways to cover her expenses. For a few years, she and her children lived rent free in an apartment in her paternal grandmother's house in Mit Uqba. She could only afford to furnish one room; the rest was not even painted. For transportation, Amal takes advantage of the cheap fares offered by the large informal microbus system that has mushroomed in Cairo since the mid-1970s. She tries to do errands by herself so as not to have to pay the extra fare for her children.

At the top of Amal's list of expenses is food. She is pragmatic and strategic, and goes for cheap items. Sometimes for breakfast she buys a quarter of a kilo of orzo (*lisān 'asfūr*) for one pound (less than 20 cents), cooks it with stock, and serves it to her children along with a pound's worth of bread. She knows how to make the most of the little she has. As food prices kept rising, more and more items became unaffordable for her. In 2014, she reported, "No one eats meat anymore. Now it's beans and falafel [*fūl wa ta'miyya*]. And lentils every day."

The second major source of expenses is school related. With four of her children in school, Amal needs to pay for uniforms, outfits for gym class, books, calculators, white board markers, geometry tools, and photocopying costs for monthly exam and answer sheets. On top of that, all children are expected to take private lessons.[7]

> If they don't take them, they get punished. Some of the teachers know about our circumstances, and they know that I can't afford lessons, so they don't punish the kids. Once a teacher was angry with Essam [Amal's oldest son] and failed him in English. I told him I can't afford lessons. He insisted that Essam needed them.

Essam was sitting with us, looking bored, but now he chimed in: "He said at the beginning of the year that whoever didn't take private lessons wouldn't pass the subject!" Amal continued:

> And, by the way, the lessons aren't even good. [The teacher] just comes and says a few words and leaves . . . You can't complain to the principal; he has an agreement with the teachers. You tell him that your children are being forced [to take private lessons], and he does nothing.

In the face of rising food prices and widespread corruption, Amal copes by cobbling together the money she needs. She receives 500 pounds (about

$85) each month from her father's pension, a state-guaranteed share that her family cannot deprive her of and one that presumably sets her apart from some of her neighbors. Sometimes she also gets support from charity organizations. Shortly after I met her, with assistance from Essam Sharaf's interim government and a microloan from Resala, she opened a kiosk (*kushk*), a small street corner store, selling cold sodas, bottled water, candies, chips, and lighters.[8] At first, the kiosk gave her a monthly income of about $65, most of which she spent on utilities, but quickly the kiosk became a burden. Business was slow, and Amal barely made what she needed to keep it going. She worked long hours, spending nights at the kiosk and taking turns with her older children, but she worried about their safety as the kiosk was surrounded by drug dealers catering to upper-class customers from Zamalek and Mohandeseen; the dealers, according to Amal, "are immune because they have made a deal with the police."

Eventually Amal gave up and began renting the kiosk to Khaled, her cousin's husband, who had moved to Cairo from Minya in Upper Egypt to search for work. But Khaled could barely make enough to pay the rent and electricity bills. Part of the problem, according to Amal, was that "the idea of the kiosk has spread. Now there are kiosks on every street!" And so, Khaled gave up too. When President el-Sisi came to power in June 2014, the state began going after minor transgressions, and things became even more difficult for small businesses. The woman who for years had been selling fruits and vegetables on the sidewalk next to the kiosk was forced to leave. Kiosks without a valid permit were shut down, including Amal's. Later she managed to get a new permit; this time she chose people to run the kiosk whom she calls "thugs," because "if *al-hayy* [the district administration] gives them any trouble, they will set *al-hayy* on fire!"

In the meantime, Amal kept looking for jobs. Earlier she had worked for a private company, serving coffee and tea to the employees, her toddler in tow. When I met her, she was hoping for a job cleaning houses or in a clothing factory. But she was cynical. Even after a minimum wage had been decreed for civil servants, private companies often paid less. "And even the minimum wage doesn't do anything," she said. "You can only live in Egypt if you hold a position [*mansib*]—if you're a minister or a director or something. And that only because you take bribes. The others can't survive."

Knowing that even a job would not ensure a livable income, Amal has become accustomed to asking for help.

"You want to see what *shu'ūn* is like? Meet me tomorrow at 9:30 A.M. in front of the fish restaurant."

I had heard much about Amal's arduous experiences in the Ministry of Social Affairs (*wizārat al-shu'ūn al-igtim'āiyya; shu'ūn* for short). She kept going back, despite her boundless frustration. I had wanted to see it in person since I met her.

"God willing," I said.

As in many other countries around the globe, the Egyptian government has been cutting back on its social services but nevertheless continues to be a place to which the poor turn to ask for assistance. What remains is the lingering promise of a caring state, despite the increasingly uncaring reality. That lingering promise is the reason why, when asked what "social justice" means, many activists continue to speak of a welfare state. And it is what leads Amal back to the Ministry of Social Affairs, again and again.

We met up a little after 10 A.M. in front of the fish restaurant, our usual spot on a busy thoroughfare that divides Mit Uqba from Mohandeseen. I asked how her morning was going. She casually responded that she had returned home from the kiosk at 7 A.M. after working all night (this was before she gave up on the project). She had rested for an hour, then made pasta for her children and sent the two older ones to the kiosk. I found myself hoping that Amal wouldn't ask about my morning: full night of sleep, a hot shower, about two hours sipping coffee and catching up on fieldnotes, then breakfast and a leisurely stroll to the restaurant. She didn't.

On the way to the Ministry of Social Affairs, we picked up a neighbor who was to testify to Amal's difficult circumstances, and who herself relies on help from governmental and nongovernmental sources. A widow raising her orphaned grandson, she had remarried in order to have someone who could take care of her and the child, but the husband, seventy years old, barely generated any income with his small store, tucked away in an alley in Mit Uqba. She joined us to support Amal but also to ask for help for her own family.

The *shu'ūn* building looked intimidating; a bureaucratic maze. But Amal knew where we had to go. We took an elevator up to the seventh floor, heading straight to the office responsible for Amal's neighborhood. The employee in the office knew Amal and seemed unhappy to see her. Amal explained her situation; she pulled back her veil to show how her skin had turned dark from working at the kiosk all day long. The employee began reading a newspaper. Amal kept talking. Eventually the employee looked up and explained to Amal that she was to blame for her problems because she had refused to sign government forms during a recent home visit by a representative from the office. Amal explained that she was afraid of signing anything because of the tricks her brother had played on her. The employee was already back in her newspaper. For the next ten or fifteen minutes Amal pleaded, cried, cursed her family, and then praised the *shu'ūn* "and all the people in it." The woman behind the desk seemed to register what Amal was saying but barely looked up.

Next, Amal elicited my help: "Amira, tell them what happened yesterday when we were walking." She almost fell, I said, aware that more drama was expected of me. Bodily signs—darkened skin, stumbling, tiredness, rings beneath the eyes—all these are put to work in the machinery of charity. I tried my best to play the part assigned to me, but I, too, stumbled.

The employee, a bit friendlier now, maybe because she had recognized that I was a foreigner, said she couldn't do anything. She suggested that Amal should find elders in the neighborhood (*nās kubbār*)—people who "know God" (*'ārfīn rabbinā*)—and ask them to reconcile (*sulh*) her with her brother without giving up her rights. It was clear that Amal would not receive any help from the office. What was less clear to me was whether this state representative thought that justice was indeed more likely to be found elsewhere, outside of the ruins of a welfare state, among people who "know God"—or whether she was simply tired of listening to Amal.

Either way, I wasn't surprised by the outcome. Neither was Amal. A few days earlier, she had described the rampant corruption in the office. Those wanting to be set up with a pension need personal connections to someone in the office, or they try to forge personal connections by giving gifts:

> Look, if you know someone in there, then they set you up with a pension the next day. If you don't, then there's absolutely nothing you can do. All the employees take bribes. I know people who give gifts to the employees. They give them car tires and I don't know what else, just to get set up with their pension. I see people who are well off and receive pensions but those who really need it don't get anything. To be honest, they only help their friends. They help each other and their families. An employee might help her brother's wife and her brother's wife's friend and the man in the same street as her brother's wife's friend and so on. They help each other. There are cases I see that don't deserve anything and they help them. For the poor they don't do anything.

Amal does not imply that the employees would not have any poor relatives. Here she uses "the poor" as a moral category: those who have no access to help; those who are forgotten or ignored. Amal's frustration is evident, though it might seem hypocritical. After all, she directed an entire bus of Resala volunteers to give food to her friends and neighbors. Yet for her there is no contradiction here. The care offered by the state should differ from an everyday ethics, in which one might well give special attention to those close by. Within a neighborhood, the moral thing might be precisely for a woman to give priority to her brother's wife and her brother's wife's friend. But honoring such relationships of proximity, if done by the institutions of the state, becomes corruption.

In Amal's view, it should be the state's priority to help the unemployed find work, offer free health care, and make sure no one lives in poverty. The state has a responsibility toward the poor. Sometimes she turns to history to make this point, to Egypt's socialist past under Gamal Abdel Nasser, or to ancient Egyptian and medieval times. Sitting by the kiosk one day, her youngest daughter asleep in my lap, she tells me: "Egypt could be the best country ever. Look, we built the pyramids when America didn't even exist yet. We have been great, and we could be great. There is lots of *khayr* in this country but some people on top are stealing from us." To recall a brighter past, she told me about the *bīmāristān,* a free hospital built by Ibn Tulun in the ninth century, where one could go, eat, and rest:

> They even had a section for psychological illnesses, and they would bring in an entertainer to cheer people up ... And when people were sick and recovered, they would give them a chicken and a piece of bread and see if they ate. If they did, it was a sign that they had recovered. This is how things should be.[9]

Sounding nostalgic and maybe naïve, Amal's account of a medieval past, similar to stories that are told about a more recent past at Tahrir Square, are best understood as a critique of the present. The contrast between past and present drives home the point that the current government does not care for its citizens. Amal had little faith in the government, both before and after 2011. But against all odds, she kept trying. Our visit to the *shuʾūn* was merely the latest in a long series of attempts.

After Amal realized that the employee was more interested in the newspaper than her story, the neighbor tried her luck. She was told that because of her husband's store, she was not entitled to permanent aid but at best a one-time token of support, for which she would need to apply in another office on a different floor. There she told her story again. I waited in the hallway with Amal, who went into a rant:

> How come Mubarak's sons were declared innocent? And he is taken to the hospital in a helicopter? And they accuse me of having some land and not having told them about it. Shouldn't the state be taking care of us? Shouldn't they be giving us an education? Shouldn't they feed us if we have nothing to eat?

About ten months had passed since Hosni Mubarak's ouster. The revolutionary enthusiasm had faded; I worried that Amal's rant might be audible to the employees. At the same time I wondered whether she was indirectly admitting to owning land she had not registered. Often Amal's stories did not match up. I was no longer irritated by these seeming inconsistencies. I had come to understand that the pressure to tell the right kind of story can be so insistent that a constant recrafting is the only sensible strategy.

PETITIONING CHARITY ORGANIZATIONS

From early on in Islamic history, direct giving seems to have played a bigger role than top-down measures. Consider this story about al-Mansur, the second Abbasid caliph, a story that takes us back about thirteen centuries: it begins with a bridge, like the story about Madame Salwa and the street cleaner. On the bridge are cripples, begging. A Byzantine emissary who has come to Baghdad sees them and says that al-Mansur should do something about them. A secretary responds that unfortunately, there are not enough resources. Al-Mahdi, who later will become the third Abbasid caliph, interrupts them. That is not the reason, he says. The real reason is that the caliph does not want to monopolize merit making. His subjects, too, should have a chance to gain rewards by giving.[10]

In this story, the ruler charitably passes on to his subjects the chance to be charitable. Maybe this is not all that different from George W. Bush, who centuries later on a different continent would declare that a "truly compassionate government" is one that rallies the "armies of compassion" in "churches and synagogues and mosques and charities."[11]

Amal, too, while not willing to let go of what she takes to be the state's responsibility, largely relies on private donations, whether received directly or channeled through charity organizations. In her view, the wealthy, just like the state, have obligations toward the poor:

> First, the simplest thing. God made Ramadan so the rich who eat well every day can feel how a poor person feels. [During Ramadan] people understand what it means to go hungry. Second, God gave the Prophet a choice. He could have had mountains of gold but he chose poverty ... If he had a guest, he would treat him very well ... Islam calls on people to help their brother, and God will help them. A true Muslim wouldn't let his neighbor sleep with an empty stomach. Whoever believes in God and Judgment Day should honor their neighbor. You give them whatever you can.

Amal frames poverty as a pious virtue (the Prophet *chose* poverty), and she echoes a common account of Muslims' moral obligations: to help the poor and to honor guests and neighbors. She grounds these obligations in the Prophet Muhammad's example and in the anticipation of Judgment Day. In her view, everyone should give whatever they can. *Zakāt,* obligatory almsgiving, according to her definition (which blends *zakāt al-māl* with *zakāt al-fiṭr*), means that the rich give to the poor, and the poor give to those who are even poorer.[12] I have seen Amal try to live up to this ideal, helping out beggars and street children as best as she can. Her volunteering with Resala, too, is an attempt to give despite not having much, usually in neighborhoods to which she has no personal connection.

But of course Amal's account is also an account of how things *should* be. Her own life has been defined by the gap between ideals and reality; her trajectory is shaped by the breakdown of family and neighborly relations. Remembering a time when Mit Uqba was still a place of solidarity, she complained that today you no longer can rely on your neighbors. Sometimes they don't even open the door when you knock, pretending not to be home, afraid of being asked for help.

Because she can't rely on relatives and neighbors, and because she has largely given up on the state, Amal spends much time petitioning charity organizations. For a while—she is, as often, vague about the exact chronology—she was receiving about $85 each month from the charity organization Misr El-Kheir (because, she says, she knew an employee there) and about $35 from another organization. But then her brother went around telling everyone that she has "a fridge and three kilos of gold," that she owns land, and that her children wear the "most fashionable" (*ashyak*) clothes, while really, as Amal put it, their clothes are all disheveled (*mubahdala*). The NGOs believed the brother and stopped supporting her. Amal complained to me that they did not even bother to investigate whether the rumors were true. Even the Subsidy Office (*tamwīn*), where those in possession of ration cards can buy fixed quantities of rationed food items such as rice, sugar, oil, beans, lentils, and tea, refused serving her after her brother told them that she was not really in need. "My brother wants to starve me to death. He took away my income [*rizq*]," says Amal, using a category that evokes both literal income and God's provisions.

Amal seems unfazed by her own complicity in an unfair system of distribution. She is fine with getting help from an NGO because of her personal connections. But when she steps out of her own trajectory, she becomes critical of the role personal connections play in most charity organizations, just as she is critical of the widespread corruption in government offices: "If you know someone, it takes a day to get help. If not, it takes years." She calls charity organizations "charity for the employees." And she claims that when Resala is distributing clothes or selling them cheaply, employees take the best pieces and put them aside to later resell them at higher prices, or they call their family and friends so they come and get the best pieces.

While employees tend to be corrupt, Amal says, the volunteers at Resala are "like angels." One day when she was at Resala, someone told the director that she was not only a volunteer but also a registered "case" with five children and that she should therefore receive six free meals. The director refused. Later, volunteers gave her the meals without any official approval, a sign of their uncorrupted, sincere, pious commitment to giving. Amal has joined Resala volunteers in a number of activities: setting up plumbing for houses in the countryside, sorting through used clothes, visiting the elderly and orphans. She is most familiar with the volunteers who distribute food and those who give free lessons to children (including hers), and she thinks highly of them:

> They don't want anything except for God to be happy with them. And how beautiful they are when they're giving lessons! Mothers come from all over and bring their kids. [The volunteers] teach them the English language and the Arabic language. From their own money they gather funds and buy things for the kids. Even though many of them aren't that well off themselves. They sometimes give a ball to a kid if he answers a question correctly, or a bag or a pencil case or a doll. They're so good at motivating them. These beautiful volunteers make us happy. They make us feel like our children are truly human and are being treated humanely.

Resala is exceptional in Amal's eyes because the volunteers' concern with the afterlife makes them give selflessly in this world. At the same time, she knows that Resala, like other charity organizations, does not give indiscriminately; slum dwellers hoping to receive help first have to convince the "exploration" team of their need and deservingness.

Amal and others like her are keenly aware that they have to perform their suffering, poverty, and need, over and over again. The term "performance" here (which is my term, not Amal's) should not be taken to indicate fakeness. I do not mean to imply that Amal's suffering, poverty, and need are somehow not real or that they are like a theatrical play. Rather, one of the remarkable things that Amal does is to skirt the line between what is real and what is exaggerated, if not outright fake. She knows that she has to perform an exaggerated version of her life and suffering because she feels that her ordinary, actual, everyday suffering is not acknowledged for what it is.

IN AN INTAKE OFFICE

I often switched sides in the field—from accompanying Amal on her rounds of petitioning, to watching over the shoulders of those who administer aid to people like her. At times, my fieldwork took me into the "social research" (al-bahth al-igtimā'ī) office at a charity organization in which cases of need are assessed.

Sitting in this office, next to an employee, I am facing a man whose name I don't know. Just like the street cleaner on the Nile bridge and like Amal, he is hoping for help, but is also used to rejection. The office is filled with stale smoke and the rattling sound of an air-conditioning unit that can barely keep up with the heat. Amal has given up on this particular organization, which is one of Cairo's largest, but about one hundred people try their luck here every day. During the three hours each day that the office is open, they come in to present their cases. There are four desks, two old, unused Dell desktops, and shelves filled with binders, some titled "new cases," others ordered by neighborhood. An employee sits behind each desk. I sit next to Tariq, who has been working in this office for more years than he would like to remember.

The man pulls back his sleeve to expose his arm. Look, he says without saying a word, staring at Tariq and me first, then down at his forearm. See the scars? See the proof? See why I need help?

And it works. The arm does look bad. Tariq breathes in audibly. He looks at the man's scars, then his face. More experienced than I am, he knows that these marks are not signs of, say, a knife fight or heroin injections, but the marks of dialysis. He takes down the man's information. From now on, the man will receive monthly support. He is lucky; usually such petitioning does not go so easily. Simply telling a story about the ordeals of dialysis might not have been enough. Of the many petitioners passing through the office on this day, only few will make it onto the list of registered recipients. Others receive a one-time token of support. Most are turned away.

Living below the poverty line is not enough. In fact, poverty and economic need are rarely evoked in this office, except for occasional remarks about the petitioners coming from a "weak class" (*taba'a da'ifa*), a vague term, infused with a sense of blame, that seems to merge "socially disadvantaged" with "morally weak." Pieces of paper stuck under the protective glass on each desk remind the employees of the abbreviations for the relevant categories of recipients: orphans (meaning children without a father), liver failure, general disability (*'agz 'am*), heart disease, lung disease. Deciding who should be helped means assessing authenticity and comparing cases. Sometimes petitioners are sent away because "there are more serious cases." Often, employees evoke a geography of need. True need, they say, can only be found in Upper Egypt, where people are "far from the eyes of the government [literally, those responsible]" (*ba'ida 'an 'uyun al-mas'ulin*).

All four employees in the office have been working for the organization for several years, but their small income renders unstable the line between those asking for help and those administering it. Like Amal, who is both a registered "case" and a volunteer at Resala, these employees, and maybe *all* people in this book, to differing degrees are both givers and receivers. But their own social position does not necessarily increase the employees' empathy. The daily grind has rendered them skeptical and cynical. Petitioners have to work hard to move and persuade the employees.

Just as donors come from afar to drop off their alms donations (both *zakat* and *sadaqa*), so petitioners travel from faraway neighborhoods or the countryside to seek help at this organization. Presenting their bodies as legible material, they expose scars, track marks, crutches, and prosthetic limbs. Others stumble as soon as they enter the office. Some bring along their sick or disabled children so they can present them to the employees. Offering up their bodily, physical performances, petitioners try to become "cases," registered recipients.

While bodies are important signs—especially those that are scarred or limping, in which need is visually obvious—even more important are papers.[13] Often the first thing the employees say is simply, "Hand me the papers" (*heeti al-wara'a*). This is a critical moment of the performance—the moment a stack of papers is placed into the employee's hand. A typical stack includes a copy of one's ID card, medical records, lease, school records of one's children, pension papers, death certificates, and an original form issued by a Social Affairs office that is based on a social background check, resulting in a document simply referred to as "research" (*bahth*). Required for applying for a pension, this document is also considered a reliable piece of evidence at charity organizations. Like papers listing one's income or pension, it needs to have been renewed within the previous six months. Social Affairs papers need to be originals; all other papers need to be copies.

You present the right papers, you might get what you want. You only have copies, wrong. Only originals, wrong. Too many papers, wrong. Illegible papers, wrong. Missing a paper, wrong. Often petitioners have to come in multiple times to get it right. They carry plastic folders stuffed with gray, dirty, crumbled papers that have been folded and unfolded countless times. In each office, whether government or NGO, bodies and papers begin the pleading process.

More exceptional is the use of photographs. One day at the same charity organization I was sitting with a director, to whom more difficult cases are referred. A young Palestinian woman came in and told her story. She was from Gaza, and her father had been shot. While she managed to make it to Egypt with him, he died (*istashhad*) the same day. They took the body back but she was not allowed to recross the border. Her brother had been killed too; her husband has been imprisoned by "the Jews" (they gave him 111 years); her children were still in Gaza. She pulled out two pictures from her purse and started crying. One showed a young man, and the other, which I did not see (first because of where I was sitting, then because I looked away), showed a body blown apart, the remains of her brother. I saw her pointing at the picture, heard her say, "This is his head." In response to the story, but especially, I think, the photograph, the director wrote a note saying she should receive 100 pounds (about $17).

Besides bodies, papers, and sometimes photographs, carefully rehearsed stories matter. Intake interviews follow a standard set of questions, including, for female petitioners, questions about the whereabouts of their husband. Having a dead husband is better than being divorced, which is better than having a husband who is merely absent. In response to the second-most-common question posed to female petitioners ("Whom do you have?" [*'andik mīn*]), they list their children's names and ages. Whereas school-age children increase one's chances of receiving help, adult offspring have the opposite effect, as they are expected to provide for their mothers. At the same time, in the case of widows or divorcées, having fewer children can mean that it is assumed it will be easier to remarry. Implied in these assessments is never an individual but a person embedded in social relationships. Accordingly, while those in need are reduced to "cases," the organization takes pride in helping ten thousand *families* each month, not ten thousand individuals. The assumption is that whatever aid is given will be redistributed within one's family network. We know from Amal's story that not all Egyptian families live up to this stereotypical expectation of cohesion and solidarity.

Petitioners work hard to offer up convincing performances. Most fail. On good days, the employees' momentary displays of kindness disrupt the boredom and cynicism, but more often there is mistrust. Those considered to be faking it are told to "stop acting" (*balāsh al-tamthīl*) or are told to leave. The employees often explicitly accuse petitioners of lying or repeat the same question multiple times: "How many children did you say you have?" People lie all the time, the director told me. "That's why our people are specialized in this. People try to fool them but they know. They see you and know you are married even if you say you're not." Employees repeatedly remind each other not to let their feelings take over. Rahma, who has been working at the organization for many years, told me about a woman who had come in to ask for diapers for her handicapped teenage son and how bad she felt for the woman (literally: how heavily she weighed on her; *sa'bat 'alayya*). Then they found out that the son had died months earlier, which meant that the woman likely intended to sell the diapers. Rahma told me this story to underscore what the organization and the government both accept as truth: that feelings should be bracketed because resources are limited and many petitioners are dishonest.

Employees explained to me that despite the lies, the boredom, and the meager pay, they like working for the organization because doing so counts as a form of *khayr*. The money that passes through their hands consists almost entirely of alms donations, rendering the employees trustees of God's provisions. The alms move through deeply bureaucratic processes before making it, in bits and pieces, to a lucky few. It is God who provides help, everyone at the organization acknowledges, but this help is administered by humans who meticulously crosscheck stories, papers, and bodily signs of hardship, and often distrust the performances they are being offered. Maybe the bracketing of compassion—a *nonhumanitarian* ethics of giving—can get us around the cruelty of charity only as long as the question of deservingness is also bracketed. While this is the case at Sufi *khidmas,* it is only partially true for Madame Salwa's mode of charity, and it is rarely true for NGOs.

DEATH AS A JOKE

Amal is one of the millions of Egyptians at the receiving end, and her story illustrates the messy social and material worlds that pierce through, and run alongside, the idea of giving to God. She is all too familiar with the widespread mistrust and cynicism that stands in tension to a Quranically ordained share for the poor. But while she knows that most times her performances won't work, she feels that she has no choice but to keep trying.

Amal performs her suffering ceaselessly. She performs it in government offices and at NGOs, to me and to herself. She tells her story so often that even her children complain, rolling their eyes, "Mama, you talk too much!" She cries. She points to her youngest daughter's word choices: "*yā 'aynī!* [Poor thing!] Looks how she talks! That's from growing up in the streets!" And when her oldest daughter refuses to be woken up close to midnight to eat *kushari* (cheap street food consisting of lentils, rice, and pasta), she says: "*yā 'aynī!* She's grown used to hunger!" Her body, her words, the many moments that make up each day, and those of her children—all are overflowing with signs of Amal's suffering.

But there is one performance that tops all others. One day, only a few weeks before I met her, Amal sat down on her kitchen floor and poured a container of gas over her clothes. Her plan was to set herself on fire. The lighter was sitting next to her. In a different version she tells, she poured gas over herself and her children, intending to set the entire family on fire. The telling of the story, in its various versions, is a performance too, and Amal is aware of the performativity of both acts—of death and its telling. She also knows that if she wants to perform the telling, the performance of death needs to be interrupted before it's too late. That day, her neighbors intervened.

I have no way of knowing what exactly happened that day and whether Amal really intended to commit suicide, or whether she counted on the interruption.[14] Regardless, after that day, death became a joke of sorts. Friends advised Amal to repeat what she had done but this time at Tahrir Square, which at the time was still a crowded protest space: "Do exactly the same: pour gas over yourself, take a lighter; we'll be right there to rescue you!" Telling me about the plan, Amal laughed: "They better be!" At that point she no longer wanted to die, or maybe she had never wanted to die in the first place. But she knows death can work; it can move people—neighbors, strangers, and also someone like me, whether I'm in Egypt or halfway around the world.

Amal knows about widely publicized deaths—cases in which death was not interrupted. In those deaths, claims for symbolic importance were made, or they were retroactively infused with meaning. She knows about Mohammad Bouazizi and Khaled Said, the two men whose deaths were credited with having set into motion the Tunisian and the Egyptian uprisings. She knows about the martyrs of the Egyptian uprising who are said to willingly have given their lives for the country's future. But she also knows that not all deaths count equally.[15] She has seen neighbors die because they couldn't afford to bribe their way into a public hospital, evading the long waiting lists. She knows that the working-class martyrs of the uprising (including ones from her neighborhood) were not celebrated and memorialized in the same way middle-class martyrs were. She has heard that when the military killed over eight hundred Muslim Brotherhood supporters at Rabaa Square in August 2013, their families received death certificates only if they signed a paper confirming that the deceased had committed suicide, which is considered sinful by Islamic standards. And there are even less heroic performances of death. When an Egyptian man hanged himself from a highway billboard on the Cairo-Ismailiyya Road in September 2014, the media accused him of having chosen such a public site because he wanted attention.

Even though not all deaths (and lives) count equally, for Amal suicide remains a possibility, sometimes real, sometimes imagined, but always cynical. Amal speaks of suicide often. One day she would tell me how she planned to put on a good show at Tahrir Square by staging a fake suicide attempt. The next day she would tell me she is tired of living. "The way my life is now, it's as if I died ten times a day." She continued speaking of the possibility of collective suicide so as not to leave her children behind. She never seemed to be fully serious, but she was not joking either. I could never be certain. I chose to understand her suicide talk as a performance, one in line with, but more tragic than, her other daily performances of suffering. Maybe I had no choice. And maybe she didn't, either.

Amal's friends often reminded her that suicide is forbidden (*harām*) in Islam, or they responded to her threats: "But why? That's wrong. God is putting you through this to make your faith stronger. Our religion is not a religion of depression. Be in the world, live! Be strong in your faith." Amal knows all this. Her favorite preachers frame Islam as a religion of optimism. They speak of trials that only strengthen one's faith, of an active engagement with the world, not a turning away from it. And yet, Amal's evocation of death is also a commentary on her life. It is addressed at the state, her family, and all those who have failed her.[16]

And maybe, I sometimes wondered, it is also addressed at God, who, too, seemingly has failed her. She only hinted at such disappointment, imploring God in times of crisis, asking why she and her children had to face such difficult circumstances, but she formulated this mostly as a sign that she did not sufficiently understand God's will, not a sign of God's injustice. And yet, I often had to think of her invocations at times when no one else was standing by her side: "I ask only God for help." The help that comes from God generally comes *through* humans. It needs to be embodied and mediated. And Amal hasn't been seeing much of it. One position to take in light of this conundrum is that of *ridā,* pious contentment, even in the face of difficult circumstances. Another is to rebel, maybe even by refusing or returning the entrustment from God that is one's life. Amal's God-orientedness is no less complicated than that of the pious donors, such as Shaykh Salah, the Resala volunteers, and Madame Salwa, who give to God by way of giving to the poor. Amal receives from God but by way of people, and often she does not receive. The triad is unstable, as much on the recipients' side as on the donors'. But the consequences are very different. While for the pious donor what is at stake is generally the afterlife, for Amal, what is at stake is her life and the lives of her children.

Shortly before one of my departures from Cairo, Amal called to ask if I could accompany her to an NGO so she could plead her case again. An employee who had been kind to her in the past had returned from a long leave. Amal thought that speaking to her might improve her chances of getting monthly support. She asked me to come along as a witness, to corroborate the account of her suffering. As usual, shortly before leaving, I found it difficult to do such favors, feeling an inability or unwillingness that had less to do with time constraints and more with the guilt that results from soon getting on a plane and returning to one's comfortable life back home. I told her I was short on time. She said she understood. While saying good-bye, she mentioned, seemingly in passing, that they had just gone through some rough days. I asked why, not expecting anything out of the ordinary. She told me her brother and bother-in-law had kidnapped her ten-year-old son, Shihab, a few days earlier. They told him his grandmother wanted to see him, and he went with them. They took him to a place somewhere outside of the city where no one could hear him scream. One held him; the other hit him with a cable. They set the field around him on fire and tried to run him over with a motorbike. He somehow got away, ran, and stopped a car that took him back to the city. He ran to his mother and told her what had happened. She took him to the police and the Agouza hospital. The police didn't do anything; a nurse at the hospital bandaged his arm.

I hung up the phone in disbelief and sprinted over to the kiosk. And there he was, Shihab, whose name means "shooting star" and for whom I have always had a soft spot. He had burn wounds on his arms, one of them large and round, one covered in dirt. His left arm was bandaged. He had a knife wound on his face, and scars on his upper arms from being hit with a cable. I sat beside him and put my arm around his shoulder. He told me he was afraid while it was happening but was OK now.

This was not the first time Amal and her children have had to cope with violence. Her brother's violence is an ongoing, looming threat, meant to deter Amal from continuing to demand her share of their father's inheritance. Her husband has been violent too. He once came to her house, grabbed one of the daughters, and held her next to a lit gas stove, threatening to burn her, to force Amal to stop demanding a divorce.

Violence is not new for Amal, but the kidnapping had clearly thrown her off. She seemed close to despair and spoke of suicide again, of wanting to kill herself and her children. On top of all that, Resala employees had been threatening that if she did not submit her monthly loan payment by a certain date, they would take the case to court. Then, seemingly implying that a court order had already been issued (I remain confused about when and whether the threat became a reality), she added that she had already been sentenced to three months in prison. "They can arrest me any moment," she said, "and my children will end up living in the streets."

I listened, and commiserated, and then, before I left, I said, "God is with you" (*rabbinā maʿāki*). To me, it sounded more like a question than an affirmation.

Then I went home, finished packing, and headed to the airport.

FIVE

All Thanks Belong to God

I STEP THROUGH THE KHIDMA'S GATE and into the courtyard. I greet Nura and her children, and sit down on the floor, resting my back against a wall. Shaykh Mahmoud saunters over from his favorite spot in the corner, sits down next to me, and tells Nura he wants tea. Then he asks me for 20 pounds, around $3. He doesn't say please or thank you, neither to me nor to Nura. "Bring me food," he says to Nura a bit later. Then, "Bring me a shisha." And to me, again: "I need money."

Shaykh Mahmoud is poor, just like Amal and millions of other Egyptians; but he is a different kind of poor. While Amal performs her suffering, he performs entitlement. While she tries to prove her worthiness, he makes demands. This is not simply an effect of how poverty is gendered. Gender does play a role, of course; it is easier to live on Cairo's streets as a man than as a woman. But I have seen many Egyptian men diligently perform their suffering in order to receive aid, and I have seen female dervishes break all rules of politeness. Ultimately, the difference between how Shaykh Mahmoud and Amal understand and inhabit their poverty has more to do with the worlds in which they move and with their relationships to Islam. She is a "case"; he is a dervish.

She goes to charity organizations and government offices; he spends most of his time at Cairo's saint shrines and its *khidmas,* both of which attract spiritual seekers and those in need of a bite to eat alike (and often the two groups overlap). Amal petitions employees and civil servants for help— a largely impersonal process. She is fully entrenched in the bureaucratic and institutional versions of performing her poverty though she, too, at times speaks a language somewhat in tune with Sufi traditions. She might say, for instance, that spiritual blessings are more important than material belongings, or that we are all indebted to God. But she is unlikely to ever end up at a *khidma,* and she is no dervisha. For that, she is too attached to her past as *bint nās* (coming from a well-to-do family), she is too worried about her children's future, and she is too drawn to a globally influenced understanding of Islam, a mix of Islamic televangelism and Salafism, promoted by TV preachers and Resala volunteers, that emphasizes the importance of work and entrepreneurship and that draws lines between the deserving poor and those who are impoverished but undeserving. Shaykh Mahmoud embodies a different form of Islam, one more fully grounded in Sufi traditions, a culmination of the logic that everything belongs to God. His Islam runs counter to an Islamic work ethic and ethos of entrepreneurship. In Shaykh Mahmoud's day-to-day life, most material support comes from, or is channeled through, Nura's *khidma,* where Shaykh Mahmoud is never a "case" but always a guest, hosted by God and the saints.

Amal and Shaykh Mahmoud occupy opposite ends of the spectrum of receiving, and they offer very different insights into an Islamic ethics of giving. Her story reminds us that even when believers ostensibly give to God, they still give to human beings, and they give in deeply human ways— selectively, sometimes disparagingly, with conditions attached, and, in this day and age, often in highly bureaucratic ways. Shaykh Mahmoud's story illustrates the other side: the backgrounding of the social transaction by way of a foregrounding of God. In his world, there is no need for the recipient to prove her worthiness or to say thank you, and there is no reason that the giver should feel pride in giving or attach any expectations. All gifts come from God and are given to God. Giving in Sufi spaces can be deeply fraught too, but, at least in theory, the framing here erases the hierarchy between human givers and human recipients. Seen differently, everyone is at the receiving end, or "poor," since it is only God who is *al-Ghanī,* or rich. This leveling is very different from saying that those who make less than $2 or $3 a day are poor, and it has profound implications for what it means to give and to receive. Such different understandings of poverty coexist in Egypt. Sometimes they blend into each other. Sometimes they seem worlds apart.

Shaykh Mahmoud describes himself as a dervish. The honorific title "shaykh," by which I have come to know him, can imply learnedness but here also indicates a certain spiritual standing, and special powers. Unlike "shaykh," "dervish" is not necessarily a positive term. For many in Egypt, the word brings to mind a particular image: a group of men, dressed in colorful costumes, whirling in circles, one hand pointed to the sky, the other to the earth, eyes closed, accompanied by the musical sounds of a tambourine, *oud* (lute), *ney* (flute), and singing. Maybe these men reach something akin to ecstasy; maybe they just put on a good show. Either way, it's an impressive spectacle. The weekly performances by a group known as the Whirling Dervishes have become a standard item on tourist itineraries and are also enjoyed by many middle-class Egyptians, the same people who tend to be wary of actual dervishes. A Salafi-leaning friend of mine once saw me talking to Shaykh Mahmoud; afterward he warned me to stay away from "people like that" and not to trust them. In his view, dervishes misrepresent Islam, falsely lay claim to spiritual and healing powers, and are only after your money.

The reality of dervishes is far different from the weekly performances offered to tourists and from such stereotypes. Dervishes (*darāwīsh*) in Egypt are pious ascetics, men and women, who gravitate toward the saint shrines and often spend time at *khidmas,* Sufi spaces of hospitality. They dress in simple *gallābiyyas,* often speak in enigmatic spiritual terms, and in ways large and small, disrespect social rules. In the most basic sense, they are seekers who have given themselves over to a spiritual path, have largely given up material possessions (though they may own a few *gallābiyyas* and maybe a cell phone), and often have abandoned their families. Effectively they are home-less. They draw on but also reinvent the early Sufi tradition's appreciation for asceticism, the voluntary embrace of poverty. And in so doing, they compli-cate our understanding of poverty itself.

The term "dervish" is of Persian origin but is also used in Turkish, Arabic, and European languages.[1] The Persian *darvīsh* literally means "poor," as does the Arabic *faqīr,* which sometimes stands in for "Sufi." The term "Sufi" is likely derived from *sūf,* the Arabic word for wool, and originally referred to a group of followers of the Prophet Muhammad who wore woolen cloaks that were cheaper and less comfortable than those in general use in the eighth century (Sedgwick 2003:5). Some early Sufi orders promoted a withdrawal from the world and emphasized voluntary poverty, recalling that the Prophet Muhammad said, "My poverty is my pride" (*faqrī fakhrī*), and in their writ-ings and poetry almost equating poverty with the ultimate goal of dissolu-tion in God (*fanā'*). The famous Persian poet Jalal al-Din Rumi frequently cited the hadith "When poverty is complete, it is God" (*al-faqr idha thamma huwa Allāh*) (Schimmel 1995:181). Asceticism still is seen by many Sufis as a spiritual tool that helps overcome worldly attachments and that enables the spirit (*rūh*) to draw closer to God. The equation of poverty and Sufism, to be clear, is not universal, and while all dervishes are Sufis, not all Sufis are dervishes.[2] Many Sufi orders instruct their followers to dress well and not to shun wealth and worldly positions. Some of the most upper-class Egyptians I know are members of Sufi orders or followers of a Sufi path.

In a world marked by a pervasive work ethic and the logic of private property, dervishes are odd characters. Many Egyptians view them as beggars or parasites; others see them as exceptionally close to God. On the surface, the dervish takes without ever giving anything in return. At Nura's *khidma,* Shaykh Mahmoud receives food, finds a place to sleep, and can enjoy a free *shīsha,* a water pipe in which one smokes crude tobacco fermented with black honey. Nura would never complain of his seeming sense of entitlement or ingratitude. She has much respect for him. And ultimately, she says, we never know who gives and who takes. The *khidma* reconfigures the very question of poverty and the relationship between giving and receiving. Perhaps more than any other aspect of Egyptian life, it most fully embraces the idea that everything—including all thanks—belongs to God.

(IN)GRATITUDE

Hadiths—that thick stack of the Prophet Muhammad's sayings—emphasize the importance of saying thank you to your fellow humans. And yet thanking humans is intimately connected to thanking God. One hadith proclaims, "He who does not thank the people has not thanked Allah." In his book on almsgiving, the medieval Sufi philosopher Abu Hamid al-Ghazali elaborates on this logic. He explains that one should always thank the giver; one should never find fault in a gift, but rather should magnify its value (1966:64). But he also explains that when saying thanks, the recipient recognizes that the giver is only an instrument through whom the grace of God is extended. The recipient owes the donor nothing, and especially when it comes to alms, the donor should be grateful to the recipient, not the other way around:

> Actually the giver should deem himself a beneficiary and [he should deem] the poverty-stricken, by virtue of accepting his gifts which are due to God, his benefactor . . . Had the poverty-stricken declined to accept his gifts, man would have remained under an obligation to give. It is his duty, therefore, to acknowledge that he is under an obligation to the poverty-stricken who has made his hand a substitute for that of God in receiving the dues [which man owes to] God. The Prophet said, "Verily alms fall into the hand of God before they fall into the hand of the beggar who receives them." Let man therefore,

know that [when he gives alms], he gives them unto God while the poor [who receives them] is receiving his livelihood from God to whom it was first given. (37–38)

Precisely because of their crucial mediating role, it is wrong to expect something from the recipients, "such as thanks, praise, service, respect, and veneration, requiring him to carry out errands for [the donor], pay him homage in assemblies, and agree with him on all subjects" (39). The test case is when the poverty-stricken commits an offense against the giver, such as insulting her. If the giver feels disgusted or outraged as a result, then the giving was not free of expectations (41).[3]

The resulting ethics is strikingly different from an etiquette of gratitude that dominates in many places. Think of Julian Pitt-Rivers's observation in the early 1990s that it is impossible for an Englishman to get "through a single day of his life without saying 'thank you' at least a hundred times" (2011:424). Think of the proliferation of thank-you cards, or of parenting websites that instruct parents to

> sit your child down [before her birthday party] and tell her, "You'll be getting gifts. Everyone will want to see you open theirs, and it's nice to say 'Thank you!' even if you don't like the present." . . . Be prepared to reinforce this habit until your child is fully grown. Writing thank-you notes doesn't come naturally to children, but as you can explain, notes make the gift-giver feel even better about giving.[4]

The giving we encounter at *khidmas*—giving without please and thank you—disrupts an etiquette of gratitude. On the rare occasions that thanks are uttered in such spaces, they are redirected: *al-shukr li-llāh* (Thanks belong to God). *Khidmas* epitomize this orientation, but thanks are also often withheld or redirected elsewhere in Egypt. Watching charitable transactions at NGOs, in slums, and on Cairo's streets, I was repeatedly struck by the *absence* of expressions of gratitude. No "thank you," no nod toward the donor, not even a gaze at the donor. Rather a simple taking and walking away, turning away, looking away. Just as Resala volunteers barely look at the recipients in the slums, the recipients barely look at the volunteers. Quite frequently, it was as if they knew that, as al-Ghazali put it, their hand was "a substitute for that of God." They knew they were needed.[5]

When recipients withhold a thank-you, they seem to drive home this point: that the donors need them, not the other way around. At the same time they drive home another point: that they are entitled to what they receive. In a Quranic economy of rights and obligations, *not* saying thank you in response to a charitable gift is not a sign of impoliteness. Rather, it foregrounds a relationship of duty that trumps mere pleasantries.

Ultimately, within this economy, giving is an attempt to cultivate gratefulness toward God—in recipient *and* giver—without any expectation or desire in this world. Instead of a vertical and hierarchical relationship between giver and recipient, the foregrounding of God reminds believers that everyone equally owes thanks to God. This pious ideal—living in a constant state of gratefulness toward God—is reflected in terms such as *ridā* (pious contentment) and *tawakkul* (complete reliance on God), and is expressed in the frequently uttered phrase *al-hamdu-li-llāh,* "all thanks and praise belong to God." In Egypt today, this is the most common response to the question, "How are you?" and can mean anything from "I'm great, thank God" to "I'm doing horribly but thank God nevertheless." Being grateful to God is a pious ideal even though, as the Quran says, God does not need our gratitude.[6] Paradoxically, gratefulness toward God should be free of expectations, but when believers *are* grateful, the Quran promises, God will bestow grace upon them: "If you are grateful [*shakartum*], I will surely increase you [in favor]."[7]

In real life, orienting oneself fully toward God is difficult, if not impossible. Maybe *al-hamdu-li-llāh* needs to be uttered so often precisely because even the most pious Muslim cannot sustain a constant foregrounding of God. Take Madame Salwa, for instance. When speaking about giving in the abstract, she emphasizes that she does not expect anything from those at the receiving end. She aspires to a kind of giving in which she needs for nothing and hopes for nothing except perhaps a place in paradise. And yet, often, she cannot help but want something more tangible as well. Paradise is distant. Once she confided in me:

> You give and give and give and never get anything in return. It's not much I want. But it's only human to want to be given something as well, at least once in a while. Even just a pat on your shoulder. Once I gave to a street cleaner, and his kid came up to me and hugged me. And even though the kid was full of garbage, I hugged him back and it made me very happy. It's hard to give and give and not receive anything in return.

The most pious kind of giving is the kind that expects nothing in return—neither from God nor from the human recipient. But this is an almost saintly ideal, unattainable for most. "I'm only human," says Madame Salwa. We find a similar tension with Shaykh Salah and his *khidma*. He, too, explains that ideally he should not expect gratitude from the recipients. He sees himself as a channel for God's gifts, and he recognizes that his guests owe him nothing. And indeed, those who receive food at his *khidma* rarely use the Arabic word for "thank you" (*shukran*). Most say nothing; some call upon God to reward Shaykh Salah, saying, "May God bless you" (*rabbinā yakrimak*), "May your hands be blessed" (*tislam īdak*), "May your good increase" (*kattar khayrak*), "May God increase [your ability to do good]" (*rabbinnā yazīdak*), or "May God widen [your ability to do good]" (*Allāh yawassaʿ ʿalaik*). Like Madame Salwa, Shaykh Salah admits that he occasionally craves tokens of appreciation, be it a word of thanks or a prayer asking for God's blessings.

> Humans are weak; they want someone to thank them. God knows that there is a weakness in us. We want thanks [*shukr*]. I need a little bit. I need a little bit of gas; otherwise I run out of gas . . . According to my belief, I should not expect thanks. All thanks belong to God. If [the person receiving the food] says "*al-hamdu-li-llāh*," he did what is required of him. I'm just a tool for God. I'm a channel; God sends His gifts through me. They don't come from me. All good things come from God.

Whether in Cairo's back alleys or at its *khidmas,* what renders pious acts of giving so complex is that a spiritual interaction with God overlaps with, and fundamentally depends on, a material, social exchange. What further complicates matters is that the pious ideal coexists with a parallel, more this-worldly ideal of giving that is based on human reciprocity and mutuality. In Egypt, too, children are taught to say thank you to parents, teachers, and friends, and an ideal of reciprocity comes to the fore when dealing with relatives and neighbors and can express itself in an economy of favors. The desire for a thank you, then, can be an echo of another moral register, but it can also be folded back into a pious economy, where it needs to be accommodated and tamed. Nura explicitly distances herself from expectations of reciprocity and the competitive hospitality that is the "stuff of everyday politics" (Meneley 1996). As she explained to me,

> The problem with our traditions is that you invite people because they invited you. You want to show that you can put lots on the table; you want to show you're a good host. What we do here [at the *khidma*] is very different. We don't care about traditions. We offer simple food, the same we eat. And we don't expect anything in return.

Nura distinguishes her Sufi way from the Egypt that surrounds it. Unlike much of Egypt, which, in her view, is caught up in an endless cycle of gifts and countergifts, she attempts to embody (or at least approximate) divine generosity.[8] On the surface, this means that, in line with al-Ghazali's prescribed ethics of giving, she expects nothing from those who eat her food or spend the night. Significantly, however, neither does she expect a countergift from God—or at least that is the pious state she actively works toward. Unlike the Resala volunteers, who are unabashed about doing good in the hope of achieving a place in paradise, Nura insists that one's fate in the afterlife depends not on one's deeds but on God's mercy (*rahma*) alone. She believes that you cannot hold God accountable; you cannot "trade with God." At times, however, she, too, speaks of her desire to see "God's face," which is commonly associated with a high level in paradise. A visitor to Nura's *khidma* echoed a familiar paradox: "It's all about giving without expecting a countergift [*muqābil*]. Only then God rewards you."

Regardless of their occasional longing for a place in paradise, Sufis like Nura try to free themselves from a worldly gift economy and from worldly attachments. For this reason, they cherish those recipients who disrupt the human desire for gratitude and, with it, the logic of charity. Such expectation-free giving is practiced most purposefully at *khidmas*. We already encountered Shaykh Salah's *khidma,* and here I turn to Nura's. Unlike Shaykh Salah, Nura does not have separate spaces for cooking, distributing, and living. She takes Sufi hospitality to a different level. Her home *is* the *khidma*.

OF SUFI HOSPITALITY

I had seen the name countless times in my mother's passport: Shibin el-Kom. My mother was born there; a small textile-producing town in the Nile Delta. Nura's mother was born there as well. I thought this was a happy coincidence. She interpreted it as a sign of our connection, which helped her cope, I think, with her ambivalence toward my fieldwork, my desire to write about practices that should best be kept secret.[9] I didn't argue.

Both of Nura's parents were from the Nile Delta, about an hour from the capital city. When Nura's father took up a job in the Ministry of Housing in Cairo, they moved into a house at the border of the City of the Dead, a large necropolis dating to the seventh century that has become a residential neighborhood to about half a million people and that is also home to a number of saint shrines.[10] After their move, Nura's parents faced a problem. Every time her mother gave birth, their newborn died. The parents performed *dhikr,* reciting praise for God and the Prophet Muhammad hundreds of thousands of times, splashing cold water onto their faces to stay awake longer to keep reciting. But nothing helped. At some point they asked a shaykh for advice, and he explained that there was something more important than *dhikr,* and that was giving to the poor. Performing *dhikr,* or speaking personal prayers (*du ʿā'*), he explained, only serves the person herself; what one needs to do instead is open one's house to other people. And so the parents opened the *khidma.* They ended up with thirteen healthy children.

Until his death in 1975, Nura's father sat with the guests, whoever they might be, while her mother cooked for them. After his death, the mother alone took charge of the *khidma* for three decades but, a few years before I met Nura, her mother had suffered a stroke. Since then, Nura has been fully in charge. When I asked her why she took over the *khidma* and not one of her siblings, she explained: "It's destiny [*nasīb*]. It comes from God." She received a sign early on in her life through a dream-vision in which her mother told her that she would eventually take over from her.[11] And that is exactly what happened. None of the siblings regularly help in the *khidma,* although one brother and one sister come by once in a while to visit. Nura seemed resigned when she told me this but there might also have been some barely noticeable pride in being the one chosen by God to take on this spiritual work.

When I met her, Nura was forty-seven years old and had a twelve-year-old son and a fifteen-year-old daughter. Her husband worked for a newspaper's film archive and was not very involved with the *khidma.* After they got married, they moved to a distant suburb and furnished an apartment there—a spacious apartment with beautiful furniture and a nice breeze, Nura recalls—but after only one week she felt drawn back to the *khidma.* They moved back.

Entering the *khidma* means passing through a large green metal gate, on which is written "*Allāh karīm*" (God is generous). Once you have passed through the gate, you are standing in a large tiled courtyard, with a one-story house ahead of you, to the right a guest room and four stall toilets, and, further submerged, a luscious garden with plants and trees. To the left are an additional two guest rooms, their floors bare except for some reed mats and pillows. The house itself has high ceilings and six bedrooms; one of them, with multiple beds, is reserved for women. The kitchen, notably, is not any better equipped than that of an average low-income family in Egypt. Like the bathroom, it is shared by all. Nura and her husband's bedroom, as well as

Nura's courtyard. Photograph by the author.

their children's room, are semi-private, though some guests (myself included) have on occasion been invited to nap on Nura's bed.

Guests show up any time of day, seven days a week. In the mornings, Nura might serve beans, cheese, and falafel to whoever is around. Later in the day, she might offer pickled eggplant, green beans, *malūkhiyya,* and bread, or rice, white beans in tomato sauce, and pickles. Sometimes meat is served. If you show up with a cold, you get peppermint tea with cumin. And regardless of what time of day it is, there is always black tea, lots of it, prepared by Nura, one of her long-term guests, or, after I had become a fixture of sorts, by me. The food at the *khidma* is plentiful and tasty. One guest explained that it tastes so good because it is given "for God. It is filled with *baraka* and can even heal you."

Nura grows guavas, zucchini, lemons, and other vegetables in her garden and keeps chickens and pigeons in a smaller interior backyard. She uses the fruit, vegetables, eggs, and poultry for the meals. To keep the *khidma* going, she also relies on her father's pension, but ultimately, she says, it is God who provides. She accepts food and money from those who visit her—as long as she feels, she says, that the gift is coming from "someone pious, not someone who takes pride in giving." Her *khidma,* like the one run by Shaykh Salah, is a space of endless and creative circulation, a space that functions as a result of collective giving. Whatever is brought to the *khidma* is immediately offered to guests or used for the next meal Nura cooks.

Some guests, like Shaykh Mahmoud, ostensibly give nothing. Other guests contribute in different ways. The most obvious contributions are the material ones. Some bring fruit, others bring bread. Some hand a few pounds to Nura's son and send him out to buy tobacco for the shishas, or cigarettes to share. Every so often, a wealthy visitor will hand Nura a 100-pound bill. Other aspects of the collective giving are less obvious. One man brings tapes with *inshād* music by famous Sufi performers. Nura then gets the extension cord and sits the old cassette player in the doorway, and everyone gathers in the courtyard and listens. Others clean the bathrooms, sweep the courtyard, or help with the construction or renovation of rooms. Nura explains that there is *baraka* at work. Like Shaykh Salah, she insists that when she has nothing, something comes to her. Ultimately, in her account, whatever is brought to the *khidma* comes from *ahl al-bayt,* the Prophet Muhammad's saintly descendants. As she puts it: "I believe that *ahl al-bayt* are around me, helping me, sending me people who buy the things we need."

The saints are spiritually present at the *khidma,* and they inspire, through their example, Nura's daily acts of giving.[12] They also guide guests to the space, which is otherwise not easy to find. Once, a group of Syrians were visiting the saint shrines in Cairo (this was in early 2011, before the war erupted in Syria). They had never heard of Nura or her *khidma* but, guided by *ahl al-bayt,* they found their way there and ended up staying for a few days. Some guests stay longer. The guest who stayed the longest was there for a whole twenty-five years—not, Nura explained, because he felt like it (*bi-mazāgu*) but because he was drawn to the place and instructed to stay by *ahl al-bayt.* In Nura's words: "It's never by choice. It's not about whether you like the saints. It's about them: whether they like you or not."

It might be difficult to imagine hosting someone for that many years. While Resala's activities and Shaykh Salah's *khidma* might be partially familiar to readers who have volunteered or worked at soup kitchens, Nura's *khidma* is probably harder to make sense of. The idea of opening up one's own house to strangers and being surrounded by a transient blend of guests over whom one has no control might seem profoundly odd. For Nura, hosting is a spiritual technique. Sometimes she says she gives out of love, and giving fills her with joy. But giving is also hard work, and often Nura is visibly tired. The only trips she takes outside of Egypt are annual pilgrimages (*'umra*) to Saudi Arabia. In Egypt, she enjoys visiting the saint shrines but is rarely able to do so. When she told me she regretted not having been to Sayyida Zaynab's shrine in a long time and I offered to accompany her there, one of her guests interrupted us: "*warāhā bayt!*" (She has a house to take care of!). This phrase is often used by the newly wed and by recent mothers to underscore their family obligations and household responsibilities. In Nura's case, the phrase takes on a broader meaning. When I first met her, her primary responsibility, besides the *khidma,* was attending to her seventy-year-old paralyzed mother—feeding her, clothing her, emptying the bedpan, combing her hair, putting up with her moods. Nura also has a husband and children and has to make sure they are healthy, fed, and that the children do their homework. But her care is not limited to her nuclear family or blood relatives. The "house" she has to take care of includes guests, friends, and strangers passing through.

There are moments when the language of love breaks down. "I don't want people," Nura told me one time when she was frustrated because of a drawn-out conflict with her siblings. "I only want God." Nura is not by nature generous and giving. Sometimes she wishes she could just be alone. But in this world at least, her closeness to God is contingent on her closeness to, and care for, people. She intentionally cultivates a generous and giving self precisely *by* giving every day. In this sense one might read the *khidma* as a space of pious self-cultivation, similar to practices like praying or listening to tape-recorded sermons (Mahmood 2005; Hirschkind 2006). The difference is that the *khidma* cultivates a pious self by caring for others. More precisely, serving and hosting here are techniques for humbling and undoing the self (*nafs*), letting go of attachments to the material world, and overcoming claims to ownership. Giving (*'atā'*), then, is intimately related to self-erasure (*fanā'*). It means shaping oneself into a medium for God's will and trying to approximate the ways of the Prophet Muhammad and the saints, all in order to draw closer to God. Because hosting, feeding, and caring for others are essential spiritual techniques, the guest plays a crucial role. I was reminded of this every time I made the mistake of thanking Nura or apologizing for having given her extra work by uttering the phrase "we've tired you out" after having been served a big meal. The response was always reprimand. No need to say thank you, no need to apologize. I was an odd guest in this space. The ideal guest is the dervish.

A range of people visits Nura's *khidma*. I met medical doctors and journalists there, along with housewives, peasants, out-of-towners, and a young woman who was having problems with her family and needed a refuge. While most visitors come by only occasionally and spend only a few hours, others stay far longer or visit more regularly. The guests most central to the texture, feel, and daily flow of the *khidma* are the dervishes.

Usually when I visited Nura, two to three dervishes would be sitting in the courtyard, smoking shisha, surrounded by about a dozen cats. In the morning and early afternoons, they often were the only guests, with other people arriving later in the evening. Usually Sayyid would be there, a thirty-year-old dervish with a big smile. After moving to Cairo from Upper Egypt, he worked random jobs around al-Haram Street, which is known for its nightclubs and cabarets. He went to casinos, drank, and smoked pot and hashish. When I met him, he had quit most drugs (except for Tramadol, a pain medication with morphine-like effects) and occasionally worked for a brick company. He showed me how he moves bricks while at the same time performing *dhikr,* reciting the phrase "There is no god but God" while swinging his head back and forth. Often Shaykh Hossam would be there too. He was in his mid-seventies, used to own a coffee shop in the downtown neighborhood of Bulaq, and now is retired. Others refer to him as a dervish; occasionally, this is how he describes himself too. He and his wife are from Sohag, he told me; they have two daughters who are both married, and a son who still lives with them, along with two grandchildren. Although Shaykh Hossam is illiterate, he can recite long passages from different Sufi writings. He has been visiting Nura's *khidma* for forty years, from its very beginnings. For him, the heart of the *khidma* is it*'ām,* the giving of food—a practice in which he joyfully participates as a recipient. People can sleep anywhere, he says, but giving food to a hungry person is better than building a mosque. Other dervishes I met at the *khidma* acted erratic, did not speak at all, or spoke words no one could understand. One dervish wore twelve *gallābiyyas* on top of each other even in the hottest summer months. More medically inclined observers likely would read this behavior as indicating mental health problems, but in a Sufi context it is interpreted as a sign of having been subjected to a divine opening (*fath*).

And Shaykh Mahmoud would usually be there too. I first met him in 2003 when my research assistant Hassan introduced us at Imam Hussain's

Shaykh Mahmoud. Photograph by Hager El Hadidi.

mawlid, the weeklong festivities in honor of the saint's birthday that run into the early morning hours.[13] Over the months, I kept seeing Shaykh Mahmoud at different *mawlids;* like other dervishes, he organized his year around the saintly birthdays, moving from shrine to shrine.

At first I had trouble understanding what Shaykh Mahmoud was talking about. I was thrown off by his enigmatic spiritual references, elaborate metaphors, and long silences. Over the years he became more direct with me, asking for money, usually whatever he needed for cigarettes or medical expenses. Sometimes, in what always seemed like a parody of the Maussian gift economy, he would offer me a small gift, such as a ring from his hand, or he would instruct me to turn on my recorder, give me a brief lecture whose mysterious tone never quite matched its not-so-mysterious content, and then ask me for money. More often, he simply demanded, reminding me of the chasm of cultural difference that separated my life from his. I say please and thank you constantly. Shaykh Mahmoud thought that layer of civility was absurd, or at least that it did not apply to him. Intrigued and irritated at once, I repeatedly would arrive at Nura's *khidma* with the firm intention of *not* giving to Shaykh Mahmoud but would end up giving something to him nonetheless—usually anything between 5 and 100 pounds (between 80 cents and $18), depending on my mood, how much I had on me, his reported health problems, and my willpower. Another strategy I tried was to purposefully bring very little money, but even on those days I would often still hand him the few pounds I had, leaving just enough for a taxi ride back home, or not even that. While I often gave in, I was outright annoyed by his demands, and I did not like how he bossed Nura around.

Hassan, too, was faced with Shaykh Mahmoud's increasing demands. He told me that when he first met Shaykh Mahmoud many years ago, he wanted to give him money, as one does with dervishes, but Shaykh Mahmoud, maybe to underline his disinterest in material things, threw the money back at him. Later he began asking Hassan for small amounts (seemingly mindful of the moderate salary Hassan's government job provided and the three children he had to take care of). Sometimes he called Hassan in the middle of the night and instructed him to come to a particular saint shrine with a particular amount. To my surprise, Hassan usually complied.

With Nura, too, Shaykh Mahmoud was direct and demanding. As far as I know, he never asked her for money, but he demanded to be served food and tea in a similarly entitled manner. She did not seem to mind. She admired and respected Shaykh Mahmoud and often told stories about him that emphasized his almost-miraculous powers. One of her favorite stories was about the time when she was pregnant and everyone was certain it would be a boy, but Shaykh Mahmoud told her, "Don't listen to them, it will be a girl, and her name will be Zaynab." Nura did have a girl but she had already promised a relative that she would name her daughter after her, and so she called her Basma. Later, at a *mawlid,* another dervish, whom she had never met, approached Nura: "How come you named her Basma when her name is Zaynab?" Nura explained to me that the stranger and Shaykh Mahmoud could both see *al-bāṭin,* the hidden spiritual reality that lies behind the visible. Another story she liked to tell was about when she was pregnant again but did not know she was (and, because of doctors' predictions, did not think she could be). Shaykh Mahmoud asked her how her boy was doing. She reminded him that she only had a daughter, but he insisted: "You have a boy, his name is Hussain, and his father is [Imam] Hussain." To honor this proclaimed spiritual connection to the Prophet Muhammad's grandson, Nura ended up calling her son Hussain. A third memorable moment revolved around a dream in which Imam Hussain gave Nura a ring, which made her so happy that she flew in the dream. After waking up, she quickly got dressed and went to visit Imam Hussain's shrine. Shaykh Mahmoud was standing by the mosque's entrance and said: "Congratulations [*mabrūk*] on the ring!" Baffled, Nura could only mutter: "You were in my dream?" He simply told her to "go and visit," to enter the shrine and read the Fatiha for Imam Hussain, the opening sura of the Quran, which one recites for the dead.

Nura treasures these memories of Shaykh Mahmoud's spiritual powers, as well as his friendship. It was obvious that she valued his company and that he brought joy to the *khidma,* along with his seemingly endless demands.

Hassan, too, had much respect for Shaykh Mahmoud. He considered him to have spiritual if not miraculous powers, and at times he excused the constant requests for money as an intentional technique—Shaykh Mahmoud's purposeful disruption of people's respect for him, to avert the danger of polytheism (*shirk*). By presenting himself as entirely human, Hassan explained to me, Shaykh Mahmoud was diverting attention from his spiritual powers. Asking for money is similar to a saint smoking a cigarette or doing something forbidden (*harām*). Seeming missteps can thus be interpreted, at least by generous interpreters like Hassan, as attempts to redirect everyone's attention to God.

ANTI-ASCETICISM

While Hassan respected Shaykh Mahmoud's spiritual abilities, he was uneasy with his refusal to work. One evening, while strolling through downtown Cairo, he told me that he could never accept Shaykh Mahmoud as his "shaykh," someone to guide him spiritually. When I asked him why, he responded with a hadith: "Once there were two brothers. One spent all his time in the mosque, praying. The other worked and supported his brother. The Prophet Muhammad was asked which is better. He said the one who works is a hundred times better than the one who prays."

Hassan interprets this hadith to mean that Islam values work and disapproves of asceticism. And that is why Shaykh Mahmoud could be his friend but not his shaykh. And it is why many Egyptians see dervishes as parasites rather than as something akin to saints.

Hassan is not alone in embracing an Islamic work ethic. We saw versions of this work ethic articulated by Shaykh Salah and even Amal. Along with them, many Muslims understand earning a living (*kasb*) to be a central religious obligation (Singer 2008:165). The emphasis on this obligation, which stands against the lifestyle of dervishes, is not a recent capitalist rendering of Islam but is grounded in the Quran and hadith. It is also reflected in the writings of medieval philosophers like al-Ghazali, who, as we have seen, wrote about the need to give to the poor, but who also underlined the importance of work:

> If he were a devotee [muta'abbid, a pious person] and work to secure a living would prevent him from fulfilling the act of worship and observing the set hours of prayer, let him work for his livelihood as much as possible because his work to earn a living is the more important. (al-Ghazali 1966:54)

More recently, this strand of the Islamic tradition, the idea that work trumps worship, has been promoted by Yusuf al-Qaradawi, an influential Egyptian theologian who is associated with the Muslim Brotherhood and who has written extensively on the principle of almsgiving. He sees social service provision as a key means of da'wa, of bringing Muslims back to their faith (as well as a means of countering Christian missionary efforts). At the same time he explicitly rejects asceticism. In *The Problem of Poverty and How Islam Has Dealt with It* (*Mushkilat al-faqr wa kayfa 'ālajaha al-Islām*), he reminds his readers that poverty is dangerous for one's faith, morals, thought, family, and society. He claims that there will always be rich and poor people—just like there is the "beautiful and the ugly, the tall and the short, the strong and the weak, the smart and the dumb"—but he opposes the intentional embrace of poverty. *Ridā*, contentment, he says, is often misunderstood; it "neither asks the poor to be content with a life of misery, nor does it ask them to refrain from aspiring to be wealthy and have a good life" (1985:21). Countering the idea that the Prophet happily lived a life of poverty, al-Qaradawi insists that the Prophet prayed to God more than once (both for himself and for his companions) to be wealthy. Contentment, he says, simply means that one should not be greedy. Faith is a mechanism that helps the believer stay on the right track and to pursue "real" wealth in the afterlife by seeking moderate wealth in this life and doing good deeds (22).

Al-Qaradawi denounces the "venerators of poverty," those who "take from life but do not give," among them "ascetics, monks, those who call for a very simple kind of life (*taqashshuf*), and Sufis, those who view poverty not as an evil to be eliminated or problem to be fixed but as a blessing [ni 'ma] that God bestows on His favored servants to attach their hearts to the afterlife" (7). He is particularly critical of ascetic Sufis, commenting: "It is not permitted to the Muslim to avoid working for a living on the pretext of devoting his life to worship or trust in Allah, as gold and silver certainly do not fall from the sky!" (2013:133).

Al-Qaradawi has been living in exile for decades (except for a brief return to Egypt during the uprising) but his books are widely available in Cairo and are in line with a broader articulation of Islam that was dominating much religious discourse in Egypt at the time of my fieldwork. In this reading of Islam, work and the pursuit of moderate wealth are essential. Yet, the Islamic tradition also contains strong anti-materialist strands. The founder of the Muslim Brotherhood, Hasan al-Banna, warned that wealth turns people into oppressors. And even though Islam recognizes private property, Muslim thinkers have for at least a century pointed out that capitalism relies on the private property of isolated individuals, and that this principle can undermine the ethical foundations of Islam "by focusing on the individual as a self-directed and autonomous being, detracting from the social being, or the worshipper in relation to God" (Tripp 2006:54). Many Muslim thinkers have been concerned with the negative impact of a capitalist ethos ('Imara 2009; Tripp 2006).

While there might be some ambivalence about private property, I have not come across any Islamic writings against work per se—something along the lines of Paul Lafargue's nineteenth-century manifesto for the "the right to be lazy" (Lafargue 2011), Bob Black's call in the 1980s for the "abolition of work" (1985), or anthropologist David Graeber's (2018) more recent critique of "bullshit jobs." Arguably, however, a similarly radical stance against work is *lived* by dervishes, who insist on their rightful share without working, and without even pretending to work.

Dervishes like Shaykh Mahmoud are generally not invested in political utopias. They disrupt a work ethic and the logic of private property not through intellectual arguments but through their very way of life. Shaykh Mahmoud is poor, but unlike al-Qaradawi, he does not see poverty as a problem. Like al-Banna, though for other reasons, he sees *wealth* as the real problem—not because it disrupts social solidarity but because it creates attachments to the material world that distract from what really matters, closeness to God and the Prophet Muhammad. Ultimately, then, the very question of poverty is transformed by Shaykh Mahmoud's way of life and, more broadly, through the space and logic of the *khidma*. Nura is not blind to the fact that the dervishes who eat at her house rely on what she provides, and yet, she insists, the *khidma* does not aim to feed "the poor" but is about "getting closer to God by feeding people, without distinguishing between those who have money and those who have nothing." When I asked her during one of my first visits whether the people she hosts are mostly poor people, she was taken aback. I had come to know the City of the Dead through previous visits with Madame Salwa when we were distributing food in the area, and I had seen many signs of what I would call poverty. When I first visited Nura, I assumed that the *khidma* played a role in sustaining some of its immediate neighbors, and that those neighbors likely were poor. Nura rejected this framing. Most of her guests, she said, have a home but have traveled far to visit the saints and need a place to spend the night, or they have a home in Cairo but enjoy being at the *khidma* because it is a spiritual place. Poverty, at least in the way I used the term, was not the right way for understanding the *khidma*. My reading was far too materialist. "It's not about them not having food or being hungry," said Nura. "It's about offering a place where you can sleep and eat and talk about the Prophet and do *dhikr*."

WE ARE ALL POOR

One afternoon at Nura's *khidma,* a dervish disrupted the calm. He was yelling, refused to take off his dirty shoes when entering the house, and woke up Nura's mother, who had just fallen asleep. Another guest, Muhammad, kicked him out. When Nura emerged from the kitchen, they told her what had happened. Muhammad reported somewhat proudly that he had taken care of the problem. Nura scolded him: "You don't know what he's carrying. People like that carry other people's problems. They carry our stuff" (*biyshilu 'annina*).

Nura here refers to the idea that dervishes often take on other people's burdens. Sometimes this is called *tahmil,* which literally translates as "making someone carry." Dervishes might appear to be parasites, but only to those who fail to see beyond the visible. It is commonly believed in the world of *khidmas* that it is the most marginal, abject person who carries the heaviest weight, someone who might look homeless, poor, and disturbed. Such people are also called *magzub* (pl. *magazib*), a term that literally means "drawn to God" and refers to someone who is entirely consumed by the Divine (and, again, someone whom medically inclined observers might diagnose as mentally ill).[14] Nura treats such people with much respect. "You have to let them be," she explained to Muhammad, and then she told us a story from a long time ago.

When her mother was still healthy and strong, about twenty years earlier, a stranger showed up. He walked through that door (she points to the gate) and sat by that wall (she points to the wall, the one right next to the gate). Her mother said no one was to touch the stranger; they should leave him alone and only bring him food and water. They brought him a plate of food; he flipped it over, spilling the food. They brought him water; the same. He sat there for three days. His face kept changing. Sometimes he looked like a person, then like a monkey, then like a *jinn,* a spirit. The mother kept insisting that they should leave him alone. The third day they again brought him food on a tray, and he said, "How come you don't bring me a table? Am I not a human being?" He stood up and left. They never saw him again. But before he left, he told Nura's mother that he was "carrying" with him two-thirds of their problems. Nura concluded the story by explaining that people like that are directed by God and carry all kinds of things for other people. One of the reasons they should be left alone is that if you bother them, they might transfer the entire weight onto you. So there is some risk involved, but really, Nura insists, we should be grateful to them.

While acting entitled ("How come you don't bring me a table?"), the stranger in this story is the one to whom Nura and her family owe gratitude. Although he does not accept their food, he demands to be treated like a proper guest. Seemingly the one who takes, he is in fact the one who gives. He might be dangerous and unpredictable but, as he walks away, he has given to those at the *khidma* by taking something from them. He performs a kind of labor that is entirely invisible to those who can only see him as a parasite. Like Nura's tireless labor in the kitchen, the stranger's labor does not register if one proceeds from a limited understanding of work, the kind that, in al-Ghazali's words, allows one to "secure a living" or the kind that, in al-Qaradawi's words, goes hand in hand with the aspiration to "moderate wealth in this life." But it is labor nevertheless, recognizable to people like Nura and her mother.

At first sight, in Nura's story, the *khidma*'s economy seems to have slipped back into a gift economy, expressed in the implicit hope that one's giving will be rewarded by the seemingly crazy person who is actually doing the donor a favor. But the strange stranger—an extreme version of the dervish—also brings into focus a divine logic by disrupting social rules and expectations, and by rupturing the visible order of things. He reminds those witnessing his behavior (and later those to whom Nura tells the story) that the visible world can be highly misleading. Seemingly lazy and parasitical people might be the ones doing the heaviest kind of lifting. And the seemingly poor and destitute might be the richest and strongest in spiritual terms. Poverty, then, here does not refer to how much income a person has, how many savings and assets, and whether they can cover their expenses and those of their dependents. Neither are "the poor" here simply those who are constituted *through* charity (Simmel 1965). At the *khidma,* poverty takes on other meanings. It can be a disguise that conceals spiritual strength or a technique used to detach oneself from worldly desires. In NGO contexts, *miskīn* means "in need"; for Nura, it refers to someone oriented toward God (*mutaggih ila-llāh*). Poverty, in her view, can also refer to the human condition more broadly. As she sees it, drawing on the Quran, all humans are in need of God or, literally, are poor toward God (*fuqarā' ila-llāh*).[15] This does not mean that Nura does not notice the relative levels of poverty or wealth of her guests. But those levels are not what dictates or guides her giving. In a profound way, material, measurable, quantifiable poverty is irrelevant to her.

Along with the metrics of material poverty and a quasi–Protestant work ethic, Nura rejects the logic of charity and of welfare. When she serves food to Shaykh Mahmoud, they are not donor and recipient but are both equally dependent on, and oriented toward, God and the saints. Nura never asks whether her guests work, or why they do not work. Their personal circumstances are none of her business. What matters is that they are here, that *ahl al-bayt* have guided them to her door. The point is precisely not saying please and thank you, because what Nura gives never belongs to her to begin with. The dervish, with his ostensibly ungrateful behavior, reminds the giver that all giving comes from God and should be directed to God. The fact that Shaykh Mahmoud is *not* grateful to her, in the end, might be the reason Nura is grateful to him.

DELAYED GRATITUDE

In October 2013, Shaykh Mahmoud died of pneumonia. The last time we spoke, a few months prior, he told me that worms would soon crawl through his body. But he was not old and his body seemed tough. His death caught me by surprise. He was buried in the City of the Dead, close to his favorite saint shrines, and not far from Nura's *khidma.*

Nura later told me how devastated she was when she learned of Shaykh Mahmoud's death. She misses him tremendously. Despite her usual insistence that we have to let dervishes act however they want, one of the rare times

I saw her get angry was during the following summer, when a dervish, without saying anything, ripped apart a poster that she had taped onto a wall in her courtyard. She had paid the equivalent of about $5 to get Shaykh Mahmoud's photograph from her cell phone printed onto the poster. Quite uncharacteristic of her usual attitude, she declared the dervish "crazy."

There are human reasons, I think, for why Nura appreciated Shaykh Mahmoud's presence. He offered her company, lent her an ear, and occasionally made her laugh. But just as important, there are reasons that have to do with human-divine relations. By playing his part—by *not* saying thank you—Shaykh Mahmoud enabled Nura to play *her* part: to serve and give humbly without expecting a countergift, to never take credit for her giving and her labor, to actively shape herself into a medium for God's generosity.

Hassan, too, misses Shaykh Mahmoud. He told me he is filled with a sense of loss but also a sense of betrayal. They had known each other for years, and Shaykh Mahmoud often visited Hassan in his home and came to know Hassan's sons quite well. Hassan never knew that Shaykh Mahmoud had children too but, after his death, Shaykh Mahmoud's daughter called Hassan, and he learned about a side of his life he had never known existed: a wife and five children. Shaykh Mahmoud had always foregrounded his relationship to God and *ahl al-bayt,* while erasing (or concealing) his this-worldly kin relations. Hassan was disappointed, I think, not so much because having a family detracted from Shaykh Mahmoud's specialness as a dervish but rather because he felt that he had been lied to and because of the lack of mutuality, given that he had opened up his own life to Shaykh Mahmoud.

I have my own feelings about Shaykh Mahmoud's death. There is sadness but also regret. During my last time in Egypt when he was still alive, I started avoiding him. Although in theory I was intrigued by an economy of giving that is not shaped by a culture of please and thank you, another part of me found Shaykh Mahmoud ungrateful and impolite. I admired his way of life, his disinterest in material things, his lack of concern with putting aside savings, and his way of disrupting rules of politeness. But I also found him pushy. Looking back, the tipping point was probably the day when I was driving back to Cairo with my mother, after having gone to visit a friend in a hospital in the city of Asyut who had gotten into a horrible car accident. Shaykh Mahmoud called while we were on the road. As usual, he did not ask any questions about how we were doing but simply insisted that we should meet later that evening and that my mother should come too (he had met her a few times and had come to expect donations from her as well). I cut the conversation short and refused to meet him. Eventually I stopped answering his phone calls. At the *khidma* I sought out other people and tried to ignore him.

My regrets about how our relationship ended now serve as a humbling reminder of the gap between the theoretical moves I am drawn to and my personal limitations. I can write against an ethos of charity with its built-in expectations of suffering and gratitude, but at least part of me still expected an occasional thank you, or at least an occasional "how are you"—an expectation that got in the way of a different encounter with Shaykh Mahmoud, a coming to know him more on his terms, and maybe the recognition that, in a not readily visible way, he gave to me too. He offered me a glimpse of a different understanding of poverty, one that does not require performances of suffering. His way of being in the world and being-with-others (including the saints and God) is very different from how Amal and many others in Egypt understand, narrate, and inhabit their poverty. In his world, and in his view, we are all poor and dependent.

I now appreciate Shaykh Mahmoud's seeming ingratitude precisely because it reminds me of how difficult it is to step out of a worldly logic of give-and-take, to shake off a humanitarian reason. In this sense, I see the figure of the dervish as an analytical, ethical, and political challenge. Again, that is not to say that Shaykh Mahmoud was particularly interested in politics. He once told me a premonitory dream-vision that he had seen months before the uprising, figuring a naked Hosni Mubarak, and he was outspoken about his dislike for the Muslim Brotherhood, as were all at the *khidma,* but, apart from that, politics did not seem to faze him much. Nura, too, is ostensibly disinterested in politics. She does not care about concepts like "social justice," and she had no interest in the uprising that was driving thousands of people to Tahrir Square only a few kilometers away from her *khidma*. When I asked her if she had been to any of the protests, she told me that protests are none of her business: "My area is food and drink" (*magālī al-akl wa al-shurb*). The fight for a better world is not what Shaykh Mahmoud and Nura are all about. Nevertheless, I cannot help but wonder what Shaykh Mahmoud would have made of the newest chapter in Egypt's recent turbulent history. What I do know is that, in the current era of austerity measures, his performances of entitlement would be as odd and disruptive as ever.

After the Revolution

SIX

Tomorrow Is Better

A NEW SUEZ CANAL. A new capital city, replete with a green space twice the size of New York's Central Park, an amusement park four times the size of Disneyland, and the largest mosque and largest church in all of Egypt. A new nuclear power plant financed through a loan from Russia. Since Abdelfattah el-Sisi became president in June 2014, there has been lots of newness. Or at least the promise of newness. Each megaproject is announced with great fanfare, and then is outdone by the announcement of another, even more fantastic project, a few months later. El-Sisi promises a stronger Egypt, a rebuilt economy, a brighter future. *"Al-ghad afdal,"* he says. *"Bukra agmal."* Tomorrow is better. Tomorrow is more beautiful.

The months I spent in Egypt during the immediate aftermath of the 2011 uprising were both unsettling and inspiring. The contrast between revolutionary and charitable spaces was jarring but also tempted me, at least at times, to read pious modes of giving as counterhegemonic, if not revolutionary, and to read certain aspects of the uprising, such as the sit-in at Tahrir Square, as sharing some traits with those modes of giving, among them a profound present-orientedness, attention to immediate needs, and commitment to sharing. It was a special time for me and for most people I know in Egypt.

In December 2011, I left Cairo only to return the following summer, in time to witness the Muslim Brotherhood candidate Mohamed Morsi win the presidency. I remember standing on my balcony when the election results were announced, relieved that the only other remaining candidate, someone aligned with the previous regime, had been defeated but unsure of what would come next.[1] I heard the fireworks and knew crowds were heading to Tahrir Square to celebrate, but decided not to join them. I thought about the Muslim Brotherhood's historical commitment to social justice but also about its increasing entanglement with a capitalist structure and ethos. I thought about Amal, who was cautiously optimistic that this change would mean more help for the poor but would soon be disappointed. I thought about Madame Salwa's unabashed classism, which had lately been finding expression in her disdain for the appearance of low-ranking Muslim Brotherhood supporters. And I thought about Nura, Shaykh Salah, Shaykh Mahmoud, and other Sufi friends and worried about what this would mean for them and their ways of life. The Muslim Brotherhood was widely understood to be vehemently anti-Sufi.[2] It was a summer filled with uncertainty.

My next visit to Egypt was in the summer of 2014, and once again I found the country transformed. While I was away, the military had ousted Mohamed Morsi, and over eight hundred Muslim Brotherhood supporters had been killed when their sit-ins in Cairo were violently dissolved. Abdelfattah el-Sisi, formerly the minister of defense, had become president. In only three years, Egypt had changed drastically. The country went from talk of revolution and justice in 2011, to talk of progress and sacrifice in 2014. These shifts have been jolting for everyone, a confirmation of the powers that be and depressing for activists and many of the poor. Through all these changes, though, there has been one constant. Lots of people still need help. And a few givers have kept right on giving. Shaykh Salah has continued going to the market every morning, cooking meals, and distributing them at the Sayyida Zaynab mosque, though, as we will see, he now worries about the increasing numbers of people he has to feed. Madame Salwa has continued distributing food in poor neighborhoods while trying to combine her charitable work with investing in the nation's future. Amal has continued looking for help or for a job, and things have only gotten harder. Egypt has changed drastically, but the giving and receiving continues. Though equally dismissed by progressive activists and by those invested in el-Sisi's megaprojects, everyday practices of giving are as important as ever. Not simply because they meet immediate needs in ways that the state does not. But also because, by highlighting dependency (on God *and* humans), they disrupt the very logic of an emancipatory (neo)liberal politics and its built-in individualism, emphasis on work, and promise of a better tomorrow.

Focusing on tomorrow itself is not a problem. Surely, people all over the globe live with an eye to some kind of future.[3] A person might be concerned with what will happen in ten minutes, or what will happen tomorrow, or what will happen in ten years. One person might save for their retirement, while another will worry about their children's future or future generations.

Many of us think about what happens after death. While the future figures in ways big and small across the globe, what is so detrimental about el-Sisi's promise of a better tomorrow is that it tends to justify a dreary today. El-Sisi's futurity invests heavily in hope and is brought into being through citizens' sacrifices and hard work; all the while, the state looms large in the background, a father figure that promises to take care of its citizens, not through distribution but by building new canals, bridges, nuclear plants, and cities, while repressing all oppositional voices. This future rides on what Lauren Berlant (2011) calls a "cruel optimism," propelled forward through an attachment to forms and fantasies of life that never bring about what they promise but that nevertheless have a powerful hold on people. It is a future that echoes post-9/11 public relations campaigns in the Arab world that popularized slogans such as "Hope," "Life," and "Optimism" and helped to facilitate (and legitimate) a neoliberalization of the economy by espousing entrepreneurialism, volunteerism, and hard work (Sukarieh 2012). With his focus on hard work and sacrifice, el-Sisi promotes an orientation toward a "better tomorrow" at the expense of the present.[4]

Describing a similar dynamic, Caroline Melly has analyzed long-term projects of growth and change in Senegal that put forth a "very particular vision of the present that rationalize[s], emphasize[s], and even celebrate[s] the everyday hardships wrought by infrastructural change" (2013:387). She speaks of a tendency "to "rationaliz[e] the impossible present as enabling an alternative future" (391). Elizabeth Povinelli (2011a), too, has written about the detrimental effects of a continuous displacement of the present in favor of the future. She argues that late liberal imaginaries tend to justify current suffering through reference to a future anterior—the idea that "it will all have been worth it." In Egypt, the continuous promise of a better tomorrow has turned the pain of today into something to be endured, celebrated, or simply ignored. As an Egyptian TV presenter put it in September 2014: "When you give people the first step toward tomorrow, they forget all the pain and brokenness."

El-Sisi's politics of hope has gone hand in hand with political repression and at the same time has involved the call for an active giving to and for the nation, a giving that is quite different from the everyday practices that revolve around giving to God, or rather offering *returns*—giving back what already belongs to God. Giving to God—in the sense of the *khidma*, Madame Salwa, and the Resala volunteers—is not about building a better tomorrow; it is about detaching oneself from the material world, drawing closer to God, and at the same time addressing immediate needs. It calls for a different kind of labor, one that does not yield monetary profit. It is about dependency, not emancipation.

To be clear, there can appear to be some overlap between our instances of giving and el-Sisi's vision of government. Some Islamic discourses, too, console those suffering in the present with the promise of a better tomorrow. They, too, seem to imply that "it will all have been worth it" by presenting hardship in reference to future salvation through the cultivation of patience (*sabr*) as a virtue, and other times they seem to rationalize, or celebrate, poverty by assuring the poor that they will be the first to enter paradise. Islam is not immune to being co-opted by neoliberal logics (Atia 2013; Rudnyckyj 2011). But there are other visions of Islam, too. Many of the people you met in previous chapters give without worrying about whether tomorrow will be better or not. "You might walk out of here and be hit by a car," Resala volunteers often say. "You could die tomorrow."

For many, giving *li-llāh,* to God and for God, is about the afterlife, but it takes the form of giving in the here and now. An eschatological temporality is seemingly about the future too, but it is not linear. Rather, each moment is connected to the afterlife. Unlike the future tied to el-Sisi's megaprojects, which promise this-and-that many jobs by this-and-that year, pious givers insist that the this-worldly future is intrinsically unknown. The stubborn present-orientendess of giving to God runs counter to an ideology of newness, growth, and improvement. Against the backdrop of el-Sisi's megaprojects, such quiet everyday practices deserve even more of our ethnographic and political attention. They point to an Otherwise, maybe despite themselves.

HOPE AND SACRIFICE

When declaring his decision to run for president, Abdelfattah el-Sisi announced that hard times were upon his countrymen. A brighter future could only be reached through hard work.

> Finally, allow me to speak about hope. Hope is the outcome of hard work. Hope is safety. Hope is stability. Hope is the dream, the dream to usher Egypt into its leading role in the world, to restore its leverage and influence and to teach the world as it did before. I cannot perform miracles. Rather, I propose

hard work and self-sacrifice. And I promise you—if I am granted the honor of leadership—that together, the leadership and the people, we can achieve stability, safety and hope for Egypt, God willing.[5]

The future here depends on God (if we take "God willing" to be more than an empty rhetorical gesture) but also on hard work and sacrifice. El-Sisi's brand of optimism is pious and patriotic. And it seems to have been effective. In May of 2014, el-Sisi won the elections, defeating the Nasserist candidate Hamdeen Sabahi. In the months that followed, he kept returning to the same themes of sacrifice: hard work and hope, safety and stability. If there was one key message during his early presidency, it was this: Sacrifice! Sacrifice for the sake of your children, for the nation, for Egypt's recovery. Sacrifice by working harder, eating less, paying higher prices, and putting up with austerity measures and subsidy cuts. Don't complain. Show that you're civilized and educated, that you know the future matters more than this current moment. Don't be shortsighted. Sacrifice today for a better tomorrow.

In his inauguration speech, el-Sisi explained his personal relationship to the sacrificial spirit:

> I have not sought a day in political office. I started my professional life in the institution of the armed forces where I learned the meaning of the nation and its value and the value of taking responsibility. I also learned that our lives and our souls are to be sacrificed for the nation.[6]

As became increasingly clear, however, in el-Sisi's vision, not only do soldiers have to embrace the spirit of sacrifice but also ordinary citizens. One month into his presidency, el-Sisi likened the subsidy cuts he had imposed to sacrifices made during times of war.[7] Speaking calmly in colloquial Arabic, occasionally smiling and placing his right hand on his heart, he addressed the nation, asking all Egyptians, rich and poor, to endure. In his speech, Egypt's past served as a resource, a tool for crafting a present-day willingness to sacrifice for a better future. He recalled the harsh economic times of war between 1967 and 1973 to underline "the resilience of the Egyptian people for the sake of the future" (sumūd al-masriyīn 'ashān al-mustaqbal). The Egyptians' steadfastness and patience, he argued, had been critical in leading Egypt to victory in the 1973 war against Israel. "Egyptians faced a lot of pain and suffering . . . they were living in a war economy for six years and never complained until victory was achieved in 1973." The same patience and perseverance, he implied, were required once again to reach stability and long-term prosperity. In these difficult times, he insisted, "there have to be real sacrifices [*tadhīyāt haqīqiyya*] that every Egyptian man and woman must make." Likening post-uprising Egypt to a time of war, el-Sisi called upon all citizens to put aside their personal needs and prioritize the nation. In war times, he reminded them, every house had a son in the army, and the parents did not think twice about whether he would return home or not. The nation took priority.

For el-Sisi, the parallel between the interwar years and his presidency consisted of two things. First, the country was under attack, in his case by "Islamist terrorism," a specter that has justified massive political repression across Egypt. Second, the country faced an economic crisis caused by the immense interest payments due on its national debt, salaries to the millions of government employees, and subsidies historically provided for certain food items, electricity, and gas. "We pay all that out of our pocket. And don't we all know that it's wrong to spend more than you have?" El-Sisi's economic lesson implicates the listener: Egypt is akin to a household, a zero-sum game. If there is not enough money coming in, we should not be spending so much. We should—individual and nation alike—tighten our belts.

Despite Egypt's dire financial situation and the grave danger it was facing, el-Sisi insisted that there was hope. It was precisely through their sacrifices that Egyptians could bring about a brighter future. "Tomorrow is better, God willing," he concluded. And so, the time of sacrifices began. And the president led by example.

As the commencement speaker at a military college graduation, with the speech aired live on national television, el-Sisi saluted these upcoming Egyptian soldiers at the beginning of Ramadan and asked them and all viewers for a month of work for the sake of Egypt. He declared that he would not agree to the proposed budget because it failed to address the country's large deficit. Egypt could not be left to future generations with this immense debt. It was time to sacrifice. And he would go first.

> There must be real sacrifices from every Egyptian man and woman. I receive the maximum salary . . . What is the maximum [monthly] salary? Forty-two thousand Egyptian pounds [about $5,900]. That's too much for me. I say in front of you all: I will do two things. I will give up half of my salary. And half of my personal wealth and even the money I inherited from my father will be given up for the sake of the nation. I want to think of the children that are coming and to leave them something good, but this way we will leave them nothing. If the debt keeps accumulating like this, we won't leave them anything good.[8]

After pledging his own sacrifice, el-Sisi called upon Egyptians inside and outside of the country to follow his example. A few hours later, a news flash announced that a new account, Tahya Masr (Long Live Egypt), had been set up at the National Bank of Egypt to collect donations in support of the country's economy.[9] Contributions started pouring in.

High-ranking politicians and businessmen made widely publicized donations, emphasizing their willingness to contribute to Egypt's development (and maybe also seeking to cleanse themselves of a long-standing reputation for corruption). A spokesperson said Prime Minister Ibrahim Mehleb was going to give up half his salary and another unspecified amount from his fortune. The governor of Port Said announced he was going to donate half of his salary. An anchorwoman tweeted: "I'm with you, president, and I will donate half of my monthly salary for our country Egypt." Mohammad al-Amin, a businessman and owner of the satellite TV channel CBC, said he was going to donate half of his cash and bonds for the initiative. The head of Nile University announced he was going to contribute his entire salary.[10] The fund became a neoliberal tax of sorts, with each individual choosing how much to give instead of the government choosing how much to take for the benefit of all. Those who did not donate—among them businessmen who were uneasy with the privileges granted to the military in a supposed "free-market economy"—ended up on a blacklist compiled by Sisi supporters (Abul-Magd 2016:36). The initiative thus created a certain amount of pressure, but it also created the opportunity for much self-congratulatory talk, which was sometimes infused with a pious flair. The Coptic billionaire Naguib Sawiris declared on TV that he would follow the "Sisi initiative." He refused to disclose the nature of his contribution, praising the secrecy of donations "because we are dealing with God and should have no other goals."

Al-Azhar and the Coptic Church made donations, too, and the head of Dar al-Ifta, a government body tasked with drafting nonbinding religious rulings (*fatwas*), announced that participation in the initiative could count as Muslims' obligatory alms donations, since alms can be used "to serve the poor, provide job opportunities for youth, and build armies." Political and religious needs could thus be merged through a redefinition of alms away from immediate needs toward long-term development and megaprojects. Stability (*istiqrār*), one of the magic words in post-uprising Egypt, became intimately tied to development (*tanmiya*).

One of el-Sisi's first major projects was the New Suez Canal, a project that, in his words, was going to be "Egypt's gift to the world."[11] When I arrived in

Cairo in the summer of 2014, this grand project of hope had already taken over the front pages of Egyptian newspapers and was dominating talk on Cairo's streets. The construction of the New Suez Canal had been inaugurated in early August, when, under the supervision of the Egyptian Army Corps of Engineers, 7,500 workers started digging.[12] A few days later, I arrived in Cairo. Driving from the airport to Mohandeseen, my taxi driver told me about how gas prices were skyrocketing; it was becoming increasingly difficult for him to get by from day to day. Then he smiled: "But I'm sure you've heard of the New Suez Canal! In two years, Egypt will be strong again." In the weeks that followed, Egyptians from various backgrounds brought up the Suez Canal project in conversations, echoing el-Sisi's promises. That the new canal would help revive Egypt's economy. That it would double the canal's capacity from forty-nine to ninety-seven ships a day. That it would increase revenues from ship traffic. That it would lure large foreign investments into the area, and jobs by the thousands.[13]

Hope, it seemed, had become a strategy of survival. The cab driver, and others struggling to get by, simply had to wait it out. Their hardship was a necessary sacrifice for a better tomorrow. It would all have been worth it.

The cost for the New Suez Canal was estimated to be $4 billion, and el-Sisi announced that he would not rely on any foreign loans.[14] Egyptian citizens would themselves pay for the megaproject. They would invest in their country's future. And so, in addition to collecting donations, the government began selling investment certificates, denominated in 10, 100, and 1,000 Egyptian pounds ($1.40, $14, and $140, respectively), with a maturity of five years at a 12 percent interest rate, a generous countergift for the citizens' gift to the nation.[15] For many pious givers a countergift can only come from God; that is the reason one should never expect anything from the recipient, not even a word of thanks. Here the countergift comes from the state, or rather from nearly miraculous capital growth, which is seemingly more predictable than divine rewards could ever be.

Countless Egyptians participated in el-Sisi's project of hope. Some traveled to the Sinai to cheer on the workers. Others donated for the New Suez Canal or bought investment certificates. Among them was Madame Salwa, who bought a stack of 10-pound investment certificates for a group of orphans she visits regularly in an orphanage.

She asked me, wouldn't it be wonderful if these orphans, too, could partake in Egypt's growth? If they, too, could own a part of the new Egypt that was being built?

I shrugged my shoulders. I was troubled by Madame Salwa's unshakeable faith in el-Sisi's megaprojects and uneasy with the collapse between her present-oriented giving and her desire to invest in the future—two orientations that I had maybe too artificially held apart in my thinking. Madame Salwa was not concerned about that distinction. For her, giving can take many forms. As I had to remind myself in such moments, neither she nor anyone else in this book is bound to a static notion of what an Islamic ethics should look like, what "Islam" is, or what "the good" (*al-khayr*) consists of.

Along with Madame Salwa, many gave. Over $8 billion—twice the target amount—was collected in donations and investments over only eight working days.[16] The mantra of development kept resounding. Soon things will be better! Hope in a better future was actively crafted in the present, through celebrating the nation's willingness to wait, through the insistent valorizing of sacrifice, and through donations and investments. The sacrificial spirit that was sweeping across Egypt was in line with state-approved interpretations of Islam and geared toward rebuilding the nation. El-Sisi had set the tone. And not only the wealthy and middle-class Egyptians like Madame Salwa donated. The poor, too, gave of the little they had, or at least so goes the story of Sayyida Zaynab.

THE POOR IN THE ERA OF SACRIFICE

Sayyida Zaynab Moustafa Saad El-Mallah was ninety years old and blind when, in July 2014, President el-Sisi invited her to the presidential palace to publicly honor her sacrificial gesture. Wanting to contribute to the Long Live Egypt fund but lacking the savings to do so, Sayyida Zaynab sold her gold earrings and donated the profits. El-Sisi allegedly learned of her donation from a newspaper. In the official video of their meeting, shot in the presidential palace, el-Sisi was dressed in a suit, smiling, facing Sayyida Zaynab, who was wearing a brownish *gallābiyya* and a loose white scarf, and seemed to be sinking into the plush golden chair, next to her a large microphone. El-Sisi leaned over to kiss Sayyida Zaynab's forehead. He asked why she had made the donation. She responded that she loves Egypt and was inspired by the president's announcement that he would donate half of his salary in support of the Egyptian economy. He asked whether she had ever performed the hajj, the pilgrimage to Mecca, which each Muslim ideally should undertake at least once in her lifetime. She had not. He said he would personally pay for her pilgrimage—not out of Egypt's funds but out of his own pocket. And when she meets the Prophet Muhammad there, could she please make supplications for Egypt? Sayyida Zaynab seemed overwhelmed and confused by what el-Sisi was saying. Or maybe she did not hear him well. He threw in an additional gift, promising to buy her a hearing aid. Then, as if needing to top it even more, he said: "I'll tell you something. Your earrings will be displayed in the museum of the presidential palace, along with your picture!" After the meeting, he walked her to a car that would take her home and again kissed her forehead.[17]

The multiple gifts offered by el-Sisi confirm a fundamental tenet of Islam, one also emphasized by Resala volunteers: that all well-intentioned good deeds will be rewarded—in this case by God, or the president, or both. El-Sisi's praise for, and memorialization of, this woman's gesture drives home the point that no one has an excuse not to sacrifice, and that everyone will be better off for doing so. Everyone should follow in Sayyida Zaynab's footsteps. If even this ailing, blind, poor woman could contribute to the long-term prosperity of Egypt, so can you.

Sayyida Zaynab belongs to "the noble poor," the kind that does not complain and the kind that gives of the little they have. The noble poor are distinct from the beggar (shahhāt) and the thug (baltagī), who together make up a vague but feared category of the lazy, untrustworthy, dangerous poor.[18] The noble poor make no demands and sometimes are not even recognizable as poor. El-Sisi had praised them already during an earlier television interview in which he promised to put an end to the Muslim Brotherhood but also showed a softer side, emphasizing his respect for his wife (and all Egyptian women) and nostalgically recalling a time when a different spirit perfused Egyptian society. He described his childhood in Gamaliyya, a neighborhood in Islamic Cairo, as one of peaceful coexistence where Muslims, Christians, and Jews lived side by side, and one could hear the church bells ring and see people visit the local synagogue; no one ever asked, "What is your religion?" This was also a time, he said, when the poor and the rich lived side by side, and "you didn't know who was what."

Later, at a time when food prices had risen by two-thirds since Mubarak's ouster, el-Sisi reported proudly: "I receive letters from people who can't find food . . . and they tell me, 'we're not eating but we accept that for your sake.'" This is the ideal poor citizen: someone who does not complain, let alone protest. Someone willing to go hungry for the sake of the nation. Someone who does not question the status quo but ritually confirms it through self-sacrifice.

The counterimage to el-Sisi's dream of the poor and the rich living together peacefully, of self-sacrifice and acquiescence, is the revolution of the poor and hungry that many in Egypt have been warning of (or anticipating), a revolution yet to come that would be far more volatile than the presumed middle-class revolution the country witnessed in 2011. Equally at odds with the "noble poor" are people like Amal, who actively, if not aggressively, seek help from wherever they can. Amal would be dismayed by the idea that sacrificing for the nation's future should take priority over meeting her children's immediate needs. She goes to great lengths to make sure that people know that she is struggling. She will never live up to the ideal of the noble poor. At the same time, things have only become more difficult for her.

Under el-Sisi, and due to pressure from the International Monetary Fund, those who do not voluntarily make sacrifices have been forced to do so. After less than a month in office, el-Sisi raised fuel prices overnight; phased electricity cost hikes were announced the same week as subsidies were being cut.[19] The changes were, not coincidentally, imposed during Ramadan, a month devoted to the spirit of sacrifice. The day after fuel prices went up, a headline in the daily *Al-Masry Al-Youm* read: "The hour of suffering has struck." El-Sisi likened the subsidy cuts to "bitter medicine."[20]

People like Madame Salwa defended the cuts as necessary measures enforced by a strong leader who was keeping his gaze firmly fixed on the future. Others complained. The Egyptian Revolutionary Socialists denounced el-Sisi's austere vision as characteristic of a "counter-revolutionary mandate" that betrayed the founding principles of the 2011 revolution and the Egyptian people at large.[21] A leader of the group wrote on Facebook: "El-Sisi, the candidate of the billionaires, is asking people to submit to austerity measures and sacrifice for one or two generations! It seems there will be no honeymoon between el-Sisi and the masses."[22] Another opposition group posted a picture on Facebook of a street child eating from garbage, next to a picture of el-Sisi and army leaders eating at a fancy banquet, to highlight the contradictions of the government's call for sacrifice.[23] An Islamist activist tweeted that Egypt has seven of the world's hundred richest people and at the same time has a high rate of corruption. Under these circumstances, he asked, how can the poor be expected to accept austerity measures? The Muslim Brotherhood called the austerity measures "mad military decrees," a "new heinous crime," and "collective punishment for the people." To them, the measures were proof that "el-Sisi and his coup collaborators were determined to increase the people's pain and suffering and to deprive them of even the most essential food, while fighting them with all their murderous military might."[24]

A symbolic image, recycled in cartoons in opposition newspapers at the time, showed a piece of Egyptian flatbread cut into four parts. It played on a suggestion el-Sisi had made in a TV interview. Instead of a person eating an entire flatbread, he said, it should be cut into four parts so there is more to go around—a daring statement in a country where many low-income families eat large amounts of subsidized bread simply to fill their stomachs. Effectively making hunger a natural, even noble, part of life, el-Sisi suggested that eating only one fourth of a typical portion meant understanding and accepting the "true reality."[25] On opposition websites, photographs circulated of a few brave protesters carrying signs to which they had attached pieces of bread, cut into four pieces.

Yet, for the most part, these critical voices were muted, at best. The anger at el-Sisi was a barely perceptible echo of the resounding calls for "bread" and "social justice" that had saturated Egypt's streets during the 2011 protests. There was an obvious reason, of course: the oppressive atmosphere. Dissent was dealt with harshly, and the risk of arrest was real. But what had also rendered the critique unstable, I think, is that el-Sisi had successfully co-opted the revolutionary rhetoric. What made his gaze to the future so powerful was precisely that it combined the ideology of state-run development, a particular reading of Islam, and the revolution's spirit of sacrifice. The uprising, too, had ridden on the promise of a better tomorrow, albeit a tomorrow differently imagined and differently crafted. Many activists reported that they were driven to the streets by the dream of a better future, a dream for which they were willing to sacrifice everything, even their lives. Throughout 2011, protesters came to Tahrir Square dressed in funeral shrouds or wearing stickers with the words "A martyr is available here" (*shahīd taht al-talab*) (Mittermaier 2015). In the months following Hosni Mubarak's ouster, American multinational corporations colonized the revolutionary future. Billboards sprang up throughout the country exhorting passersby: "Make tomorrow more beautiful" (Coke); "Think, participate, dream" (Pepsi). New political parties called themselves "Revolution's Tomorrow Party," "Egyptian Hope Party," or "The Beginning." The revolu-

"Make tomorrow more beautiful," Coke ad in Cairo, August 2011.
Photograph by the author.

tion's hopefulness was quickly reappropriated by capitalism, the state, and conventional party politics.

Hoping for a better future can be revolutionary; it can also be deeply conservative. Both forms of hope, in their own way, betray the present. They draw attention away from the here and now, and make practices such as food distribution and almsgiving seem parochial and shortsighted. Just as consequential was that in the months after the uprising, the many meanings of "social justice" began to narrow. A broad and impossibly optimistic panoply of demands was slowly reduced to one: equal work opportunities. One of the initial strands of the uprising, a fundamental questioning of the way the country's resources are distributed, faded into the background and was replaced by a notion, shared among revolutionaries and counterrevolutionaries alike, that what was most valuable was a good work ethic combined with fair work opportunities. It was but a short step from the demand for more work to the demand for more belt tightening.

GIVING A MAN A FISH

At the same time as they had to cope with subsidy cuts, Egypt's poor were called upon to eat less and work more. Intimately related to the sacrificial spirit is the ideology of hard work. "From Egyptian to Egyptian: Work is our only solution," mysterious billboards proclaimed on Cairo's streets in the months following the uprising, both in English and Arabic. During el-Sisi's presidential campaign, the message resurfaced full force. Billboards in run-down neighborhoods featured el-Sisi's stern face, and next to it the words "Hard work is all I have, and all I will ask from you," or "With work the people live," or even just "With work."

Faith in work is, of course, not unique to el-Sisi. From the very beginnings of capitalism, one of its key imperatives has been "to drive people into labor" (Ferguson 2015:xi). Faith in work, as Max Weber (2001) famously argued, can also have an elective affinity with religious beliefs. In Weber's reading, Calvinist Protestantism, which encouraged hard work and the pursuit of profit, aided the development of a capitalist ethos. But Christianity does not hold exclusive rights to capitalism. We find faith in work also among Muslim Brotherhood thinkers like Yusuf al-Qaradawi, Sufis like Shaykh Salah, and even those struggling to get by, like Amal. We find it in those Islamic NGOs that embrace a "pious neoliberalism" (Atia 2013) and that have shifted from handouts to microloans in an effort to "help the poor help themselves."

In Egypt, one such organization is Dar al-Orman. Founded in 1993 and originally focused on orphan care, over time Dar al-Orman has turned its attention to funding micro-enterprise projects. During my first visit to the organization, one of its directors put it to me bluntly: "In the army they say, 'Dig or die.' Here we say: 'Work or die!'" He handed me a leather-bound book filled with dozens of fatwas, nonbinding Islamic legal rulings, that justified a reorientation of alms from handouts to microloans. The fatwas cite hadiths that emphasize the value of work and encourage self-reliance, such as one in which the Prophet Muhammad says, "Verily, for a man to carry a rope and gather firewood, then come to sell it in the market and make himself independent thereby such that he can spend on his needs, that is better for him than asking people who might give him or deprive him."

Along with hadiths in favor of self-reliance, there are a number of resources in the Islamic tradition that point to long-term horizons. The institution of *waqf*, for instance, an endowment or trust, refers to donations of privately owned property for a charitable purpose with long-term effects, such as in the form of a school, hospital, or fountain. The goal of a *waqf* is to keep on giving toward a charitable purpose, which in turn enables the donor to continue receiving rewards past her lifetime. The concept is derived from a number of hadiths, and the practice dates from early Islamic history, the Abbasid period if not earlier. As Nada Moumtaz notes, this long history problematizes the assumption "that before its colonization by development discourses, charity emphasized the here and now and was not geared towards sustainability."[26] In Egypt, under Gamal Abdel Nasser, all *waqfs* were dismantled and nationalized, but, since the early twenty-first century, development-oriented NGOs have tried to revive the concept.[27] More widely used in Egypt today is the principle of *sadaqa gāriyya* (continuous, or literally, "running" charity), a type of voluntary donation that is given with an eye to long-term effects. *Sadaqa gāriyya* projects can involve digging a well for a village, giving a cow to a poor family, or planting palm trees. An employee at one NGO told me a typical success story. Once they gave a cow to a poor woman as *sadaqa gāriyya;* the cow gave birth, and the woman kept the calf and returned the cow so it could be given to another family. During a follow-up visit, they found the woman distributing rice pudding, made from cow's milk, to the poor of the village. From being a recipient, someone in need, the woman had been transformed into someone who was able to give. The employee concluded, "This is the best kind of giving: the kind that helps the poor stand on their own feet."

In this story, and in similar long-term gifts, an orientation to a future horizon merges with the more immediate imperative to give. The idea in giving a cow to a poor woman is to help *now* with the intention that the gift grows so that the future can be better too. This is not a story of "it will all have been worth it." Nevertheless, the story of the cow emphasizes the value of entrepreneurialism and the responsibility of the poor. It praises those who stand on their own feet, those who are not dependent.

Pious logics of giving can be varied and multilayered. Madame Salwa, as we have seen, eagerly bought investment certificates for the New Suez Canal to gift to orphans. Shaykh Salah, despite his commitment to offering food every day, applauds el-Sisi's megaprojects, and ideally he would like to not only cook for the poor but to also teach them how to become more self-reliant. Resala does not just send volunteers into slums; it also gives out microloans. Likewise, el-Sisi's own faith in development and sacrifice is not in conflict with Islam but rather a particular elaboration of it. Think of the blind woman who donated her earrings and was rewarded with a pilgrimage and the promise that she would meet the Prophet Muhammad. Think of the austerity measures being introduced during Ramadan, a month of spiritual purification and sacrifice. Think of Dar al-Ifta's declaration that donations to the national development fund could count as obligatory alms. The NGOs' turn toward development and el-Sisi's project of hope are not the same, but they share a number of features. Both promise that tomorrow will be better; both place responsibility on the shoulders of individuals rather than the government or society at large; and both maintain that "work is our only solution." Both, not surprisingly, are deeply suspicious of handouts.

As the director at Dar al-Orman sees it, handouts only create more beggars. And begging, he says, is a particularly pressing problem in Egypt, where people are unnaturally lazy—almost by nature. "Look, you go by any café, and you see them sitting there, smoking shisha, doing nothing. There are thousands of young guys sitting in cafés. This laziness is unnatural [*kasal ghayr ṭabīʿī*]! But people are like that [*al-nās kida*]."

The trope is familiar: lazy, tea-drinking young men "killing time" (Ralph 2008). In light of this ostensible moral crisis, the director then cited what James Ferguson (2015:35) calls "perhaps the world's most widely circulated development cliché": "Give a man a fish and you feed him for a day. Teach a man to fish and you feed him for a lifetime." The proverb is used around the globe to illustrate a seemingly obvious point: that sustainable development is preferable to handouts. As Ferguson notes, across the political spectrum, "the stubborn idea seems to persist that while production is primary, structural, and material, distribution is somehow secondary, derivative or ephemeral" (45).

In Egypt, too, the proverb circulates widely. "I don't want to give people a fish, but want to teach them how to fish," then–presidential candidate Mohamed Morsi said in a TV interview in 2012.[28] He promised to use obligatory alms donations to provide not handouts, but rather financial support and training for young Egyptians to help them find jobs. Secularist intellectuals cited the proverb to me to explain what they dislike about charitable giving. To many, the proverb seems to imply that it is better to look to the future than to address present needs. It is better to create autonomous, self-sufficient subjects than to reinforce dependencies. It is better to work and make a living than to extend one's hand and rely on other people.

Commonly, this is taken to be the "progressive" view; it is forward looking. It is a view that not all Egyptians embrace, as Ghada knows all too well. The founder of a small charity organization in one of Cairo's slums, Ghada complains that her fellow citizens are far too immersed in a "culture of charity." She tells me she feels frustrated that few donors are willing to support projects in education, health, and employment. The right balance in her view would consist of putting 70 percent of all donations toward education and job creation, and 30 percent toward the distribution of goods such as food and clothes. "But what is happening in Egypt is that 95 percent go into distribution," Ghada added with a sigh. "If you want to fund-raise for a project, you get nothing. If you ask for money for food, you get ten times more than what you need!"[29]

I have watched Madame Salwa laboriously collect alms from relatives and friends to support her charitable work. She texts me every year to remind me when it is time to send my Ramadan contribution. I am not sure Ghada is right in her assessment that Egyptians give more than enough in alms and food donations. But regardless of how accurate her assessment is, her complaint represents the "progressive" view: that handouts don't do much, and that we instead should help the poor help themselves. Given how common-sensical this view has become, it is easy to join in Ghada's sigh. As we know from Amal's story, however, not all attempts to help the poor stand on their own feet end well. Amal's microloans, which she combined with other forms of aid, allowed her to open a kiosk but this enterprise quickly became a burden. Her inability to repay the loans meant that she had to live with the constant fear of arrest and imprisonment.

This is not to say that Amal likes her dependency on charity. For her, the uprising brought with it the promise of autonomy and pride, expressed in the constantly repeated slogan: "Raise your head up high, you're Egyptian!" In line with this ideal of pride and dignity, activists, too, sometimes evoked the trope of the self-reliant fisherman. I recall a lively gathering in downtown Cairo—a so-called Flash Hub—in September 2011, where young Egyptians shared their visions for a postrevolutionary Egypt. Most were in their twenties or early thirties, but there were also two or three older people, among them a butcher known for his political and intellectual sophistication. Attendees took turns sharing their ideas. A young man proposed excitedly that leftover food should be collected from hotels and restaurants and given to the poor. Someone pointed out that this idea was already being implemented by the

Egyptian Food Bank, an organization founded by Egyptian businessmen in 2006 that has the ambitious goal of eradicating hunger in Egypt by 2020. Interrupting the exchange, the butcher stood up and gave a short but passionate speech:

> I reject the Food Bank entirely! I'm against encouraging any kind of begging. That's all the Food Bank does. It's a thousand times better to help the poor find a way to get even the simplest food on the table from their own land or through their own work than to give them a meal or leftovers from a hotel … It's all about dignity. You don't give dignity to people through handouts. Instead of giving them cooked fish, give them a fishing rod so they can fish for themselves in the Nile!

The butcher's interjection might seem naïve. The Nile is contaminated, and not everyone lives near the Nile or knows how to fish. Few people have their own land. But regardless, his interjection reminds us that the idea of self-sustainability, of growing one's own food and fishing for oneself (and one's family or community), is not inherently capitalist or neoliberal. It can also follow a different logic, one that envisions communal forms of life that circumvent the reliance on existing bureaucracies and economies.

What the butcher and the director at Dar al-Orman have in common, despite their presumably radically different politics, is their objection to handouts. Their insistence on self-reliant "fishermen" is a direct attack on the work of the givers throughout this book, and a direct attack on what many poor people rely on to survive. It is a stance that valorizes the kind of work that leads to an income or at least a visible outcome (fish on the table) and disregards other forms of labor—the countless hours Madame Salwa, Shaykh Salah, and Nura spend cooking, giving to God, and serving the poor. It also devalorizes the many hours people like Amal spend running from charity organization to charity organization, or what James Ferguson (2015:94ff.) calls "distributive labor," which for him includes everything from begging to panhandling and pickpocketing. A deep suspicion toward "handouts" has come to be shared across the political spectrum, and is echoed by secularists and pious Muslims alike.

Some, though, are critical of the ideal of the self-reliant fisherman. Dr. Sherif Abdelazeem, the founder of Resala, says, "Yes, it's a good thing to help people find a job but you can't turn everyone into a fisherman. Not everyone is able to fish. Many are too old, or too young, or handicapped. So what do you do then? Helping is extremely important."

Though not fundamentally questioning the ideal of self-reliance, Dr. Sherif emphasizes that people have different capacities. A more profound unease was expressed by an employee at a center for the study of philanthropy at the American University in Cairo, a young Muslim man who confided in me his ambivalence, or what he calls "feeling schizophrenic at times." Whereas his daily work revolves around strategic development and involves spreadsheets and sustainability studies, on a personal level he believes that "it's not about needing more fishermen but about distributing the fish more evenly." In an article from 2011, Yussuf Ghishan, a Jordanian journalist, made a similar point. He argued that the famous proverb does not offer a solution to poverty because it assumes that poverty results from a lack of skills or education while ignoring the enormous power of class structures, and the oppression and exploitation that nearly inevitably results from class difference.[30] He asks questions that are both literal and metaphorical: "If you teach [the poor] how to fish, who will provide the sea? And if there is a sea, who can guarantee that it will not be turned into a port for commercial ships?"

This critique resonates with ones put forth by anthropologists such as Tania Li (2010), who reminds us that we no longer live in a world where everyone can find work, even if they wanted to, and James Ferguson (2015), who directly takes on the infamous proverb in his work on basic income programs. Building on an idea first articulated in the eighteenth century, basic income programs have been giving out cash payments since the 1980s. These are not conditional grants, and, importantly, they go not only to classical welfare recipients (women, children, the elderly, the disabled) but also to young, able-bodied men. The reason such programs are so crucial, Ferguson argues, is that it is no longer the case (if it ever was) that we should simply teach everyone to fish. The "productionist paradigm," which has long dominated development programs, as well as discourses of the radical left, is outdated. Simply put, and again in literal *and* metaphorical terms, there are not enough fish left in the ocean for everyone to become a fisherman (or a fisherwoman for that matter); mass fishing has decimated our waters. What we need instead is a new politics of distribution. In response to the common claim that "giving a man a fish" does not lead to real structural change, Ferguson argues that there is no reason to treat efforts at distribution as any less "real" (or any less "structural") than efforts at production.[31]

In el-Sisi's Egypt, there is no sign of a basic income program on the horizon.[32] The state continues cutting back on social services and subsidies, investing in megaprojects instead. The latest of these projects is the New

Administrative Capital, a project to be completed by 2020. Promotional videos show something akin to a large-scale gated community populated by light-skinned, mostly nonveiled women and shorts-wearing men who smile as they ride bikes along luscious green lawns. Critics have pointed to the neoliberal logic that underpins this project and renders the city of Cairo dispensable and replaceable. A professor of political science at Cairo University, in an open letter to el-Sisi, emphasized the connection between the development of such megaprojects and the deprivation of the Egyptian people. Ultimately, the New Administrative Capital, he says, will be for Egypt's elites while the costs will be "borne by the Egyptian people with limited income."[33] Again, such voices of criticism are rare. Many seem ready to jump on the bandwagon of hope and optimism—even of the cruel kind. Madame Salwa dreams of moving to the New Administrative Capital even though she could never afford a home there.

El-Sisi, in the meantime, has continued to uphold the spirit of self-sacrifice, even bemoaning the fact that he cannot sell himself for the nation.[34] At the same time, the tightening of belts has continued. In November 2016, in the hope of receiving an IMF loan, the Central Bank of Egypt floated the Egyptian pound, devaluing the currency by almost 50 percent. When I was in Egypt last, in February 2018, prices had skyrocketed.

In many ways, this feels like more of the same, and many are disappointed and disillusioned by what has come of the uprising. A working-class Egyptian in the summer of 2014 succinctly summed up his disappointment:

> In my opinion, and I'm sorry to say this, the revolution has failed completely. It didn't accomplish a single demand. Its demands were forgotten. Morsi came and made us feel that we made the revolution so we can pray—as if Mubarak didn't allow us to pray. And the current regime [el-Sisi's government] makes us feel that we made a revolution to save money and stay on a budget—as if we had so much money and lived in so much luxury that we decided to revolt to stop spending money!

To this man, the models that have been put forth since the uprising—by the Muslim Brotherhood and el-Sisi—do not point in any new directions, or at least not those the revolutionaries fought for. People did not take to the streets in order to be able to pray or tighten their belts. They hoped for a better life, whatever that might be.

While politics are more of the same, what we do find in Egypt is a long-standing commitment to a kind of distribution that is fundamentally embodied and that points to other forms of life. The distribution that is practiced in Cairo's alleys, slums, *khidmas,* and saint shrines does not call for each and every body to sacrifice, but rather calls for each body to be taken care of, to be provided whatever it needs right now. Academic critiques of a "productionist paradigm" would be unfamiliar to people like Shaykh Salah or Nura. And yet the giving that I witnessed day after day in their *khidmas* shares a great deal with these theorists' interventions. Their endless cooking reveals a profound recognition of the fundamental fact that each of us is reliant on other people every single day. Even more obvious is the resonance between the basic income idea and Shaykh Salah's concept of a divine minimum wage, which frames food as a basic God-given right. As such, an Islamic ethics of giving has something in common with the anthropologist's call for a politics of distribution. My interlocutors recognize human needs even as they say they give to God. In their daily practice, they give—day after day, and without asking questions about the recipients' deservingness. Like the state-based practices described by Ferguson, their perpetual efforts point beyond the "hegemony of work" and a "productionist common sense [which] has too often rendered distribution subsidiary, invisible, or even contemptible" (2015:21, 23). Their efforts, too, are not grounded in pity-driven charity but in the concept of a rightful share (24), in their case the Quranic idea of the "right of the poor" (*haqq al-faqīr*).[35] They, too, proceed from the idea that humans are fundamentally dependent (on each other and, most important, on God), an idea that runs counter to an emancipatory liberal politics. They, too, speak to questions of distribution, ones that too often get backgrounded—if not violently erased—but that are of critical importance in today's world.

THE BULLDOZER

One afternoon in August 2014, I was sitting on a metal bench at Abdel Munim Riyad Square, a major transportation hub adjacent to Tahrir Square. In 2011, both squares had witnessed fierce battles. Now Tahrir Square was guarded by tanks; a daily flow of buses and microbuses had returned to Abdel Munim Riyad. In front of me a bus stopped. Some got off the bus; a crowd rushed toward it. The call to prayer, resounding from a megaphone, temporarily drowned out the sound of traffic. About two dozen men headed toward a small outdoor prayer space, lining up for the afternoon prayer. Likely, most of them were strangers to one another; they had gotten off one bus and were about to board another. I sat and watched the gentle movement of their prayer, lost in thought. I was supposed to meet Amal to accompany her to meet the lawyer who was assisting with her divorce case. As always, she was late. As usual, I was not. I waited while the buses came and went, and the men completed their prayer.

Then something jolted me out of my afternoon lethargy. I saw a young muscular man, with wide shoulders, dressed in jeans and a hooded T-shirt. I saw a machine gun in his hand. I instinctively began to search for an escape route. Then I noticed dozens of policemen, similarly armed but in uniform. The man with the machine gun must have been a plainclothes police officer. I scanned the square for a fuller picture. Two policemen were stopping buses as they came into the station, to create a lane for a large yellow bulldozer. The bulldozer rolled toward an area by the side of the station that normally was crowded with small makeshift stands selling tea, candy, cold drinks, and chips. That day the stands were strangely deserted. The bulldozer knocked down a fence and grabbed whatever came into its view: boxes, tables, merchandise. Then it turned around to deposit its prey into the back of a truck. Policemen guarded both vehicles. I wondered about the whereabouts of the vendors; maybe they had been arrested? Amid this terribly fast destruction one stand was spared; it sold newspapers and magazines, and looked more permanent than the others. The owner stood next to his stand, as if proud of it. Probably he was the only one who had a permit and paid taxes. He made a point of greeting the policemen. As the bulldozer kept moving back and forth, crushing one stand and then another, a crowd formed. Two or three men held up their cell phones to film what was happening. One policeman carried some merchandise—a wooden crate filled with bags of chips—toward the truck. A man who looked worn out and hungry ran up to him to ask if he could have the chips. The policeman conceded and handed over the tray.

An army tank, right outside of the bus station, reminded those watching that this was not a random act of destruction. The bulldozer was, in fact, landscaping el-Sisi's new Egypt. There had been lots of buzz in the media around the restructuring and reordering of Cairo. El-Sisi had been calling for everyone to work, yet clearly not any kind of work would do but only the kind regulated by the state and the kind that yields profit. Part of the attempt to streamline and strengthen the economy consisted of trying to formalize Egypt's vast and essential "informal" economy. Unauthorized street vendors were a key target and were removed from the streets en masse. Some had been relocated to officially approved spaces, such as the Turguman garage, which had been turned into a temporary home for three thousand street vendors. Those enchanted with el-Sisi's iron fist told me that ultimately all would benefit, including the vendors; that this was an act of reorganization, not elimination. "Look how much more orderly the new spaces are," Madame Salwa said. "Now they have proper stands, a roof that protects them from the sun, and clean toilets." A number of vendors told me that they were in fact better off selling merchandise without a permit, but Madame Salwa insisted that "illegal vendors" needed to be forced into the order of the state, whether they liked it or not.[36] It would all have been worth it.

That afternoon, at Abdel Munim Riyad, I watched the bulldozer for almost an hour. I could not help but think of this scene as emblematic of how the government was, well, *bulldozing* the parts of Cairo that did not fit in its vision of the future. About how it was crushing alternate ways of doing things, and seeking out some kind of standardized and regulated form of life. That sense of control seemed at odds with the spirit of the revolution, and also with the spirit of many of the givers and recipients I had come to know who, by and large, have much more of a live-and-let-live approach to life.

Then Amal showed up. I told her what had happened. She grumbled: "May God destroy el-Sisi and his people [*rabbinā yikhrib baytu*]. What are the poor supposed to do? Commit suicide? What are they supposed to live from?" There it was again: despair, anger, talk of suicide. But now Amal was not speaking about her own life (and hypothetical death). She was speaking about the poor at large, a broad category with which she identified while still allowing for empathy for, and solidarity with, those even worse off. The street vendors, in her view, were being hit particularly hard. They deserved our collective outrage. Given her own experience with the kiosk, Amal knows that attempts at partaking in capitalist entrepreneurialism do not always end well. She knows that hustling, panhandling, and informal economies that evade state control can enable one's survival, and belonging, in ways that capitalist entrepreneurialism does not. She also knows about—or insists on—a divinely ordained share for all, regardless of what they do for a living, whether they pay taxes, and even whether they work at all.

A few days later I sat with Shaykh Salah at his *khidma*. Through his daily work, Shaykh Salah has come to know many of the vendors who are scattered around the Sayyida Zaynab mosque; they come each morning with beat-up folding tables and sell chickpeas, plastic toys, religious books, prayer beads, spices, and towels. When I told him about the bulldozer, he said that the vendors at Sayyida Zaynab, too, would soon be removed. They had been told that they had only one month left. Some of them are his friends and help with the food preparation. He worried about what would happen to them, and he knew what this cleansing process meant for the *khidma*. He would have to increase the amount of food he cooks every day. As a supposedly better tomorrow was being crafted around him, actively and violently, Shaykh Salah's reaction was to stick to his own work—work that would only be in greater demand, as former vendors would now be unable to provide for their families. In the face of the state's demands, and in the midst of el-Sisi's painful grandeur, Shaykh Salah stuck to his own temporal logic, one of continuous daily giving.

Postscript

THE EGYPTIAN UPRISING HAD LONG BEEN IN THE MAKING.
Behind it lay decades of corruption and oppression, workers' strikes and
grassroots organizing, and everyday acts of "quiet encroachment" (Bayat
2013). Yet what unfolded at Tahrir Square during the eighteen decisive days
exceeded all these prehistories and all the planning. The sit-in itself, to many,
became a source of inspiration, a self-organizing of "the people" outside of the
framework of the state, a collective and spontaneous inventing of alternative
ways of being, and the embodied, living proof that a more just world could
be manifested right here, right now.

But the Tahrir moment could not last. Like Occupy and similar movements, it was haunted from the beginning by what would soon seem inevitable, by the "decline and fall into structure and law" (Turner 1977:132). To
some, the magic of Tahrir began to crumble when disagreements had to be
managed, when the need to formulate collective statements silenced some
while giving voice to others, when street children stole from activists who
had tried to make them feel welcome, when harassment was reported, when
those disturbing the peace at the square were kicked out or punished, when
a space defined by its openness needed to have its entry points policed. In
other words: when Tahrir Square became a little bit like the state it was fighting against, replete with its own police and border guards.[1] To others, the
Tahrir moment ended later, after Hosni Mubarak's ouster, when the military
reclaimed the space and cleansed it of protesters, slogans, and graffiti, when
activists started to be publicly demonized and Egyptians were told to keep
the wheel of production turning, when the ballot box and elections became
the only legitimate political path forward.[2]

Against the seeming inevitability of that slide from anti-structure to structure, from spontaneity to commodification, from openness to exclusion, many activists have tried to keep alive the spirit of Tahrir.[3] For more privileged activists, this has meant, among other things, opening new community spaces, learning about urban farming, attending yoga retreats, and organizing music festivals in the desert. More recently, a number of former activists have also turned to Sufism and joined Sufi orders. I hope to tell the story of these activists-turned-Sufis another time, as part of my next endeavor, an "ethnography of God."[4] For now I suggest that such an unexpected crossing-over resonates with what this whole book is about. It is about the thinking-spaces that open up when we put into conversation seemingly apolitical practices and the revolutionary moment. It is about the spiritual reach for a beyond *and* the worldly reach for a beyond. It is about *khidma* and Tahrir. It is about affinities, resonances, and frictions.

My goal in putting an Islamic ethics of giving and the revolution together on the same page was to disrupt the certainty with which we dismiss "charity" as shortsighted, ineffective, selfish, and nonpolitical. We cannot simply throw out concepts like "social justice," but we can draw into view what they erase, and we can try to open them up to new meanings. In Egypt, the revolution's call for social justice was quickly reduced and contained. The justice that drives, and is embodied in, an Islamic ethics of giving is less easily co-opted, in part because it works on a different register. People like Madame Salwa and the Resala volunteers don't "care" in the way we might want them to care, but they give continuously, day after day, and with profound devotion. And so, instead of smirking at their meticulous point counting, we might ask: To whom, why, and under what circumstances does "caring" matter? When might "caring" become its own form of violence? What does it mean to think of giving as a duty and obligation, not an act of kindness?

We encountered different strands of Islam, along with a singularity of purpose: an orientation toward God. It is difficult to overestimate the role of God, however conceived, in this giving. Within this godly orientation, there are many different ways of dealing with the poor—ranging from befriending them (as Shaykh Salah does) to intently looking away from them (as Resala volunteers often do). At the same time, even for my most pious interlocutors, the foregrounding of God is always an ambition and never stable. People like Amal cannot afford to constantly think about God; they have to think about getting food on the table. Madame Salwa says that she does not care about the poor, but whether she likes it or not, she comes face to face with them, sees them, hears their stories. Clearly she does care, at least some of the time, or she is made to care when being confronted with extraordinary hardship. While speaking extensively of paradise, Resala volunteers head into the slums, and some of them break down, or have become activists, as a result of those trips. Shaykh Salah says he is spiritually guided by Sayyida Zaynab, but at the same time he has to deal with the increasingly complex logistics of the growing numbers of people relying on his meals, not to mention the police, the mosque administration, and conflicts among vendors and beggars around the mosque. A lot of the work at the *khidma* is tedious, mundane, and utterly this-worldly. The foregrounding of God never fully lifts people out of the material and social worlds they inhabit; in fact, the practice of giving to God embeds the giver all the more firmly within this world.

This central paradox—becoming more fully embedded in the here and now by looking to a beyond—is closely related to the radical potential I see in the ethics of giving I have described. This ethics is not radical or progressive in the way activists might use the term—in the sense of boldly pointing to a different future. It is radical precisely because it disrupts a future-orientedness and instead stubbornly addresses need in the here and now. It foregrounds distribution, relationality, and interdependency rather than entrepreneurship and the individual's right to work and make a living. It is neither about economic growth nor about compassion toward, or the deservingness of, the poor. It is not even about human rights. It is to and from and because of God.

People like Shaykh Salah, Madame Salwa, and the Resala volunteers attend to the most basic bodily needs of humans by distributing food in Cairo's most densely populated neighborhoods. At the same time they orient themselves away from humans and toward God. Put differently, they attend to the human while *decentering* the human. They attend to need in this world while thinking of this world as temporary and fleeting. By not taking "the human" too seriously, they evade what Hannah Arendt (1965) calls a "politics of pity," and they do not get caught up in programmatic visions of how to overthrow the current order of things. They simply give.

Of course, regardless of how my interlocutors frame it, one could ground a utopian vision in this kind of giving. In a sense, Marcel Mauss has done just that. In his conclusion to *The Gift,* he cites several verses from the Quran that emphasize the obligation to give. He then boldly proposes to replace "God" with "society" (1967:75–76). As should be clear by now, I am wary of such acts of translation. My pious interlocutors do not give to the poor *instead of* giving to God. They give to the poor *in order to* give to God. The way they see it, because God asks us to give, we should give even when—perhaps especially when—we are not in the mood, when we are not feeling compassionate, when we doubt the recipients' deservingness. You should give *despite* yourself. That is not to say that one cannot think of duty, obligation, and dependency apart from religion, but conversations are far richer, I find, when they do not subsume or erase difference.

Admittedly, in the midst of my fieldwork, the very idea of a conversation between charity and revolution at times seemed plain ridiculous. Recall the activists insisting that handouts only reinforce social inequalities. Recall Nura saying that protests are none of her business. Revolution and *khidma* often seemed worlds apart, and Nura's refusal of the political poses a challenge to my search for political potentials in unexpected places. Despite these tensions, I could not help but look for openings and resonances, such as between Nura's present-orientedness—an "ethics of immediacy"—and accounts of the sit-in at Tahrir Square that foreground a being-with-others in the here and now (Mittermaier 2014b). Occasionally I also met people who were equally interested in unlikely conversations, among them Hamid, an activist in his late twenties, keen, as were many others, on finding ways to "live Tahrir" more permanently. At first drawn to a language of development, rebuilding, and entrepreneurship, Hamid eventually found this language too pre-scripted and began looking for alternatives. He started traveling throughout Egypt with like-minded friends to learn about local "customs and traditions," hoping to draw inspiration from the traditions of hospitality in the Western Desert, and from the collective decision-making processes in villages in Upper Egypt. He had never been to a *khidma* but could immediately see its appeal for a (post)revolutionary imagining of what it is to be with, and toward, others. Only time will tell whether the activist-turned-Sufis, too, end up folding their spiritual path into their politics, and vice versa, or not.

It is possible, of course, that Hamid romanticizes Upper Egyptian life—and that I romanticize an Islamic ethics of giving. In the end, critical readers might say, people like Shaykh Salah, Nura, the Resala volunteers, and Madame Salwa do not aim for a world free of poverty. They *need* the poor as their gate to paradise, and they justify suffering in this world through the prospect of an otherworldly reward for the poor.

It is true that for the most part, my pious interlocutors do not see poverty as a problem, something that needs to be overcome. When asked if they could imagine a world free of poverty, almost all answered no. Their goal is not a world revolution or a restructuring of society. They are invested in piously giving to the poor, not in eradicating poverty. But while they do not aim for a world free of poverty, I think that something can be learned from how they engage with need—the orientations, sensibilities, and ethics that they embody in their acts of giving and that push back against common assumptions about how poverty should best be dealt with. For one, their ethics of giving renders the very call for an "end to poverty" unstable. Sufis insist that we are all poor and dependent. This is very different from, say, Wael Ghoneim praising himself for having sacrificed his carefree life in his Emirati villa for the sake of Egypt's poor. It is also very different from wanting to push the poor over the edge for the sake of a revolution. Even those, like Madame Salwa, who give while being invested in class differences, reconfigure "the poor" by fore-grounding God. Giving to God is neither about feeling bad for the poor nor about wanting to help the poor help themselves. It is about distribution and circulation, which are not grounded in a Marxist desire to level all class distinctions or to overthrow the status quo, but rather are about preventing the resources required to meet the daily needs of life from being hogged by the rich, even in the midst of vast inequality. From this vantage point, the things we own are ultimately meaningless, and what is actually valuable is our ability to keep the wealth of the world moving, from our hands to the hands of those who need it a little bit more than we do. As in other places in the world, the central moral problem here is not inequality but rather what one *does* from one's position within a given hierarchy (Scherz 2014:97).

The commitment to circulation, to continuous giving, is particularly important now, at a time when the revolutionary impulse in Egypt has been co-opted by a regime that tells the poor to tighten their belts, proclaiming that "work is our only solution." A time when the (post)revolutionary imagination has reached an impasse, when secular critics dismiss religion's political potentials out of hand, and when violent oppression stifles all debate. A time, moreover, when the continued divergence of income inequality, and the frightening appeal of strongman authoritarian leaders, has relevance far beyond Egypt.

I anticipate another objection; one that has to do with scale. One of my key sites for imagining an Otherwise is the Sufi *khidma*. Such places of distribution are limited in space and often also time. *Khidmas* can consist of a carpet on the floor, a tent that is put up during a *mawlid*, or a spot next to a mosque.

Even the giving that is practiced in more permanent *khidmas* unfolds on a day-to-day basis. What I describe sounds nice and idyllic, I am told, but could it ever be scaled up? In 2011, a time still marked for me by idealistic enthusiasm, I insisted the answer was yes. Drawing together strands of Islam that are usually held apart, I cited Islamist thinkers such as Sayyid Qutb (2000), who formulated a Quranically grounded political program of social justice.[5] I said that while *khidmas* and Madame Salwa's kind of giving exist somewhat apart from the state and political structures, one could easily imagine a state, or *umma,* or world organized around the same sensibilities and principles. I added that I had noticed that young Muslim Brotherhood members were largely unfamiliar with Sayyid Qutb's book on social justice, and when asked about their own vision of social justice, they vaguely referred to the principle of *zakāt.* There is not much left of the Islamic left. And that, I used to say, is the reason I look to everyday practices and not political programs.

Over time, I have become more skeptical. I have watched Resala struggle against the crackdown on NGOs under el-Sisi. The more political an Islamic practice appears to be, the more it will be oppressed. In the meantime, Nura, Shaykh Salah, and Madame Salwa go right on giving. I now think that the most radical thing about the kind of giving I describe might be that it can only exist on a small scale, that it cannot be blown up, co-opted, branded, or put to profit. The *khidma* refuses to be institutionalized and commodified. It could never be turned into a bureaucratic machinery of giving, an NGO, or a state project; doing so would undermine its very philosophy and spiritual underpinnings. But precisely for that reason, it is also not subjected to political upheavals or other changes that characterize politics.

Maybe, in the end, we need to resist the temptation of reading such spaces as a source of political inspiration. Maybe doing so is itself an act of violence that counteracts their radical potentiality. The very question of institutionalization (how to draw a more durable, far-reaching, systematic politics out of something like Tahrir Square or a *khidma*) might in fact point to the limits of our political imagination.

The revolution will not be televised, and the *khidma* will not be revolutionized. And maybe that is a good thing.

I leave you with a final scene.

On one of a seemingly endless number of hot Cairo afternoons, Madame Salwa and I are shopping in a busy outdoor market, somewhere in Gizeh, about seven kilometers southwest of Tahrir Square. We have taken multiple microbuses to reach this market. Prices here are low, and, as always, Madame Salwa is concerned with making the most of the alms friends and relatives have entrusted to her. Today we are going to use these donations to buy pasta, beans, cooking oil, canned tomato sauce, zucchini, and black tea, so we can distribute them later, in food bags, in the City of the Dead. We are moving swiftly through the market, stopping here and there, comparing prices. Then we pass a beggar. We are used to this. We have already passed many beggars on our way to the market today, just like every day. And this day, just like every day, some of these beggars exposed their bodily ailments; one pulled back his *gallābiyya* to offer us a good look at his amputated leg. Others told us of their difficult circumstances: sick relatives, hungry children, urgently needed medical interventions. What these beggars offered were performances of suffering, not that different from those occurring every day in the intake offices of charity organizations across the city.

This beggar is different. He does not exhibit his frail body. He does not tell us a story. He does not perform his suffering. He does not even *beg*. What he says is simple: "*hāga li-llāh.*" Something for God. With this one phrase he stops us. He turns himself into a medium, into an embodiment of God's hand. He takes to its logical conclusion the idea that nothing truly belongs to any of us, and that therefore we ought to give continuously. All comes from God and ought to continuously be returned to God. This is neither about compassion nor about suffering. It is about the obligation to give.

Madame Salwa prefers giving food to giving money, and she tends to be skeptical of beggars. She prefers traveling deep into the slums or the City of the Dead in order to seek out those she perceives to be truly in need.

But today, she hears this man's voice and stops. She lowers her shopping bags to the ground, pulls her wallet out of her purse, and takes out a crumbled bill. Regardless of her disdain for beggars, of how she feels about this man, she gives to him.

She gives to God.

NOTES

INTRODUCTION

1. Fasting throughout the month of Ramadan—abstaining from food, drink, and sexual relations from sunrise to sunset—is one of the five pillars of Islam. Because the Islamic calendar is lunar, months move back by eleven days a year in relation to the Gregorian calendar. Ramadan is also a key time for charitable giving, including in the form of Ramadan tables (*mā'idat al-rahmān*), literally "tables of the Merciful," indicating that the guests are "God's guests." Ramadan tables have become ubiquitous in Cairo since the late 1980s (Denis 2006:57). I was told that the idea was imported from Saudi Arabia, inspired by the practice of feeding pilgrims during the *'umra* and *hajj;* others say the practice dates back to the Fatimid era. Ramadan tables in Cairo are run by Sufi orders, business owners, mosques, and, in post-uprising Egypt, also the military. Some put up such tables for purposes of spiritual purification; others, it is rumored, for money-laundering purposes. Other forms of giving in Ramadan include informal food distribution, as practiced by Madame Salwa, and a small obligatory donation to the poor, given by each family at the end of the month (*zakāt al-fitr*).

2. The dollar equivalent for Egyptian pounds throughout this book reflects the exchange rate of each moment. Over the course of my fieldwork, and especially after the Central Bank of Egypt floated the pound in November 2016, the Egyptian currency increasingly lost value.

3. See Oxfam's 2017 report, "An Economy for the 99%," www.oxfam.org/en /research/economy-99. A recent report on global inequalities states that income inequality is highest in the Middle East. http://wir2018.wid.world/files/download /wir2018-summary-english.pdf.

4. Egypt's socialist experiment under Gamal Abdel Nasser in the 1960s was followed by Anwar Sadat's "open door" (*infitāh*) policy and embrace of free-market reforms in the 1970s. Beginning with Hosni Mubarak's structural adjustment policies in the 1980s, and driven by pressure from the International Monetary Fund (IMF) and the World Bank, Egypt's path of development has taken an increasingly

neoliberal turn, marked by widespread privatization, reduced subsidies, a shift to microloans, and the rise of a small wealthy group of businessmen and a wealthy military. Accelerated neoliberalism, importantly, does not imply a dismantling of the state; rather, the Egyptian state is increasingly playing the role of facilitator of capitalist profit-making at the expense of the working class (Alexander and Bassiouny 2014:6). The military is a key player in Egypt's economy and has retained a hegemonic status since the 1950s, surviving the transition from socialism to neoliberalism and continuously expanding its business empire. The military owns a large number of enterprises that produce a range of products and services and that enjoy exceptional privileges in the form of free land, tax breaks, and tax exemptions (Abul-Magd 2016, 2018; Alexander and Bassiouny 2014). On the army's entanglements with Egypt's business and financial world, or the "army going civilian," see also Abaza (2006). On its increasing investment in megaprojects, see chapter 6 and Amar (2018).

5. "Middle class" is a vague term and in Egypt can include both members of the bourgeoisie and the upper class, as well as rather poor people who have higher education and a government job. Throughout this book I use the term, despite its vagueness, because it is a common tool of self-identification. On the middle class's longstanding involvement in charitable giving in Egypt, see Clark (2004).

6. On Egypt's billionaires becoming even richer after the uprising, see www .madamasr.com/en/2015/05/05/news/economy/egypts-billionaires-80-richer-than-before-the-revolution/. On the role of international aid in consolidating the power of Egypt's dominant classes, see Hanieh (2012).

7. China Scherz (2014) and Erica Bornstein (2012) similarly characterize charity as the despised Other of sustainable development, in Uganda and India respectively. The former speaks of an "ethics of unsustainable charity"; the latter speaks of "disquieting gifts." For anthropological critiques of the ideology of development, see, e.g., Ferguson (1994) and Li (2007).

8. Needless to say, this is a stereotypical depiction of Christianity that primarily serves the purpose of highlighting Islam's difference. The idea that the compassionate subject lies at the heart of Christian charity can be complicated through the very etymology of the word "charity," which foregrounds God's grace (*caritas*) working *through* the subject (Muehlebach 2013:456). In some Catholic contexts, charity is also understood as a way of enacting one's love and devotion to God, a form of prayer (Scherz 2014:72). In Christian communities in Egypt, almsgiving, charity, and service (*khidma*) are variously understood. During my fieldwork I spoke to a range of Copts about their charitable practices, but, to avoid tokenism and the flattening of differences, I decided against including "Coptic examples" in this book.

9. For lack of a better term and for the sake of recognizability, I nevertheless use the word "charity" throughout this study. Egyptians themselves often use the term *'amal al-khayr* ("good deeds"), which is easily and often translated as "charity." Madame Salwa, too, sometimes uses this phrase; other times she refers to her practices as *tawzī'a* (distribution) or *it'ām* (the giving of food).

10. On the "rights of the poor," see the Quranic verses 17:26, 51:19, and 70:24–25, which speak of a rightful share (*haqq*). Almsgiving, accordingly, is best understood

as a web of "entitlement and obligation" (Singer 2008:3). In a widely cited book on almsgiving, the Egyptian theologian Yusuf al-Qaradawi (2006:103) similarly points out that in Islam, giving to the poor is not a "good deed" (*'amal tayyib*) but an obligation. For Sayyid Qutb, the principle of rights and obligations is what raises Islamic almsgiving "above the stage where it is merely a mark of the superiority and pre-eminence of the rich over the poor" (2000:107).

11. That is, of course, not to say that Islam is inherently non-compassionate. British author Karen Armstrong, who in 2008 launched the Charter of Compassion, calls the Quran a "cry for compassion," and told the thousands of Muslim attendees at the Reviving the Islamic Spirit conference in Toronto in 2012 that "compassion lies at the core of [their] religion." William Chittick (2013), who has written extensively on Sufi thinkers, makes the related point that love lies at the heart of the Islamic tradition. He criticizes approaches to Islam that overemphasize jurisprudence and depict God as the supreme law-giver, and he reminds us that nearly every chapter of the Quran begins with the formula *bismillāh al-rahmān al-rahīm,* a phrase that roughly translates as "In the Name of God, the All-Compassionate, the All-Merciful." The latter two words are derived from *rahma,* which means "mercy, compassion, or benevolence," and is related to *rahim,* which means "womb." The attribute *al-rahmān,* the All-Compassionate, is generally taken to refer to universal mercy, to God's bestowal of existence. *Al-rahīm,* the All-Merciful, refers to a more particular manifestation of mercy, God's response to human efforts. Some of my interlocutors explained that human mercy is merely a fraction of God's mercy; whatever we do out of kindness is an attempt to partake in the Divine's infinite kindness.

12. Indebted to a mainstreaming of revivalist habits, the phrase *li-llāh* has come to be used in many contexts. Today in Egypt, the most common answer to the question "How are you?" is "Praise be to God" (*al-hamdu-li-llāh*). Those offering condolences say, "Eternity belongs to God" (*al-baqā' li-llāh*), whereas in the past they might have said, "The rest will be in your life" (*al-ba'ia fi 'umrik*). When someone is thanked, instead of a simple "You're welcome" (*'afwan*), a pious response is "All thanks belong to God" (*al-shukr li-llāh*). When an injustice has occurred, one can say, "From them directly to God" (*minhum li-llāh*), meaning that God will hold them accountable. Through all these phrases, divine generosity and divine justice are continuously rendered present in this world. The visible world is continuously enfolded in an invisible order.

13. As Mona Atia (2013:6) notes, the concept of *amāna* is commonly understood to mean that humans are never the absolute owners; everything is merely entrusted to them by God. They have the right to private property but this right is contingent on their moral and spiritual responsibility. The implications can be variously understood and connected to different Islamic moral economies, ranging from capitalist to socialist (Tripp 2006).

14. To the extent that neoliberalism dictates deregulation, the restriction of public spending, and the erosion of the welfare state, it seems by definition opposed to national development (Edelman 2013; Elyachar 2012). But the two orientations

can also converge, for instance in the construction of megaprojects and the simultaneous call for citizens' sacrifices for these projects (see chapter 6).

15. The quotes are from Patricia Crone and Josef van Ess, both cited in Lange (2016:10).

16. Comparatively, Robert Orsi (2016) describes how, in Christianity with the rise of Protestantism, the gods were increasingly removed from the world of humans.

17. This was reported to me by Mustafa Mahmoud's daughter, who emphasized his deep respect for Sufism (along with his dislike for an ascetic withdrawal from the world). She told me that before the dream-vision, he had wanted to use his savings to buy a yacht.

18. Jon Bialecki (2014:43), who calls for more ethnography that does not avoid God as an ethnographic presence, notes that "God acts with the same kind of stochastic wildness that is usually allocated to the other human agents who stand in the centre of so much of contemporary anthropological writing." He offers the example of a divine directive that "informs the believer of a duty or obligation to which they would not normally feel beholden" (42). Taking a cue from Bialecki and other anthropologists of Christianity who have thought about the "problem of presence" (Engelke 2007; Luhrmann 2012; Orsi 2016; Robbins 2016), my next project will draw on fieldwork among Egyptian Muslims to work toward what I call an "ethnography of God."

19. Note that I consider the rich anthropological literature on the gift relevant to Islamic charity despite Amy Singer's (2008:9) helpful reminder that Muslim law makes a clear distinction between charity and gifts. In everyday religious contexts, I find, the lines are blurry.

20. Comparatively on this triadic model of giving, see Emanuel Schaeublin's thesis on almsgiving in Palestine (2016).

21. The gifts in this book are mostly considered *sadaqa* but also include *zakāt*. The latter, almsgiving, is one of the five pillars of Islam and is mentioned in eighty-two Quranic verses, often alongside prayer. Some scholars have emphasized the continuity between pre-Islamic values of generosity (*karāma*) and hospitality (*diyāfa*), and the Quranic imperative to give alms and attend to the poor (Bonner 2003; Izutsu 2002). Literally, *zakāt* means "purity," often understood to imply that by donating the obligatory 2.5 percent of one's assets (and 10 percent of one's crop, and one out of forty animals), one purifies and protects one's remaining wealth. In verse 9:60, the Quran lists eight categories of people who are entitled to receiving alms: the poor, the needy, administrators of *zakāt* funds, recent or potential converts, freed slaves or those in bondage, overburdened debtors, those following the cause of God (today often interpreted to not only refer to warfare but also to building a society's infrastructure), and travelers who need to return to their homes (for details, see al-Qaradawi 2006). In addition to obligatory alms, Muslims give voluntary donations, referred to as *sadaqa*. The line between the two kinds of donations is often blurry, although some Muslim scholars insist that *zakāt* can only be given to Muslims, whereas *sadaqa* can also go to non-Muslims. Over the centuries Islamic charity has taken many different forms, some more centralized than others.

Umayyad rulers distributed cash payments and in-kind support to the blind and disabled so they would not have to beg (Crone 2004). In medieval Egypt, Mamluk sultans set aside funds for distributing bread and water to the poor (Sabra 2006), and a central source of poverty relief consisted of charitable endowments (*waqf*). In the nineteenth century, the Egyptian state opened government-run shelters and criminalized begging, seeking to take control of the poor, who had become an eyesore at the same time as they had become a much-needed source of labor power (Ener 2003). In the twentieth century, state-run efforts at poor relief were increasingly complemented by private initiatives. Partially in response to the charity work of Christian missionaries (Baron 2014), the Islamic organizations Al-Gam'iyya al-Shar'iyya and the Muslim Brotherhood were founded in 1912 and 1928, respectively, and quickly became key players in Egypt's economy of assistance. On Islamic charity generally, see Singer (2008) and Benthall (1999, 2016).

22. In Arabic, Sayyid Qutb (2009:73) speaks of *raf' al-nufūs,* the "lifting of selves," which is quite different from a breaking of the self or liberation from the self that many Sufis aim for by giving.

23. Hassan Hanafi, trained at the Sorbonne, launched a project called "The Islamic Left," whose goal it was to "uncover the revolutionary elements inherent in religion, or, if you wish, to show the common grounds of one and the other; that is, interpret religion as revolution" (cited in Kassab 2010:202). 'Abd al-Rahman al-Sharqawi (1965) described the Prophet Muhammad as the defender of the oppressed and the poor, and Mustafa Mahmoud wrote, "Islam came as a revolt against the rich, the money-hoarders, the exploiters, and the oppressors. It expressly enjoined that wealth should not be monopolized and exchanged among the rich alone but it should be open for all as a right" (1994:46f.; see also Mahmud 1975, 1976, 1978). The Marxist historian Ahmad 'Abbas Salih (1973) read Islamic history as a struggle between revolutionary and conservative forces. To him, the socialist trend that he finds in Islam from its very beginnings reflects the principle that "the core of the relationship between God and humans [rests] on how humans treat other humans" (6).

24. This is not a recent development. Muslim Brotherhood support for entrepreneurship, a market economy, and development was already prominent in the 1980s (Utvik 2006). Nefissa Naguib (2015) offers an ethnographic counterview by carefully tracking a lived commitment to the equitable distribution of food, or a "food jihad," among Muslim Brotherhood members before and during the uprising.

25. Depending on who you ask, anything from 17 million to more than half of Cairo's population lives in what, since the 1990s, have been called *'ashwā'iyāt,* often translated as "informal areas" or "unplanned areas." Largely obscured from maps (literally, as they are represented as blank spaces), these areas gained prominence in the Egyptian media in the early 1990s, when they came to be considered breeding grounds for fundamentalists. Public awareness of their existence and scope increased with new infrastructures, such as the building of the 26th of July Corridor and the Ring Road, completed in the early 1990s and in 2011, respectively. Countering common media portrayals of these areas as typical "Third World slums," David Sims (2010) points out that in Cairo these areas do not match the stereotypical

expectations of the ever-expanding "world of slums" described by authors such as Mike Davis (2007). While they started out without any infrastructure, most of these areas managed over time to get electricity, water, and sewerage. In Egypt, 99 percent of households have electricity, 97 percent have water connections, and over 80 percent have sewerage (Sims 2010:277). Sims argues that "Cairo has generated its own logics of accommodation and development [which] operate largely outside the truncated powers of government or are at best in a symbiotic relation with its weakness" (4; see also Bayat 2013). I nevertheless use the term "slums" to approximate how my interlocutors—people who live there or go there to deliver meals—talk about and understand these areas.

ONE. REVOLUTIONS DON'T STOP CHARITY

1. Despite their disillusionment, all the activists I know insisted on calling the 2011 uprising a "revolution" (*thawra*). As they point out, revolutions are not defined by their outcome. Rather, the revolution "was made through the act that took place," the fact that "people rose up." Maybe it was a failed or betrayed revolution, they conceded, but it was a revolution nevertheless. Comparatively, for an ethnography of postrevolutionary affects in Serbia, and particularly on a politics of disappointment, see Greenberg (2014).

2. For thinking about an ethics grounded in the recognition of this fundamental dependency, see Judith Butler (2005). Other anthropologists, too, describe an ethics of interdependency and patronage that stands against the ideal of the autonomous subject (e.g., Ferguson 2015; Scherz 2014).

3. These numbers are not entirely correct. In Egypt, no taxes are paid below a certain income threshold (in 2017, the equivalent of about $400 annually), and there are different brackets for incomes above that threshold, ranging from 10 to 22.5 percent. In France, counter to what Marwa is about to say, the income tax rate ranges from 14 to 45 percent, depending on income.

4. The interviews were conducted and recorded for me by my research assistant, Mariam Aboughazi, in 2014 and 2015. Mariam comes from a politically active family and had no trouble locating self-declared revolutionaries. She knows some of the interviewees through her social networks and her own activism, including from Tahrir Square, or they are friends of friends. Others she knows through her work at an Egyptian NGO. Most of them self-identified as "liberal," some as socialist, and three as followers of the Muslim Brotherhood. Different trajectories led these fifteen people to Tahrir Square. Some had become involved in politics in college; others had participated in demonstrations for Iraq or the Second Intifada, or were involved with the oppositional Kefayah movement. Others had been members of the communist movement in the 1970s and 1980s. All activists' names are pseudonyms. For other ethnographic accounts of the uprising, see Samuli Schielke's blog, "You'll Be Late for the Revolution," http://samuliegypt.blogspot.ca, and the *Cultural Anthropology* HotSpot on the uprising (Elyachar and Winegar 2012).

5. Despite the media's overall disregard for the workers' movement, workers played a critical role in the uprising (Beinin 2016). On the various roads leading to the uprising, see Beinin (2012), Hirschkind (2011), Mahmood (2011), and Armbrust (2012).

6. "Utopia" might not be the right name since it means "no-place" and Tahrir is very much a place. I nevertheless use the term because many people in Egypt used it (in English) when speaking about the Tahrir experience. On Tahrir as utopia, see also Kapp (2014).

7. On the disappearances and tortures, see Amnesty International reports, for example, www.amnesty.org/en/latest/news/2016/07/egypt-hundreds-disappeared-and-tortured-amid-wave-of-brutal-repression/. Mona El-Ghobashy (2018) sums up the situation six years after the uprising: "Egypt has become the kind of place where a teacher turns in a student for having a political insignia on his ruler; police fatally shoot an activist commemorating the January 25 revolution with flowers; and an 18-year-old student spends 800 days in pre-trial detention, for wearing a T-shirt that reads, 'A Nation Without Torture.'"

8. Though other stories could and have been told about the Tunisian uprising, Bouazizi came to occupy a central place in national and international narratives about this historical event. See Rozen (2015).

9. The precise class and gender breakdown of the Egyptian uprising will never be known. Some statistics suggest that the protesters were indeed largely middle class and disproportionately male (http://foreignpolicy.com/2013/04/15/the-anatomy-of-protest-in-egypt-and-tunisia/). Sherine Hafez (2012), by contrast, cites eyewitness reports that put the number of female protesters at Tahrir Square at 20 to 50 percent. Jessica Winegar (2012a) reminds us of the Egyptian housewives who were stuck at home, caring for their kids and cooking, while the men were out and about, marching and throwing rocks. Revolution is a privilege, as she puts it. Along the same lines, a number of working-class Egyptians told me that they did not participate in the protests because they had more pressing concerns to attend to.

10. On the ultras and their role in the uprising, see Woltering (2013) and El-Zatmah (2015). One critical event occurred in February 2012, when more than seventy Al-Ahly fans were killed in a stampede at the Port Said stadium. Ultra groups accused security officials and the police of being complicit or at least failing to intervene.

11. Sometimes instead of (or in addition to) "social justice," protesters also called for "human dignity" (*karāma insāniyya*). On the Tunisian slogans, see Beinin (2016).

12. When I asked Egyptians whether they considered the "bread riots" to be a prelude to the 2011 uprising, most responded that the 1977 riots were "not political" and did not involve a "language of rights." One civil servant who had lived through the riots explained: "It's as if you stepped on someone's foot, and they say, 'Ouch.'" In line with E. P. Thompson's writings on the eighteenth-century "riots" in England (1971), we might be skeptical of such portrayals, but regardless of their accuracy, the proclaimed contrast emphasizes the politicized language of rights pervading the 2011 uprising.

13. For a genealogical critique of "social justice," see Chakrabarty (2008), who emphasizes the concept's Eurocentric underpinnings and its inability to make space for gods and spirits, and Fleischacker (2005), who notes that common claims to continuity obscure the decisive break that happened at the end of the eighteenth century. Counter the modern aspiration to equality, "it was widely believed for a long time that certain kinds of people *ought* to live in need" (Fleischacker 2005:2).

14. Quran 3:37.

15. The blog post was published in the independent newspaper *Al-Badil* and posted on 7 June 2011 on Abu El-Gheit's Facebook page. See http://gedarea.blogspot .ca/2011/06/normal-0-false-false-false.html.

16. Others cite higher numbers for those living in slums—anything from half to two-thirds of Cairo's population. On living in Cairo's cemeteries, see Watson (1992), Nedoroscik (1997), and Singerman and Amar (2006:21–23).

17. The campaign coincided with a growing number of industrial strikes by underpaid workers and protests demanding jobs and proper housing.

18. Ibrahim Eissa's article "Freedom Is More Important than the Poor" was published in Arabic in the *Tahrir* newspaper on 4 July 2011.

19. The op-ed was published in *al-Masry al-Yawm* on 27 June 2011. It is no longer accessible online. On the afterlife of the blog post, see also Mellor (2014).

20. After the Free Officers' Coup in July 1952, Egyptians gathered at Tahrir Square to celebrate the birth of their new republic. In 1977, the bread riots drove protesters to the square, and in 2003, it was witness to large rallies against the Iraq war—despite the emergency laws, which since 1981 had been making it difficult and dangerous for protesters to gather.

21. https://antonionegriinenglish.files.wordpress.com/2012/05/93152857-hardt-negri-declaration-2012.pdf.

22. The Tahrir experience itself, by contrast, arguably was not concerned with the religious/secular question, but was what Hussein Agrama (2011) calls "asecular."

23. Wilde published his essay in 1891 amid a spirited debate about a postcapitalist society, and his utopian vision involved a society without private property. Žižek (2009) takes up the critique at a time of neoliberal capitalism. He finds the spirit of charity all around him—in the growth of charitable institutions around the globe but also in phenomena such as "fair trade," which calm the consumer's conscience while effectively maintaining the status quo. See also the RSA Animate at www .youtube.com/watch?v=hpAMbpQ8J7g.

24. As was pointed out by James Ferguson during the Q&A after his lecture "A Rightful Share: The Politics of Distribution beyond Gift and Market," Development Seminar, University of Toronto, 9 October 2015.

25. Although most activists I know were critical of the Muslim Brotherhood, they thought that the military coup in 2013 had undermined the possibility of a popular movement that could have democratically defeated Mohamed Morsi. Some had participated in anti–Muslim Brotherhood protests but were left with a feeling of betrayal and the sense that "the street was no longer ours."

1. The demand for a national minimum wage of 1,200 Egyptian pounds dates back to the December 2006 strikes in Mahalla. For more details, see Charbel (2014) and Abd al-Ghani (2011).

2. For overviews and histories of Sufism, see Chittick (2007), Knysh (2017), Sedgwick (2003), and Schimmel (1995).

3. On eating (and fasting) in Sufism more broadly, see Hoffman-Ladd (1995a). On Ottoman soup kitchens, see Singer (2005) and Algar (1992).

4. Shaykh Salah distinguishes between moving and fixed *khidmas*. At the fixed *khidmas* found at saint shrines such as Sayyida ʿAisha, Imam Shafiʿi, and Imam Laithi, the food is served on site, whereas Shaykh Salah prepares the food in one location and serves it in another. This way, he says, he can reach more people.

5. For a detailed ethnography of Sayyida Zaynab's shrine, see Abu Zahra (1997).

6. According to Shaykh Salah, all saintly descendants of the Prophet were known for distributing food and for their hospitality (*ikrām al-dayf*). They would bring guests to their homes from afar, and they would give away food even if it meant that nothing was left for them. Generosity is a saintly virtue, and one that Sayyida Zaynab in particular was known for.

7. Among these Sufi parties are the Egyptian Liberation Party (*al-tahrīr al-masrī*), with mostly members of the Azmiyya Sufi order, and the Voice of Freedom Party (*sawt al-huriyya*), founded by the Rifaʿiyya order.

8. Ties between some Sufi orders and the regime survived from the Mubarak era into the Sisi era. One key player in this alliance is Ali Gomaa, former Grand Mufti, who has stated that obeying President el-Sisi is a religious duty, and who in 2018 founded a new government-aligned Sufi order, the Shadhliyya al-ʿUliyya. State support for Sufism also has to do with its proclaimed fight against "extremism."

9. Shaykh Salah alternates the location to stay out of the sun (especially in the summer months) and to accommodate other people who distribute food around the mosque, as well as vendors who compete for the best spots on the sidewalks.

10. To break the *nafs* (self), many Sufis turn to serving food or cleaning bathrooms. Drawing on sixteenth-century texts, Francisco Rodriguez-Mañas (2000) points out that in Moroccan Sufism, serving others was understood to lead to a state that one could not reach through self-mortification or periods spent in spiritual retreat. Many Sufis in Egypt emphasized to me the spiritual benefits that result from cleaning public bathrooms, especially bathrooms attached to saint shrines.

11. Shaykh Salah pointed out that at the Prophet's time, those without a home could sleep in mosques; they were called *ahl al-suffa* (*suffa* means "roof"). Today, he says, mosques are generally only used for the five daily prayers. He believes mosques should stay open continuously so street children can sleep in them. According to Shaykh Salah, the Ministry of Religious Endowments and the mosque administration oppose this idea because they believe the children would steal things.

12. This applies to cooked food. Sometimes Shaykh Salah stores frozen meat.

13. Mariam's father was a member of the Dostour Party, literally "Constitution Party," which was founded in 2012 by Mohamed ElBaradei and other liberal politicians with the aim of protecting the principles of the 2011 revolution. In 2013, the party supported the Tamarod movement and the removal of Mohamed Morsi. ElBaradai was temporarily appointed vice president but resigned in August 2013 to protest against the violence against Muslim Brotherhood supporters. In the 2014 elections, the party endorsed the leftist-Nasserist candidate Hamdeen Sabahi. By 2016, because of the extensive oppression of oppositional forces, the number of party members had gone down from thirty thousand to two thousand.

14. Unlike the original organization, the Muslim Brotherhood's Freedom and Justice Party lacked closeness to the people, Shaykh Salah said. "They have their heads in the books."

15. At some point Shaykh Salah managed (through his personal connections to a charity organization at the Sayyida Zaynab mosque) to secure subsidy (*tamwīn*) papers that allowed him to obtain a certain number of bread loaves at the discounted price—a minimal token of state participation in his daily food distribution. Ideally, he thinks, the state should do far more.

16. Other times Shaykh Salah distinguishes between basic needs (which might be met by individual donors) and more elaborate needs (which should be met by the state): "Look, you see the poor and give them what? Food and shelter. You won't give them clothing, a job, or help them get married. That is the responsibility of the state—if there is a state. Employment and marriage are the responsibilities of the state but the *khidma* gives the minimum: food and shelter."

17. Shaykh Salah believes that the Mamluk and Ottoman era caused fundamental damage to Egypt and at the same time increased the importance of a parallel spiritual government. In his account, one effect of Egypt's long-term exposure to exploitative rulers and oppression was that people started turning to the saints for protection. They would ask the saints to prevent injustice, and the saints would appear to rulers and warn them. On the other hand, Shaykh Salah speaks highly of the nineteenth-century ruler Muhammad Ali, who, he says, cared about his people and "would go out and see everything for himself, and if a field was not used for agriculture, he would make sure it was used."

18. Quran 76:8; Sunan Ibn Majah 1334.

19. Shaykh Salah tries to reread the *Ibrīz* at least once a year. He says that it must be read in the right spiritual state and not with the mind (*bil-ḥāl wa laysa bil-'aql*). For a while, Shaykh Salah invited people to gather at one of the mosque's gates in the late afternoon so he could explain sections of the book. He dreams of reviving these lessons. Sometimes he would walk me through a few pages, unpacking the hidden, inner (*bāṭin*) meanings of hadiths. In his view, the *Ibrīz* can help us understand how particular deeds increase the light in one's body, how they affect the color and smell of one's blood, and how pure faith can kill microbes.

20. The phrase Shaykh Salah used is ambiguous. Commonly understood to refer to a minimum wage, *al-ḥadd al-adnā* literally only means "minimum" (without the wage).

1. The question of the houris has long figured in anti-Islam polemics. Muslim scholars have interpreted the houris as rejuvenated wives, or virgins whose hymen is continuously restored. A largely discredited view, promoted by some Western scholars, is that the Quran does not actually speak of houris but of grapes.

2. To my knowledge, to date the only extensive study of Resala is Sara Lei Sparre's doctoral thesis (2013). Sparre acknowledges that Resala volunteers often speak of God, but she argues that the pervasive God-rhetoric conceals other interests, such as their search for marriage partners at the NGO. She suggests, "The powerful narrative about good deeds and God's rewards veils other important considerations, some more conscious than others" (148). I agree that a multiplicity of motivations and desires are at play but, at least for the volunteers I know best, God was far more than a pretext. Interviews with Resala volunteers also figure in an article by Ibrahim, Mesard, and Hunt-Hendrix (2015). On Resala, see also Mittermaier (2014a).

3. When one Resala volunteer wanted to create an image of paradise for a Facebook post, he used a photograph of the Sanssouci castle. Built in Potsdam in the eighteenth century, this castle was the summer palace of Frederick the Great, king of Prussia, and is often considered a German Versailles. That the volunteer chose this image of European aristocracy speaks to the limited repertoire available to volunteers trying to imagine paradise. This stands against a rich textual tradition of Muslim writings on paradise and hell. See for instance Ibn al-Jawzi's *What Paradise Is Like,* Ibn Rajab's *The Terrors of the Graves,* and al-Suyuti's *The Shining Full Moons of Eschatology.* For a detailed account, see Lange (2016), a study I rely on extensively in this chapter.

4. See also Jonathan Parry (1986), who explains that the ongoing appeal of a selfless gift is due to its being an almost-mythical counterpoint to market ideologies.

5. Quran 4:74.

6. The afterlife has come in and out of focus over the centuries, and hell and paradise have not always received equal attention. Western studies of the Muslim afterlife generally foreground paradise, perhaps, suggests Lange (2016:27), "because the notion that the god of Islam is essentially merciful has proven more palatable to liberal scholars of religion than the terrifying spectre of a punisher deity." In pious circles up until the Islamic third century (the ninth century CE), however, hell was more important. ʿUmar ibn al-Khattab, the second caliph, instructed a preacher in the mosque of Medina to "frighten us" (*khawwifnā*), and it is reported that several ascetics (*zuhhād*) of the first two Islamic centuries wept, fainted, or even died on the spot when passing blacksmiths working a forge, overwhelmed by the thought of hellfire (ibid. 221). Later, longing (*shawq*) for paradise gained ground. In the nineteenth century, reformist thinkers bracketed both hell and paradise, calling upon believers to focus on *this* world and social issues instead (Smith 1981). The Islamic Revival has partially reversed this trend, bringing the afterlife back into the foreground.

7. See Lange (2016:227).

8. Both *hasanāt* and *thawāb* literally mean "rewards." I additionally use the word "points" to capture the calculative spirit that is actively embraced by Resala volunteers. On pious point counting, see also Mittermaier (2014c), Schielke (2012a, 2015), and Tobin (2016).

9. "Salafism" is a broad umbrella term for reformist movements seeking to return to the ways of the Prophet Muhammad and the early generations, known as *al-salaf.* I explain my use of the term in more detail below.

10. For all Egyptians, unemployment rates are high, but they reach their peak of 30 percent for those between the ages of fifteen and twenty-nine, particularly college graduates. www.brookings.edu/wp-content/uploads/2016/07/en_youth_in_egypt-2.pdf.

11. Of course, not everyone is after piety. One young woman complained to me about the more conservative branches. She disliked the pressure she had felt during a trip to Fayyoum: "The entire time they were giving religious lessons. It gave me a headache!" Subsequently she decided to go out of her way and volunteer at other branches because "they're more fun." At my branch, such criticism was rare.

12. Resala volunteers go to Cairo neighborhoods such as Batan al-Baqara, Imbaba, Mit ʿUqba, Bulaq, and al-Marg al-Gedida, places called ʿashwāʾiyāt in Arabic, often translated as "informal areas." I opt for the term "slums" because it comes closer to how the volunteers describe and imagine these areas, but also because, despite their infrastructure, they are abject areas, disregarded by the state, and rarely set foot in by middle- and upper-class Egyptians.

13. On *istikhāra,* see Mittermaier (2011:95–98).

14. As Yasmin Moll notes, however, the stress on entrepreneurialism on the part of the New Preachers also comes with a continued stress on charitable giving. For their main target audience—middle-class professionals and university graduates—being proactive about improving one's lot is presented as a divine obligation, while the poor are still positioned as the recipients of charity (personal communication, December 2016).

15. Mona Atia, by contrast, underscores similarities between Dr. Sherif and Amr Khaled, one of the most famous of the New Preachers (2013:78). She comments on Dr. Sherif's tendency to evoke success, satisfaction, and social networks along with the hereafter: "The linking of material and spiritual benefits is one of the hallmarks of pious neoliberalism" (144).

16. On the cleaning campaigns, see Winegar (2012b).

17. Nasser implemented a pan-Arab brand of socialism, giving ordinary citizens unprecedented access to affordable housing, education, jobs, and health services. Concurrently, he promoted a reorientation from the afterlife to *this* life. An excerpt from one of his speeches, which circulated widely on Facebook in 2011, begins with a close-up of the president saying, "Paradise belongs to the poor" (*al-fuqarāʾ lihum al-ganna*). There is applause. A smile appears on Nasser's face. And he begins again: "Paradise belongs to the poor. But those poor, don't they also have a share

[*nasīb*] on earth? Is their fate only in the afterlife? They also want a small share of life. [In turn] they will give you a share of paradise after death." Nasser hints at frequently cited hadiths assuring the poor that they will enter paradise years ahead of the rich (some say forty years; others five hundred). While seemingly echoing these promises, he flips things around and turns the poor into a social and political problem.

18. In the United States, thousands of volunteers work in urban soup kitchens (Allahyari 2000), and evangelical megachurches promote new forms of "organized benevolence" (Elisha 2011). "Voluntourism" has become a lucrative branch of the travel industry, and in India visiting volunteers search for transformative experiences through the "shock of poverty" (Bornstein 2012). Andrea Muehlebach argues that in neoliberal Italy (and elsewhere), voluntarism has placed "pity at the center of social life; a life now structured around inequality, not equality" (2012:226). Writing about Shiʿi Beirut, Lara Deeb calls Islamic voluntarism "a critical thread in the social weft of the pious modern" (2006:169).

19. Quran 6:160: "Whoever shall come [before God] with a good deed will gain ten times the like thereof; but whoever shall come with an evil deed will be requited with no more than the like thereof; and none shall be wronged."

20. This dual temporal orientation resonates with a hadith that Sayyid Qutb cites in his book on social justice: "Work for this world as if you were going to live forever, but work for the future world as if you were going to die tomorrow" (2000:29).

21. For hell images, see, for instance, the Quran 22:19 and 14:50. In his study, Christian Lange does not shy away from graphic depictions of hell but also notes that they hardly reach the level of gory violence one finds in Jewish and Christian Late Antique texts (2016:63). Ephrem, for instance, depicts the sinners in hell as madmen who practice cannibalism.

22. Christian Lange, who spent years studying Islamic portrayals of paradise and hell, argues that it is misleading to speak of a here*after, after*life, or *after*world. He disagrees with Western scholars who have argued that the rigorous distinction between *al-dunyā* (this world) and *al-ākhira* (the afterlife) is as central to Islam as the mind/body dyad is for the intellectual history of the West (2016:10), and he suggests that the reformist criticism of the *otherworldliness* of traditional Islam misses the point. In much premodern Islamic eschatology, he notes, "*al-ākhira* does not aim to eclipse *al-dunyā* [the world]. Rather, it informs the present and provides it with layers of religious meaning. In Islam, the enduring promise of paradise and hell is not the escape to an unreal world of dreams, nor is it the apocalyptic imminence of the world to come, but the ability of the otherworld to sanctify life in the here and now" (2016:289; see also Smith 1981). For critiques of the trope of an "Islamic culture of death," see also Hirschkind (2006) and Asad (2007).

23. From Hassan Hanafi's book on mysticism and development, cited in Lange (2016:281).

1. There is some tolerance for "pious ascetics" in the Islamic tradition (see chapter 5), but a common view holds that Islam does not condone begging. The medieval Shafi'i scholar Subki even called for the punishment of "professional beggars" (Sabra 2006:46), and the Egyptian state in the nineteenth and twentieth centuries became increasingly concerned with the "nuisance" caused by beggars (Ener 1999, 2003). The British Orientalist E. W. Lane attributed the large number of beggars in Cairo to the fact that "benevolence and charity to the poor are virtues which the Egyptians possess in an eminent degree, and which are instilled into their hearts by religion" (1895:370). On a "Quranic economy of poverty," see Bonner (2005).

2. For ethnographies of low-income and poor neighborhoods in Cairo, see Ghannam (2013), Hoodfar (1997), Singerman (1995), and Wikan (1996).

3. Imam Ali was the cousin and son-in-law of the Prophet Muhammad. The Quranic verse is 2:268. The hadith can be found in Bukhari's Book of Zakat, 1429.

4. In the southern, smaller area, dubbed Mit Uqba Island, most of the neighborhood services can be found, such as bakeries, the fire department, and the school. Amal's kiosk, to which I return shortly, is located in this part. The northern part, where Amal used to live, is larger and more densely populated; here one also finds a youth center and the market. For more information on Mit Uqba, see www.tadamun.info/?post_type=city&p=260&lang=en&lang=en.

5. I borrow the idea of disrupted reciprocity from China Scherz's work on charitable giving in Uganda (2014).

6. For an analysis of similar situations of having to produce certain stories or scripts in North American and French social assistance contexts, see Carr (2011) and Fassin (2012). For a historical perspective, see Cohen (2013) on paupers' petitions from the Cairo Geniza archives.

7. On private lessons in Egypt, see Farag (2006) and Singerman (1995).

8. Amal took out a loan of 4,000 pounds (about $670) from Resala for the merchandise, promising to pay back 200 pounds ($32) per month. The microloan she received from Resala speaks to a neoliberalization of Islam and is tied to an ethos of self-help and entrepreneurialism (Atia 2013; Elyachar 2005). Two years later Amal still owed half of the loan. I take this as a sign not of her personal failure but rather of the failure of the neoliberal model.

9. On bimaristans, see Sabra (2006:74ff.).

10. I borrow this story from Patricia Crone (2004:307f.).

11. G. W. Bush (2001), "Rallying the Armies of Compassion," https://georgewbush-whitehouse.archives.gov/news/reports/faithbased.html.

12. It is not uncommon for these two categories to get confused. *Zakāt al-māl* is due on a person's surplus wealth and therefore only paid by those who have money set aside. *Zakāt al-fiṭr* is a small set amount paid by the head of a household for each member of the family before the Eid al-Fitr Prayer at the end of Ramadan. For the past few years, an amount roughly equivalent to $1 was required in Egypt.

13. Comparatively, on the role of papers and documents in bureaucracies, see Hull (2012) and Messick (1992).

14. I am aware of the ethical questions this story might raise. Had this occurred in a North American context, I would arguably have been expected to call a crisis center or to refer Amal to a suicide hotline, or to call social services because of the possible danger to her children. In Egypt, no such resources are available.

15. Notably, at least ninety-four Tunisians attempted or succeeded in burning themselves to death between 1992 and 1995 without their deaths having the kind of effect Bouazizi's death did (Beinin 2016:100). On the uneven valuation of life, see also Butler (2006).

16. Of course, the contours of "the state" kept shifting. Amal supported the uprising but had mixed feelings about the Muslim Brotherhood. She enjoys attending religious study groups (though she rarely has time for them) and thinks some pressure is good. She appreciates the Muslim Brotherhood's commitment to religious discipline. Although the presidency of Mohamed Morsi disappointed her, she was uneasy with the quickly rising anti-Muslim Brotherhood sentiments. A Muslim Brotherhood shaykh from her neighborhood had helped her by giving her some merchandise for the kiosk and by buying clothes for her children. In her view, the Muslim Brotherhood did more for poor people (*al-ghalāba*) than el-Sisi's government. Her positive experiences with the Muslim Brotherhood, however, were mostly confined to individual members, not the organization's political party.

FIVE. ALL THANKS BELONG TO GOD

1. For a historical perspective on dervishes as antinomian, anti-institutional, if not anarchist characters, see Karamustafa (2006). Brief ethnographic engagements with the figure of the dervish can be found in Schielke (2012b) and Biegman (1990, 2009). Reflecting on the figure of the dervish in medieval Egypt, Adam Sabra (2006:31) notes that there is no simple way of drawing a line between voluntary and involuntary poverty. On dervishes in Orientalist literature and paintings, see Sedgwick (2016:114ff.).

2. Shaykh Mahmoud, the dervish most central to this chapter, is a Sufi in the sense that he practices a form of Islam that places emphasis on hidden, spiritual truths (*al-bātin*), not the visible world (*al-zāhir*). His father, who was a shaykh of the Hamdiyya Shadhiliyya Sufi order, was a Sufi in a more narrowly defined sense.

3. Comparatively, see Richard Lee's account of the !Kung San in Botswana, where insulting the hunter who brings meat to the group is a leveling mechanism (1969). To James Ferguson (2015), the ability to insult the giver indicates an ethics of *sharing* rather than a *gift* economy.

4. www.babycenter.com/o_how-to-teach-your-child-to-say-thank-you-and-be-polite-when_10305049.bc.

5. A thought experiment can help us grasp the profound dependency of donors on recipients. Imagine the people of Cairo waking up one sunny morning and

finding the city free of beggars. Not a single beggar in the streets or on the sidewalks, or pleading for help on subways and buses, or sleeping in front of saint shrines, cemeteries, mosques, and churches, or lining up wherever free food is provided. A city completely free of beggars, free of those "black holes in our daily galaxy" (Augé 2002:48). In her novel *The Beggars' Strike,* Aminata Sow (1981) describes an unnamed West African country that decides to violently cleanse the capital city of beggars to increase tourism. Mour, the man behind the campaign, hopes to be rewarded with the position of vice president. Outraged by the violence, the beggars decide to go on strike. But then a marabout, a holy man, instructs Mour to distribute food to beggars to ensure he will become vice president—and the beggars are nowhere to be found. Their withdrawal leads to a very specific kind of crisis, a panic of benevolence. The country asks: to whom do we give now? I imagine a similar kind of crisis would happen in Cairo. Almsgivers and alms administrators, people running *khidmas,* businessmen who like to be filmed while performing their generous gestures—they all would be at a loss if those in need disappeared from Cairo's streets. The employees at Cairo's charity organizations would lose their jobs. Resala volunteers would lose their well-traveled path to paradise. Madame Salwa, I imagine, would be equally outraged by the sudden disappearance of beggars as she is by their seasonal multiplication. To be able to enact her piety, she *needs* orphans to visit, hungry people who line up with their bowls, beggars who extend their hands. Shaykh Salah and Nura need guests to whom they can serve food in order to be able to channel divine generosity and to humble themselves.

6. See Quran 39:7, 31:12.

7. Quran 14:7. The difference between *hamd* and *shukr* in relation to God is discussed in theological works. Some note that *hamd* is for spiritual things whereas *shukr* refers to material blessings. Alternatively, *hamd* is taken to refer to a more general state of gratitude, while *shukr* refers to thankfulness toward God for a concrete gift. Again, others say *hamd* is thanking by tongue whereas *shukr* is by action. God's Ninety-Nine names include *al-hamīd,* the One Always Deserving of Praise, and *al-shakūr,* the Most Grateful.

8. Comparatively, on nonreciprocal gifts in India, see Bornstein (2012) and Laidlaw (2000).

9. Nura faced a conflict through my presence. Everyone is welcome in her space, including nosy anthropologists, but my desire to write about the *khidma* ran counter to the idea that pious giving should be done in secret. Our biggest enemy (even bigger than the Devil), Nura explained, is the *nafs,* the self, which craves pride and recognition. Over time Nura and I found a compromise, avoiding certain topics, deflecting attention to Nura's mother when she became uncomfortable talking about her own life story, and sometimes simply sitting and eating together. To honor her pious secrecy, I use a pseudonym.

10. On life in the City of the Dead, see Watson (1992) and Nedoroscik (1997). For a critique of romanticizations of the City of the Dead, see Singerman and Amar (2006:21–23).

11. When Nura thinks ahead to who might one day take over the *khidma* from her, she assumes it will be her son, Hussain. Her daughter, she said, is a very kind person, but her son was special from the beginning. He would say things that later came true, and one day when he was still a toddler and could barely speak, he somehow communicated to Nura that the *khidma* would grow one hundred times bigger. From a young age, he wanted to participate in the *hadra,* the weekly spiritual gathering held in the courtyard. And, perhaps most importantly, she had seen in a vision that he would take over. (Hussain himself told me that he wanted to become a police officer.)

12. In the *khidma*'s courtyard, countless stories are told and retold that highlight the saints' generosity and care for others. How concerned al-Sayyid al-Badawi was with people in need and especially widows. How Sayyida Nafisa and Fatima al-Nabawiyya prepared food for the poor and orphans. How Rabiʿa al-ʿAdawiyya did good deeds simply out of love for God. How Ali Zin al-ʿAbidin used to go around at night, accompanied by a man who wore a mask and handed money to people without anyone knowing their identity, and people only found out when the money flow stopped after his death. How Hasan and Hussain, the Prophet Muhammad's grandsons, "did exactly what [Nura] is doing. They had a house, gave away food, offered people a place to sleep. For three days in a row they gave food away to people without having anything to eat for themselves."

13. On *mawlids,* see Schielke (2012b) and Waugh (1989).

14. In classical Arabic, the equivalent term is *majzūb.* Valerie Hoffman-Ladd (1995b:99, 109) distinguishes the *magzūb* from the dervish: the former has lost his understanding whereas the latter travels from *mawlid* to *mawlid* and lives off charity. Barbara Drieskens (2006:148) notes, by contrast, that the term "dervish" in Cairo is used for both groups, as both live "in the love of God." Some also understand the *magzūb* as a victim of the *jinn* (ibid. 149).

15. The phrase stems from the Quran (35:15), translated by Muhammad Asad as "O men! It is you who stand in need of God, where He alone is self-sufficient, the One to whom all praise is due." Nura used the words "in need of God's mercy" (*faqīr ilā rahmat Allāh*).

SIX. TOMORROW IS BETTER

1. This was the second round of the 2012 elections. The only other remaining candidate at that point was Ahmed el-Shafiq, who had been prime minister under President Hosni Mubarak.

2. I refer here to how my Sufi interlocutors perceive the Muslim Brotherhood. Historically, the relationship between the Muslim Brotherhood and Sufism is complicated. Hasan al-Banna, the organization's founder, had some Sufi training, along with orthodox training, and praised early Sufi asceticism. The Muslim Brotherhood's structure and practices of self-discipline actively borrow from Sufi traditions.

Sayyid Qutb, on the other hand, denounced "the lazy and superstitious Sufi shaykhs and their murīds" and insisted that they should be excluded from the government of an Islamic state (Sirriyeh 2016:161).

3. To counteract the discipline's classical focus on the present, a range of anthropologists have considered how futures have in many places begun "replac[ing] the past as a cultural reservoir" (Piot 2010:16; see also Guyer 2007; Munn 1992; Shaw 2013), or have turned their attention to different forms of hope (e.g., Crapanzano 2003; Miyazaki 2004).

4. Lila Abu-Lughod (2005) describes a broad shift in Egypt from a developmentalist to a capitalist-consumerist paradigm. Things look somewhat different under President el-Sisi, who embraces a strong developmentalist rhetoric, one closely tied to neoliberalism but also paired with oppression.

5. www.bbc.com/news/world-middle-east-26764201.

6. www.youm7.com/story/2014/6/9/تنصيبيه-بحفل-الرئيس-خطاب-نص-ننشر-بالفيديو/أسمح-لن-السيسى/1713855.

7. This speech was given during the yearly presidential address marking the anniversary of the October War.

8. https://www.skynewsarabia.com/varieties/670692-السيسي-يتنازل-راتبه-نصف. See also www.reuters.com/article/2014/06/24/us-egypt-sisi-economy-idUSKBN0EZ16A20140624.

9. The fund was preceded by the Support Egypt Fund, which was launched in July 2013 and had the identification code 037037 to refer to the day when el-Sisi declared Mohamed Morsi's ouster. On the Tahya Masr fund, see www.almasryalyoum.com/news/details/471017.

10. www.almasryalyoum.com/videos/details/7718.

11. This article includes a link to el-Sisi's 2014 address to the United Nations, where he presented a "comprehensive development plan" and in particular spoke about the New Suez Canal project. http://egyptianstreets.com/2014/09/25/egypts-president-sisi-addresses-the-united-nations/.

12. Abul-Magd (2016) highlights the close involvement of former military personnel in el-Sisi's various megaprojects. This is in line with a broader "blending of military and capital expansion" (Amar 2018:82).

13. Economists have raised doubts about the New Suez Canal's economic benefits. Here I am less interested in actual outcomes than in a politics of hope.

14. Earlier, in 2012, Salafi preacher Muhammad Hassan had issued a similar, much-publicized call, asking Egyptians to donate enough money to make U.S. aid unnecessary.

15. Originally the plan was to sell stocks, allowing partial ownership. This plan was changed to interest-bearing investment certificates that do not confer any ownership rights to investors, but in public discourse these different forms of investments were blurred, inciting people to speak of "owning" a part of the canal. Yasser al-Borhami and other Salafists opposed the purchase of investment certificates on the basis that banking interest is forbidden in Islam. Dar al-Ifta and al-Azhar ruled that it is not forbidden. Having himself earlier declared banking interest un-Islamic,

the former grand mufti Ali Gomaa now argued that modern banking interest was different from usury because "usury is restricted to gold and silver, while banks deal with money."

16. The new canal was inaugurated in a flashy ceremony in August 2015. The remainder of the donations was used for constructing four tunnels underneath the canal.

17. Sections of the video can be found on www.youtube.com/watch?v= P3BC38jmtqU.

18. Turkish in origin, *baltaci* means "a person skilled with an axe" and was adopted into Arabic during the Ottoman era. In modern Egypt, the Arabic *baltagī* has come to mean "thug." The term was used widely during the 2011 uprising to refer to regime supporters who were hired to attack and disperse protesters. After Mubarak's fall, it came to refer to anyone who continued protesting. Some dismissed the "martyrs of the revolution" (particularly those from working-class backgrounds) as thugs, claiming that they were killed while looting, not while fighting for freedom and social justice. Countering such classism, protesters reappropriated the term, wearing T-shirts with the words "I'm a thug."

19. The poor were hit particularly hard. The price of gasoline used for old cars was increased by 80 percent. Diesel, which is used for most taxis, buses, and micro-buses, went up 64 percent. Gasoline used for higher-end cars only went up 7 percent. See also www.aljazeera.com/programmes/insidestory/2014/07/sisi-fuel-backlash-20147615242446900.html.

20. http://egyptianstreets.com/2014/07/08/egypts-president-sisi-explains-subsidy-cuts-warns-religion-is-being-used-to-destroy-the-region/.

21. global.revsoc.me/2014/07/sisis-government-lifts-fuel-subsidies/.

22. The post was from 7 March 2014. It is no longer accessible.

23. The Facebook group is called "Baradai, the Conscience of the Revolution." The photo was accompanied by a comment calling on the military to distribute a percentage of its own wealth to the poor. The post is no longer accessible.

24. http://ikhwanweb.com/article.php?id=31699&ref=search.php. The article is in English and was published in the name of the Anti-Coup Pro-Legitimacy National Alliance.

25. www.reuters.com/article/2014/05/28/us-egypt-election-boycott-idUSKBN0 E81TF20140528.

26. I cite from a draft that Nada Moumtaz kindly shared with me of her forth-coming book, *Reviving the Waqf.*

27. Notably, Sahar El-Daly (2006:66), who conducted a large-scale study of philanthropy in Egypt in the early 2000s, found that many of her interviewees did not even know what the term *waqf* means.

28. www.irinnews.org/printreport.aspx?reportid=95655.

29. By contrast, in the context of Ugandan charity organizations, China Scherz (2014) reports on an overabundance of international donors' contributions toward development projects, and a lack of people wanting to give consumables. Of course, this difference might also have to do with geography. Donors living halfway around

the globe might be more likely to give to "development" when giving from afar but at the same time might donate to charity in a local context.

30. Yussuf Ghishan, " 'an al-samak wa al-bahr wa al-faqr" (About Fish, Sea, and Poverty). *Dustour,* 19 January 2011.

31. Q&A with James Ferguson, *News from Duke University Press* (blog), https:// dukeupress.wordpress.com/2015/05/06/qa-with-james-ferguson/.

32. As part of its Takaful and Karama program, and supported by the World Bank, the Egyptian government has experimented with providing cash transfers to some of its most vulnerable groups, but this is not a basic income program. www.worldbank .org/en/news/feature/2017/03/30/transforming-livelihoods-through-cash-transfers-to-more-than-15-million-families-in-egypt.

33. Mostafa Kamel, "The Need to Open the Discussion again about the New Capital Project," http://www.shorouknews.com/columns/view.aspx?cdate= 19102015&id=ad48ca49-d7c2–4fe6-acfe-590447785067, 19 October 2015. The "New Capital" and the "New Administrative Capital" refer to the same project. An upper-class Sisi supporter told me that the name was changed "out of respect for Cairo."

34. www.latimes.com/world/middleeast/la-fg-egypt-sisi-20160224-story.html.

35. For James Ferguson, what matters are not abstract rights but *rightfulness,* doing something because it is right (2015:50). For my pious interlocutors, the Quranic concept of rights (*haqq*), which include God's rights upon humans, is markedly different from the idea of "rights" circulating in contemporary political and development discourses.

36. El-Sisi had talks with the Peruvian economist Hernando de Soto, a famous proponent of the formalization of "black economies" to unlock "dead capital" in assets that can then be used as collateral for loans to invest and grow. After the model had been put to work in Peru, other countries imported it, among them Egypt, long before el-Sisi. In one of their most widely cited statistics, de Soto's researchers said that the dead housing capital in Egypt represented more than fifty-five times the amount of all direct foreign investments ever recorded in modern Egypt. Against the promise of miraculous economic transformation, Timothy Mitchell (2004) argues that de Soto's proposal reaffirms the tenets of neoliberal economics. He also notes that de Soto's proposed remedy has been tried before. In the 1850s, a series of laws introduced a modern system of private property in Egypt that brought along its own courts, property registers, and enforcement mechanisms. "The result," writes Mitchell, "was a disaster. In rural Egypt small farmers faced rapidly rising prices. Tax payments increased sharply, to cover mortgage payments on the estates of the ruling family." See also Mitchell (2002).

POSTSCRIPT

1. On Tahrir becoming like a miniature-sized Egypt (but one without a central-ized government), see "Tahrir: An Exercise in Nation-Building," by the Egyptian

blogger and activist Sandmonkey. www.sandmonkey.org/2011/07/16/tahrir-an-exercise-in-nation-building/.

2. On this impasse, see also Sabea (2014).

3. On the search for a more lasting anti-structure in Egypt, see also Peterson (2015). On inevitable foreclosures, or the impossibility of sustaining the ethical practice that lies at the heart of activism, see Dave (2011).

4. Having long been struck by how absent God is from the "anthropology of Islam," I seek in my next research project to move God even farther into the foreground than I have done in this project and in my previous work on dreams. Seeking to grapple with God not theologically but ethnographically, I plan to explore how ordinary Muslims in present-day Egypt (re)turn to, engage with, imagine, speak to, listen to, interact with, or turn away from God. This project begins with the insistence that anthropologists must step outside of their secular comfort zone, both analytically and methodologically, if they want to grasp and describe religious life-worlds such as those that lie at the heart of this book.

5. See also Yusuf al-Qaradawi (1995), who describes an Islamic economy that grounds justice in the concept of successorship (*istikhlāf*), the idea that humans are God's deputies on earth and that ultimately everything belongs to God.

GLOSSARY

AHL AL-BAYT People of the house; the Prophet Muhammad's descendants, who are venerated as saints; many of them are buried in Cairo; people visit their shrines to ask for intercession with God.

'AMAL AL-KHAYR Doing good deeds, an umbrella phrase for all kinds of charitable activities.

AMĀNA Trust; refers to the responsibility to fulfill one's obligations to God.

BARAKA Blessing, spiritual power, divine grace, or sanctity; associated with individuals, places, or objects.

AL-BĀTIN Hidden secret, inner reality; opposite of *al-zāhir,* the external visible reality.

DARWĪSH Dervish; ascetic Sufi.

DHIKR Invocation of God; repetitive prayer with the objective of remembering (always being mindful) of God; a central Sufi ritual.

FANĀ' Self-annihilation, passing away from worldly reality, becoming one with God; a central goal of Sufi practice.

GALLĀBIYYA Traditional Egyptian garment worn by both men and women.

HADĪTH Hadith; authoritative records of words or actions of the Prophet Muhammad or his companions; besides the Quran, the second major source from which Islamic law and ethical guidelines are derived.

HASANĀT Good works, which will be weighed against one's bad deeds on Judgment Day.

IT'ĀM Giving food, feeding.

JINN Supernatural but physical creatures mentioned in the Quran; can be good or evil; along with angels and humans, understood to be one of the three sapient creations of God.

KHAYR The good; good deeds; can also refer to charity or welfare.

KHIDMA Service; a Sufi space of hospitality in which food is served and sometimes a place to sleep is offered.

LI-LLĀH To God or for God; a central phrase in Islamic pious economies in which all gifts are directed toward God.

MAWLID Saint day commemorating the birth or death of a saint, usually celebrated at his or her shrine.

NAFS Self; distinct from the soul/spirit (*rūh*); Sufis seek to break it.

RAHMA Mercy or compassion, often associated with God.

AL-RAHMĀN AND AL-RAHĪM All-Compassionate, All-Merciful; two of God's ninety-nine names.

RIDĀ Pious contentment, even in the face of difficult circumstances.

RIZQ Provisions by God; income.

SADAQA Voluntary alms.

SADAQA GĀRIYYA A specific type of *sadaqa* given with an eye to generating long-term benefits.

TAWAKKUL Trust in God; intentional and willful dependence on God.

THAWĀB Merit or credit arising from a pious deed, connected to the hope for a place in paradise.

WAQF Islamic charitable endowment or trust.

ZAKĀT Mandatory almsgiving; one of the five pillars of Islam.

BIBLIOGRAPHY

Abaza, Mona. 2006. "Egyptianizing the American Dream: Nasr City's Shopping Malls, Public Order, and the Privatized Military." In *Cairo Cosmopolitan: Politics, Culture, and Urban Space in the New Globalized Middle East,* edited by Diane Singerman and Paul Amar, 193–220. Cairo: American University in Cairo Press.

Abd al-Ghani, Muhammad Fathi. 2011. "Al-abʿād al-iqtisādiyya lil-hadd al-adna lil-ujūr: dirāsāt wa tajārib dawliyya lil-tatbīq fī masr." *Shorouk Journal of Commercial Sciences* 5: 95–170.

Abdel Ghaffar, Mansour. 2011. "It Took Us All Day to Break through the Barricades." In *18 Days in Tahrir: Stories from Egypt's Revolution,* edited by Hatem Rushdy, 49–64. Hong Kong: Haven Books.

Abul-Magd, Zeinab. 2016. "Egypt's Adaptable Officers." In *Businessmen in Arms: How the Military and Other Armed Groups Profit in the MENA Region,* edited by Elke Grawert and Zeinab Abul-Magd, 23–42. New York: Rowman & Littlefield.

———. 2018. *Militarizing the Nation: The Army, Business and Revolution in Egypt.* New York: Columbia University Press.

Abu-Lughod, Lila. 2005. *Dramas of Nationhood: The Politics of Television in Egypt.* Chicago: University of Chicago Press.

———. 2012. "Living the 'Revolution' in an Egyptian Village: Moral Action in a National Space." *American Ethnologist* 39: 21–25.

Abu Zahra, Nadia. 1997. *The Pure and Powerful: Studies in Contemporary Muslim Society.* Reading, U.K.: Ithaca Press.

Agrama, Hussein. 2011. "Asecular Revolution." The Immanent Frame 2011. http://blogs.ssrc.org/tif/2011/03/11/asecular-revolution/.

———. 2012. *Questioning Secularism: Islam, Sovereignty, and the Rule of Law in Modern Egypt.* Chicago: University of Chicago Press.

Alexander, Anne, and Mostafa Bassiouny. 2014. *Bread, Freedom, Social Justice: Workers and the Egyptian Revolution.* London: Zed Books.

Algar, Ayla. 1992. "Food in the Life of the Tekke." In *The Dervish Lodge: Architecture, Art, and Sufism in Ottoman Turkey,* edited by Raymond Lifchez, 296–303. Berkeley: University of California Press.

Al-Ghazali, Abu Hamid. 1966. *The Mysteries of Almsgiving: A Translation from the Arabic, with Notes, of the Kitāb Asrār Al-Zakāh of Al-Ghazzāli's Ihyā 'Ulūm Al-Dīn.* Beirut: American University of Beirut.

Allahyari, Rebecca Anne. 2000. *Visions of Charity: Volunteer Workers and Moral Community.* Berkeley: University of California Press.

Al-Qaradawi, Yusuf. 1985. *Mushkilat al-faqr wa kayfa 'ālajaha al-Islām.* Beirut: Mu'assassat al-Risala.

———. 1995. *Dawr al-qiyam wa al-akhlāq fi al-iqtisād al-islāmī.* Cairo: Maktabat Wahbah.

———. 2006. *Fiqh al-zakāt: dirāsa muqārina li-ahkāmiha wa falsafatiha fi daw' al-Qur'ān wa al-sunna.* Cairo: Maktabat al-Wahba.

———. 2013. *The Lawful and the Prohibited in Islam.* Kuala Lumpur: Islamic Book Trust.

Amar, Paul. 2013. "Egypt." In *Dispatches from the Arab Spring: Understanding the New Middle East,* edited by Paul Amar and Vijay Prashad, 24–62. Minneapolis: University of Minnesota Press.

———. 2018. "Military Capitalism." *NACLA Report on the Americas* 50(1): 82–89.

Arendt, Hannah. 1965. *On Revolution.* New York: Viking Press.

Armbrust, Walter. 2012. "The Revolution against Neoliberalism." In *The Dawn of the Arab Uprisings: End of an Old Order?,* edited by Bassam Haddad, Rosie Bsheer, and Ziad Abu-Rish, 113–23. London: Pluto Press.

Asad, Talal. 1993. *Genealogies of Religion: Discipline and Reasons of Power in Christianity and Islam.* Baltimore: Johns Hopkins University Press.

———. 2003. *Formations of the Secular: Christianity, Islam, Modernity.* Stanford: Stanford University Press.

———. 2007. *On Suicide Bombing.* New York: Columbia University Press.

Asad, Talal, Wendy Brown, Judith Butler, and Saba Mahmood. 2013. *Is Critique Secular?: Blasphemy, Injury, and Free Speech.* New York: Fordham University Press.

Atia, Mona. 2013. *Building a House in Heaven: Pious Neoliberalism and Islamic Charity in Egypt.* Minneapolis: University of Minnesota Press.

Augé, Marc. 2002. *In the Metro.* Minneapolis: University of Minnesota Press.

Badawi, El-Said, and Martin Hinds. 1986. *A Dictionary of Egyptian Arabic.* Beirut: Librairie du Liban.

Badiou, Alain. 2012. *The Rebirth of History: Times of Riots and Uprisings.* London: Verso.

Baron, Beth. 2014. *The Orphan Scandal: Christian Missionaries and the Rise of the Muslim Brotherhood.* Stanford: Stanford University Press.

Bayat, Asef. 2013. *Life as Politics: How Ordinary People Change the Middle East.* Stanford: Stanford University Press.

Beinin, Joel. 2012. "The Working Class and the Popular Movement in Egypt." In *The Journey to Tahrir: Revolution, Protest, and Social Change in Egypt,* edited by Jeannie Sowers, 92–106. London: Verso.

———. 2016. *Workers and Thieves: Labor Movements and Popular Uprisings in Tunisia and Egypt*. Stanford: Stanford University Press.

Benthall, Jonathan. 1999. "Financial Worship: The Qur'anic Injunction to Almsgiving." *Journal of the Royal Anthropological Institute* 5(1): 27–42.

———. 2016. *Islamic Charities and Islamic Humanism in Troubled Times*. Manchester: Manchester University Press.

Berlant, Lauren Gail (ed.). 2004. *Compassion: The Culture and Politics of an Emotion*. New York: Routledge.

———. 2011. *Cruel Optimism*. Durham: Duke University Press.

Bialecki, Jon. 2014. "Does God Exist in Methodological Atheism? On Tanya Luhrmann's *When God Talks Back* and Bruno Latour." *Anthropology of Consciousness* 25(1): 32–52.

Biegman, Nicolaas. 1990. *Egypt: Moulids, Saints, and Sufis*. London: Kegan Paul International.

———. 2009. *Living Sufism: Rituals in the Middle East and the Balkans*. Amsterdam: KIT.

Black, Bob. 1985. "The Abolition of Work." In *The Abolition of Work and Other Essays*, 15–34. Port Townsend, WA: Loompanics Unlimited.

Boltanski, Luc. 1999. *Distant Suffering: Morality, Media and Politics*. New York: Cambridge University Press.

Bonner, Michael. 2003. "Poverty and Charity in the Rise of Islam." In *Poverty and Charity in Middle Eastern Contexts*, edited by Michael Bonner, Mine Ener, and Amy Singer, 13–30. Albany: State University of New York Press.

———. 2005. "Poverty and Economics in the Qur'an." *Journal of Interdisciplinary History* 35(3): 391–406.

Bornstein, Erica. 2012. *Disquieting Gifts: Humanitarianism in New Delhi*. Stanford: Stanford University Press.

Bornstein, Erica, and Peter Redfield, eds. 2011. *Forces of Compassion: Humanitarianism between Ethics and Politics*. Santa Fe: SAR Press.

Butler, Judith. 2005. *Giving an Account of Oneself*. New York: Fordham University Press.

———. 2006. *Precarious Life: The Powers of Mourning and Violence*. New York: Verso.

———. 2015. *Notes toward a Performative Theory of Assembly*. Cambridge: Harvard University Press.

Carr, E. Summerson. 2011. *Scripting Addiction: The Politics of Therapeutic Talk and American Sobriety*. Princeton: Princeton University Press.

Chakrabarty, Dipesh. 2008. *Provincializing Europe: Postcolonial Thought and Historical Difference*. Princeton: Princeton University Press.

Charbel, Jano. 2014. "Falling Short: Egypt's New Minimum Wage, the Haves and Have Nots." Mada Masr. www.madamasr.com/sections/economy/falling-short-egypts-new-minimum-wage-haves-and-have-nots.

Chittick, William C. 2007. *Sufism: A Beginner's Guide*. Oxford: Oneworld.

———. 2013. *Divine Love: Islamic Literature and the Path to God*. New Haven: Yale University Press.

Clark, Janine A. 2004. *Islam, Charity, and Activism: Middle-Class Networks and Social Welfare in Egypt, Jordan, and Yemen*. Bloomington: Indiana University Press.

Clark, Roy Peter. 2006. "Climb Up and Down the Ladder of Abstraction. In *Writing Tools: Fifty Essential Strategies for Every Writer*, 107–11. New York: Little, Brown.

Cohen, Mark R. 2013. *The Voice of the Poor in the Middle Ages: An Anthology of Documents from the Cairo Geniza*. Princeton: Princeton University Press.

Crapanzano, Vincent. 2003. "Reflections on Hope as a Category of Social and Psychological Analysis." *Cultural Anthropology* 18(1): 3–32.

Crone, Patricia. 2004. *God's Rule: Government and Islam*. New York: Columbia University Press.

Dave, Naisargi. 2011. "Activism as Ethical Practice: Queer Politics in Contemporary India." *Cultural Dynamics* 23(1): 3–20.

Davis, Mike. 2007. *Planet of Slums*. New York: Verso.

Deeb, Lara. 2006. *An Enchanted Modern: Gender and Public Piety in Shi'i Lebanon*. Princeton: Princeton University Press.

Denis, Eric. 2006. "Cairo as Neo-Liberal Capital? From Walled City to Gated Communities." In *Cairo Cosmopolitan: Politics, Culture, and Urban Space in the New Globalized Middle East*, edited by Diane Singerman and Paul Amar, 47–72. Cairo: American University in Cairo Press.

Douglas, Mary. 1990. "Foreword." In *The Gift: The Form and Reason for Exchange in Archaic Societies*, by Marcel Mauss, ix–xxiii. London: Routledge.

Drieskens, Barbara. 2006. *Living with Djinns: Understanding and Dealing with the Invisible in Cairo*. London: Saqi Books.

Edelman, Mark. 2013. "Development." In *Handbook of Sociocultural Anthropology*, edited by James Carrier and Deborah Gewertz, 259–79. Oxford: Berg.

El-Daly, Marwa. 2006. *Philanthropy in Egypt: A Comprehensive Study on Local Philanthropy in Egypt and Potentials of Directing Giving and Volunteering towards Development*. Cairo: Center for Development Studies.

El-Ghobashy, Mona. 2018. "Sisi's Plebiscitary Election." *Middle East Research and Information Project*. www.merip.org/mero/mero032518.

Elisha, Omri. 2011. *Moral Ambition: Mobilization and Social Outreach in Evangelical Megachurches*. Berkeley: University of California Press.

Elyachar, Julia. 2005. *Markets of Dispossession: NGOs, Economic Development, and the State in Cairo*. Durham: Duke University Press.

———. 2012. "Before (and after) Neoliberalism: Tacit Knowledge, Secrets of Trade, and the Public Sector in Egypt." *Cultural Anthropology* 27(1): 76–96.

Elyachar, Julia, and Jessica Winegar. 2012. "Revolution and Counter-Revolution in Egypt a Year after January 25th." *Cultural Anthropology*, 2 February 2012. culanth .org/fieldsights/208-revolution-and-counter-revolution-in-egypt-a-year-after-january-25th.

El-Zatmah, Shawki. 2015. "From Terso into Ultras: The 2011 Egyptian Revolution and the Radicalization of the Soccer's Ultra-Fans." In *Soccer in the Middle East*, edited by Alon Raab and Isaam Khalidi, 183–95. New York: Routledge.

Ener, Mine. 1999. "Prohibitions on Begging and Loitering in Nineteenth Century Egypt." *Die Welt des Islams* 39(3): 319–39.

———. 2003. *Managing Egypt's Poor and the Politics of Benevolence, 1800–1952.* Princeton: Princeton University Press.

Engelke, Matthew. 2007. *A Problem of Presence: Beyond Scripture in an African Church.* Berkeley: University of California Press.

Farag, Iman. 2006. "A Great Vocation, a Modern Profession: Teachers' Paths and Practices." In *Cultures of Arab Schooling: Critical Perspectives from Egypt,* edited by Linda Herrera and Carlos Torres, 109–34. Albany: State University of New York Press.

Fassin, Didier. 2012. *Humanitarian Reason: A Moral History of the Present.* Berkeley: University of California Press.

Ferguson, James. 1994. *The Anti-Politics Machine: "Development," Depoliticization, and Bureaucratic Power in Lesotho.* Minneapolis: University of Minnesota Press.

———. 2015. *Give a Man a Fish: Reflections on the New Politics of Distribution.* Durham: Duke University Press.

Fleischacker, Samuel. 2005. *A Short History of Distributive Justice.* Boston: Harvard University Press.

Ghannam, Farha. 2013. *Live and Die like a Man: Gender Dynamics in Urban Egypt.* Stanford: Stanford University Press.

Graeber, David. 2018. *Bullshit Jobs: A Theory.* New York: Simon & Schuster

Greenberg, Jessica. 2014. *After the Revolution: Youth, Democracy, and the Politics of Disappointment in Serbia.* Stanford: Stanford University Press.

Guyer, Jane I. 2007. "Prophecy and the Near Future: Thoughts on Macroeconomic, Evangelical, and Punctuated Time." *American Ethnologist* 34(3): 409–21.

Hafez, Sherine. 2011. *An Islam of Her Own: Reconsidering Religion and Secularism in Women's Islamic Movements.* New York: New York University Press.

———. 2012. "No Longer a Bargain: Women, Masculinity, and the Egyptian Uprising." *American Ethnologist* 39(1): 37–42.

Hanieh, Adam. 2012. "Egypt's Orderly Transition: International Aid and the Rush to Structural Adjustment." In *The Dawn of the Arab Uprisings: End of an Old Order?,* edited by Bassam Haddad, Rosie Bsheer, and Ziad Abu-Rish, 124–38. London: Pluto Press.

Hirschkind, Charles. 2006. *The Ethical Soundscape: Cassette Sermons and Islamic Counterpublics.* New York: Columbia University Press.

———. 2011. "The Road to Tahrir." The Immanent Frame. http://blogs.ssrc.org/tif/2011/02/09/the-road-to-tahrir/.

Hoffman-Ladd, Valerie J. 1992. "Devotion to the Prophet and His Family in Egyptian Sufism." *International Journal of Middle East Studies* 24(4): 615–37.

———. 1995a. "Eating and Fasting for God in the Sufi Tradition." *Journal of the American Academy of Religion* 63(3): 465–84.

———. 1995b. *Sufism, Mystics, and Saints in Modern Egypt.* Columbia: University of South Carolina Press.

Hoodfar, Homa. 1997. *Between Marriage and the Market: Intimate Politics and Survival in Cairo.* Berkeley: University of California Press.

Hull, Matthew. 2012. *Government of Paper: The Materiality of Bureaucracy in Urban Pakistan.* Berkeley: University of California Press.

Ibrahim, Barbara, Betsy Mesard, and Leah Hunt-Hendrix. 2015. "Youth-Led Pathways to Social and Political Change: Faith and Service in Contemporary Egypt." *Global Studies of Childhood* 5(2): 158–77.

Ibrahim, Barbara, and Dina Sherif, eds. 2008. *From Charity to Social Change: Trends in Arab Philanthropy.* Cairo: American University in Cairo Press.

'Imara, Muhammad. 2009. *Al-hall al-islāmī li-azmat al-ra'smāliyya al-'ālamiyya.* Cairo: Dar al-Salam.

Ingold, Tim. 2014. "That's Enough about Ethnography!" *HAU: Journal of Ethnographic Theory* 4(1): 383–95.

Izutsu, Toshihiko. 2002. *Ethico-Religious Concepts in the Qur'ān.* Montreal: McGill-Queen's University Press.

Kapp, Caram. 2014. "The Utopian State of Tahrir." In *Walls of Freedom: Street Art of the Egyptian Revolution,* edited by Basma Hamdy and Don Karl, 48–49. Berlin: From Here to Fame Publishing.

Karamustafa, Ahmet. 2006. *God's Unruly Friends: Dervish Groups in the Islamic Middle Period, 1200–1550.* London: Oneworld.

Kassab, Elizabeth Suzanne. 2010. *Contemporary Arab Thought: Cultural Critique in Comparative Perspective.* New York: Columbia University Press.

Knysh, Alexander. 2017. *Sufism: A New History of Islamic Mysticism.* Princeton: Princeton University Press.

Lafargue, Paul. 2011. *The Right to Be Lazy.* Chicago: C. H. Kerr.

Laidlaw, James. 2000. "A Free Gift Makes No Friends." *Journal of the Royal Anthropological Institute* 6(4): 617–34.

Lane, Edward William. 1895. *An Account of the Manner and Customs of the Modern Egyptians: Written in Egypt during the Years, 1833–1835.* London: A. Gardner.

Lange, Christian. 2016. *Paradise and Hell in Islamic Traditions.* Cambridge: Cambridge University Press.

Lee, Richard. 1969. "Eating Christmas in the Kalahari." *Natural History* 78(10): 60–64.

Li, Tania Murray. 2007. *The Will to Improve: Governmentality, Development, and the Practice of Politics.* Durham: Duke University Press.

———. 2010. "To Make Live or Let Die? Rural Dispossession and the Protection of Surplus Populations." *Antipode* 41(1): 66–93.

Luhrmann, Tanya M. 2012. *When God Talks Back: Understanding the American Evangelical Relationship with God.* New York: Knopf.

Mahmood, Saba. 2005. *Politics of Piety: The Islamic Revival and the Feminist Subject.* Princeton: Princeton University Press.

———. 2011. "The Architects of the Egyptian Revolution." *Nation.* www.thenation.com/article/ 158581/.

Mahmoud, Mustafa. 1994. *Dialogue with an Atheist.* London: Dar al-Taqwa.

Mahmud, Mustafa. 1975. *Al-mārksiyya wa al-Islām.* Cairo: Dar al- Maʿarif.

———. 1976. *Li-mādha rafadt al-mārksiyya.* Cairo: Dar al-Maʿarif.

———. 1978. *Ukdhubat al-yasār al-islāmī.* Cairo: Dar al-Maʿarif.

Mauss, Marcel. 1967. *The Gift: Forms and Functions of Exchange in Archaic Societies.* New York: Norton.

Mellor, Noha. 2014. "Who Represents the Revolutionaries? Examples from the Egyptian Revolution 2011." *Mediterranean Politics* 19(1): 82–98.

Melly, Caroline. 2013. "Ethnography of the Road: Infrastructural Vision and the Unruly Present in Contemporary Dakar." *Africa* 83(3): 385–402.

Meneley, Anne. 1996. *Tournaments of Value: Sociability and Hierarchy in a Yemeni Town.* Toronto: University of Toronto Press.

Messick, Brinkley. 1992. *The Calligraphic State: Textual Domination and History in a Muslim Society.* Berkeley: University of California Press.

Mitchell, Timothy. 2002. *Rule of Experts: Egypt, Technopolitics, Modernity.* Berkeley: University of California Press.

———. 2004. "The Properties of Markets: Informal Housing and Capitalism's Mystery." Institute for Advanced Studies in Social and Management Sciences, University of Lancaster. Cultural Political Economy Working Paper Series. www.lancs.ac.uk/ias/polecon/workingpapers/2mitchell.doc.

Mittermaier, Amira. 2011. *Dreams That Matter: Egyptian Landscapes of the Imagination.* Berkeley: University of California Press.

———. 2012. "Dreams from Elsewhere: Muslim Subjectivities beyond the Trope of Self-Cultivation." *Journal of the Royal Anthropological Association* 18(2): 247–65.

———. 2014a. "Beyond Compassion: Islamic Voluntarism in Egypt." *American Ethnologist* 41(3): 518–31.

———. 2014b. "Bread, Freedom, Social Justice: The Egyptian Uprising and a Sufi Khidma." *Cultural Anthropology* 29(1): 54–79.

———. 2014c. "Trading with God: Islam, Calculation, Excess." In *A Companion to the Anthropology of Religion,* edited by Michael Lambek and Janice Boddy, 274–94. London: Wiley-Blackwell.

———. 2015. "Death and Martyrdom in the Arab Uprisings: An Introduction." *Ethnos* 80(5): 583–604.

Miyazaki, Hirokazu. 2004. *The Method of Hope: Anthropology, Philosophy, and Fijian Knowledge.* Stanford: Stanford University Press.

Muehlebach, Andrea. 2012. *The Moral Neoliberal: Welfare and Citizenship in Italy.* Chicago: University of Chicago Press.

———. 2013. "The Catholicization of Neoliberalism: On Love and Welfare in Lombardy, Italy." *American Anthropologist* 115(3): 452–65.

Munn, Nancy D. 1992. "The Cultural Anthropology of Time: A Critical Essay." *Annual Review of Anthropology* 21: 93–123.

Nagi, Saad Z. 2001. *Poverty in Egypt: Human Needs and Institutional Capacities.* Oxford: Lexington Books.

Naguib, Nefissa. 2015. *Nurturing Masculinities: Men, Food, and Family in Contemporary Egypt.* Austin: University of Texas Press.

Nedoroscik, Jeffrey A. 1997. *The City of the Dead: A History of Cairo's Cemetery Communities.* Westport, CT: Bergin & Garvey.

O'Neill, Kevin. 2013. "Left Behind: Security, Salvation, and the Subject of Prevention." *Cultural Anthropology* 28(2): 204–26.

Orsi, Robert A. 2016. *History and Presence.* Cambridge: Belknap Press of Harvard University Press.

Parry, Jonathan. 1986. "The Gift, the Indian Gift and the 'Indian Gift.'" *Man* 21(3): 453–73.

Peterson, Mark Allen. 2015. "In Search of Antistructure: The Meaning of Tahrir Square in Egypt's Ongoing Social Drama." In *Breaking Boundaries: Varieties of Liminality,* edited by Agnes Horvath, Bjorn Thomassen, and Harald Wydra, 164–82. New York: Berghahn.

Piot, Charles. 2010. *Nostalgia for the Future: West Africa after the Cold War.* Chicago: University of Chicago Press.

Pitt-Rivers, Julian. 2011. "The Place of Grace in Anthropology." *HAU: Journal of Ethnographic Theory* 1(1): 423–50.

Povinelli, Elizabeth A. 2011a. *Economies of Abandonment: Social Belonging and Endurance in Late Liberalism.* Durham: Duke University Press.

———. 2011b. "Routes/Worlds." *e-flux,* no. 27. www.e-flux.com/journal/27/67991/routes-worlds/.

Qutb, Sayyid. 2000. *Social Justice in Islam.* Oneonta, NY: Islamic Publications International.

———. 2009. *Al-ʿadāla al-ijtimāʿiyya fī al-Islām.* Cairo: Dar al-Shorouk.

Ralph, Michael. 2008. "Killing Time." *Social Text* 26(4): 1–29.

Robbins, Joel. 2013. "Beyond the Suffering Slot: Toward an Anthropology of the Good." *Journal of the Royal Anthropological Association* 19: 447–62.

———. 2016. "What Is the Matter with Transcendence? On the Place of Religion in the New Anthropology of Ethics." *Journal of the Royal Anthropological Institute* 22(4): 767–81.

Rodriguez-Mañas, Francisco. 2000. "Charity and Deceit: The Practice of Itʿam Al-Taʿam in Moroccan Sufism." *Studia Islamica* 91: 59–90.

Rozen, Joel. 2015. "Civics Lesson: Ambivalence, Contestation, and Curricular Change in Tunisia." *Ethnos* 80(5): 605–29.

Rudnyckyj, Daromir. 2011. *Spiritual Economies: Islam, Globalization, and the Afterlife of Development.* Ithaca: Cornell University Press.

Rushdy, Hatem. 2011. "Life under Mubarak." In *18 Days in Tahrir: Stories from Egypt's Revolution,* edited by Hatem Rushdy, 39–46. Hong Kong: Haven Books.

Sabea, Hana. 2013. "A 'Time out of Time': Tahrir, the Political and the Imaginary in the Context of the January 25th Revolution in Egypt." Hot Spots, *Cultural Anthropology* website. culanth.org/fieldsights/211-a-time-out-of-time-tahrir-the-political-and-the-imaginary-in-the-context-of-the-january-25th-revolution-in-egypt.

———. 2014. "'I Dreamed of Being a People': Egypt's Revolution, the People, and Critical Imagination." In *The Political Aesthetics of Global Protest: The Arab*

Spring and Beyond, edited by Pnina Werbner, Martin Webb, and Kathryn Spellman-Poots, 67–92. Edinburgh: Edinburgh University Press.

Sabra, Adam. 2006. *Poverty and Charity in Medieval Islam: Mamluk Egypt, 1250–1517.* New York: Cambridge University Press.

Salih, Ahmad ʿAbbas. 1973. *Al-yamīn wa al-yasār fī al-Islām.* Beirut: Al-Muʾassassa al-ʿArabiyya lil-Dirāsāt wa al-Nashr.

Schaeublin, Emanuel. 2016. "Zakat in Nablus (Palestine): Change and Continuity in Islamic Almsgiving." PhD diss., University of Oxford.

Scherz, China. 2014. *Having People, Having Heart: Charity, Sustainable Development, and Problems of Dependence in Central Uganda.* Chicago: University of Chicago Press.

Schielke, Samuli. 2012a. "Capitalist Ethics and the Spirit of Islamization in Egypt." In *Ordinary Lives and Grand Schemes: An Anthropology of Everyday Religion,* edited by Samuli Schielke and Liza Debevec, 131–45. Oxford: Berghahn.

———. 2012b. *The Perils of Joy: Contesting Mulid Festivals in Contemporary Egypt.* Syracuse: Syracuse University Press.

———. 2015. *Egypt in the Future Tense: Hope, Frustration, and Ambivalence before and after 2011.* Bloomington: Indiana University Press.

Schimmel, Annemarie. 1995. *Mystische Dimensionen des Islam: Die Geschichte des Sufismus.* Frankfurt: Insel Verlag.

Sedgwick, Mark. 2003. *Sufism: The Essentials.* New York: American University in Cairo Press.

———. 2016. *Western Sufism: From the Abbasids to the New Age.* Oxford: Oxford University Press.

Sharqawi, ʿAbd al-Rahman. 1965. *Muhammad rasūl al-hurriyah.* Cairo: Dar al-Hilal.

Shaw, Rosalind. 2013. "Provocation: Futurizing Memory." *Cultural Anthropology.* www.culanth.org/fieldsights/376-provocation-futurizing-memory.

Simmel, Georg. 1965. "The Poor." *Social Problems* 13(2): 118–40.

Sims, David. 2010. *Understanding Cairo: The Logic of a City out of Control.* New York: American University in Cairo Press.

———. 2015. *Egypt's Desert Dreams: Development or Disaster.* New York: American University in Cairo Press.

Singer, Amy. 2005. "Serving Up Charity: The Ottoman Soup Kitchen." *Journal of Interdisciplinary History* 35(5): 481–500.

———. 2008. *Charity in Islamic Societies.* Cambridge: Cambridge University Press.

Singerman, Diane. 1995. *Avenues of Participation: Family, Politics, and Networks in Urban Quarters of Cairo.* Princeton: Princeton University Press.

Singerman, Diane, and Paul Amar. 2006. "Introduction: Contesting Myths, Critiquing Cosmopolitanism, and Creating the New Cairo School of Urban Studies." In *Cairo Cosmopolitan: Politics, Culture, and Urban Space in the New Globalized Middle East,* edited by Diane Singerman and Paul Amar, 1–46. Cairo: American University in Cairo Press.

Sirriyeh, Elizabeth. 2016. *Sufis and Anti-Sufis: The Defence, Rethinking and Rejection of Sufism in the Modern World*. New York: Routledge.

Smith, Jane I. 1981. *The Islamic Understanding of Death and Resurrection*. Albany: State University of New York Press.

Sow, Aminata. 1981. *The Beggars' Strike; Or, The Dregs of Society*. Essex: Longman.

Sparre, Sara Lei. 2013. "A Generation in the Making: The Formation of Young Muslim Volunteers in Cairo." PhD diss., Department of Anthropology, University of Copenhagen.

Sukarieh, Mayssoun. 2012. "The Hope Crusades: Culturalism and Reform in the Arab World." *PoLAR: Political and Legal Anthropology Review* 35(1): 115–34.

Sullivan, Denis Joseph. 1994. *Private Voluntary Organizations in Egypt: Islamic Development, Private Initiative, and State Control*. Gainesville: University Press of Florida.

Thompson, E. P. 1971. "The Moral Economy of the English Crowd in the Eighteenth Century." *Past and Present* 50(1): 76–136.

Ticktin, Miriam. 2011. *Casualties of Care: Immigration and the Politics of Humanitarianism in France*. Berkeley: University of California Press.

Tobin, Sarah A. 2016. *Everyday Piety: Islam and Economy in Jordan*. Ithaca: Cornell University Press.

Tripp, Charles. 2006. *Islam and the Moral Economy: The Challenge of Capitalism*. Cambridge: Cambridge University Press.

Turner, Victor W. 1977. *The Ritual Process: Structure and Anti-Structure*. Ithaca: Cornell University Press.

Utvik, Bjørn Olav. 2006. *Islamist Economics in Egypt: The Pious Road to Development*. Boulder: Lynne Rienner.

Watson, Helen. 1992. *Women in the City of the Dead*. Trenton, NJ: Africa World Press.

Waugh, Earle H. 1989. *The Munshidin of Egypt: Their World and Their Song*. Columbia: University of South Carolina Press.

Weber, Max. 2001. *The Protestant Ethic and the Spirit of Capitalism*. New York: Routledge.

Wikan, Unni. 1996. *Tomorrow, God Willing: Self-Made Destinies in Cairo*. Chicago: University of Chicago Press.

Wilde, Oscar. 1891. *The Soul of Man Under Socialism*. New York: Humboldt.

Winegar, Jessica. 2012a. "The Privilege of Revolution: Gender, Class, Space, and Affect in Egypt." *American Ethnologist* 39(1): 67–70.

———. 2012b. "Taking Out the Trash: Youth Cleaning Up Egypt after Mubarak." In *The Journey to Tahrir: Revolution, Protest, and Social Change in Egypt*, edited by Jeannie Sowers and Chris Toensing, 64–69. London: Verso.

Woltering, Robbert. 2013. "Unusual Suspects: 'Ultras' as Political Actors in the Egyptian Revolution." *Arab Studies Quarterly* 35(3): 290–304.

Žižek, Slavoj. 2009. *First as Tragedy, Then as Farce*. London: Verso.

———. 2011. "For Egypt, This Is the Miracle of Tahrir Square." www.theguardian.com/global/2011/feb/10/egypt-miracle-tahrir-square.

INDEX

Atia, Mona, 9, 84–85, 168, 189n13, 198n15
austerity measures, 16, 151, 159, 165–166, 170.
    See also subsidies
authoritarianism, 16, 183

Badiou, Alain, 36
baltagiyya. See thugs
baraka. See blessings
basic income programs, 173–175, 206n32.
    See also minimum wage
Battle of the Camel, 25–26, 37, 44
Bayat, Asef, 179, 192n25
beggars, 52, 107, 119, 132, 181, 185; The Beg-
    gars' Strike, 202n5; as medium to God,
    89, 132, 185; negative views on, 41–42,
    105–106, 111, 164, 170, 185, 200n1. *See
    also* poor; poverty; "the poor first"
being-with-others, 11, 16, 40, 151, 182
benevolence, 189n11, 199n18, 200n1, 202n5.
    See also blessings; generosity
Berlant, Lauren, 5, 157
Bialecki, Jon, 190n18
bimāristān, 117, 200n9. *See also* healthcare
blessings, 43, 91, 94, 112, 129, 135, 138–139,
    145, 202n7. *See also* benevolence;
    generosity
Bornstein, Erica, 5, 42, 188n7, 199n18
Bouazizi, Mohammad, 27–28, 126, 193n8,
    201n15
bread, 69, 113, 166; in charitable contexts,
    55–56, 117, 138–139, 191n21, 196n15; riots
    (1977), 29, 193n12, 194n20; subsidies, 29,
    160; in the uprising, 32–36. *See also*
    "bread, freedom, social justice"
"bread, freedom, social justice," 4, 9, 25–26,
    29, 166. *See also* protests; revolution
bureaucracy, 7–13, 69, 92, 115, 124, 129–130,
    172, 184, 201n13. *See also* intake office
Butler, Judith, 36, 192n2, 201n15

Cairo: Abdel Munim Riyad, 36, 175, 177;
    City of the Dead, 136, 147, 149, 185,
    202n10; Gizeh, 84, 184; Islamic, 1, 106,
    164; Mit Uqba, 14, 109–111, 113, 115, 119,
    200n4; Mohandeseen, 109, 114–115, 162;
    Zamalek, 70, 114. *See also* class differ-
    ences; New (Administrative) Capital;
    Tahrir

Calvinism, 66, 168
capitalism: corporate, 37; and hope, 167,
    172; military, 3, 188n4; relation of
    Islamic practices to, 41, 73, 76, 145–146,
    156, 168, 189n13; and social justice, 44,
    177, 194n23; state, 10, 188n4, 204n4. *See
    also* neoliberalism; property; social
    justice; socialism
care, 90, 115; for *vs.* about the poor, 1–7, 11,
    13, 16, 60–61, 140, 175, 180–181, 196n17,
    203n12; in humanitarianism, 5; and
    social justice, 36–37, 70, 83, 151; of the
    state, 67, 70, 117–118, 157. *See also*
    healthcare; humanitarian reason;
    li-llāh; welfare state
case, charity, 10, 13–14, 107–110, 116, 120–
    130. *See also* bureaucracy; performance
Catholicism, 89, 188n8
Chakrabarty, Dipesh, 16, 194n13
charitable organizations. *See* al-Gam'iyya
    al-Shar'iyya; bureaucracy; Dar al-
    Orman; Egyptian Food Bank; Muslim
    Brotherhood; Mustafa Mahmoud
    Association; Resala
charity. *See* care; case; gift economy; *khayr;*
    rights; *sadaqa;* self-cultivation; social
    justice; *zakāt;* individual charity
    organizations
Christianity and Christians, 3, 83, 145, 164,
    168, 190n16, 190n18, 191n21, 199n21;
    compassion of, 4–5, 88, 101, 188n8;
    solidarity in the 2011 uprising, 35, 37. *See
    also* Catholicism; Coptic Church and
    Copts; Protestantism
circulation, 16, 29, 36, 65, 139, 183. *See also*
    distribution; economy; gift
citizens, 171, 198n17; abandoned by state,
    112, 117; productive/sacrificing, 42, 62,
    85, 157–164, 190n14. *See also* elections;
    welfare state
City of the Dead, 136, 147, 149, 185,
    202n10
class differences: and charity, 4, 173, 183;
    endorsing, 13, 30, 156, 183; in the upris-
    ing, 27–29, 32, 35–38, 43, 126, 193n9,
    205n18. *See also* elitism; inequality;
    middle class; Tahrir; working class
commodification, 44, 65, 180, 184

donors *(continued)*
    107, 110, 118, 127. See also *amāna;* case;
    dependency; economy, of circulation;
    endowment; *sadaqa;* trading with God;
    triadic giving; voluntarism
Dostour Party, 196n13
Douglas, Mary, 4
Dr. Sherif. *See* Abdelazeem, Sherif
dreams, 7–8, 55, 62–63, 69, 137, 143–144,
    151, 190n17, 199n22, 207n4; *istikhāra,*
    82, 198n13. *See also* invisible realm
dunyā (this world), 43, 94, 199n2; rewards
    in, 94–95. *See also* afterlife
duty. *See* obligation; responsibility

economy: of circulation, 16, 29, 36, 65, 139,
    183; divine, 68, 73, 94; gift, 8, 76, 136,
    142, 148, 201n3; pious, 15, 36, 45, 108,
    135. *See also* afterlife; capitalism; distri-
    bution; neoliberalism; socialism
Egyptian Food Bank, 172
Egyptian Revolution (1919), 10
Egyptian Revolutionary Socialists, 49, 165
Eissa, Ibrahim, 33, 194n18
El-Daly, Sahar, 205n27
El-Ghobashy, Mona, 27, 193n7
El-Shaarawi, Mohamed Metwally, 64
El-Sisi, Abdelfattah: heightened persecu-
    tion under, 27, 114, 157, 177, 184, 195n8,
    204n4; ideology of sacrifice/develop-
    ment, 11, 27, 155–170, 173–178, 204n4,
    204n9, 204n11, 204n12, 206n36; politi-
    cal fatigue under, 45, 201n16; support
    for, 2, 27, 161–166. *See also* austerity
    measures; coup; elections; megaprojects
ElBaradei, Mohamed, 67, 196n13, 205n23
elections, 32–33; 2012, 2, 9, 26, 44, 85–86,
    155, 179, 203n1; 2014, 159, 196n13;
    2018, 27
elite, 3, 10, 33, 174. *See also* class differences;
    poor; poverty
elitism, 33–34, 67. *See also* class differences
emancipation, 45, 156, 158, 175
endowment (*waqf*), 169, 191n21, 195n11,
    205n26, 205n27
equality, 30, 38, 43, 194n13, 199n18. *See also*
    class differences; inequality
eschatology. *See* afterlife

ethics: of giving, 4–5, 9–10, 15–16, 24, 27,
    43–45, 52, 73, 125, 130, 136, 175, 180–183;
    of immediacy, 182; of secrecy, 12, 51, 161,
    202n9. *See also* dependency; justice;
    nonhumanitarian ethics
everyday: charitable giving, 7, 10–11, 24, 51,
    135, 156–158, 190n19; ethics, 82, 117; *vs.*
    exceptional time, 7, 37; *vs.* revolutionary
    practices, 40, 184; suffering, 121, 157, 179
extremism, 195n8
Ezzat, Amr, 33

Facebook: as site of critique, 165, 194n15,
    205n23; during 2018 elections, 27;
    during the 2011 uprising, 24, 49, 198n17;
    Resala's use of, 77, 87, 90, 97, 197n3; "we
    are all Khaled Said," 28, 32
faking poverty, 105–106, 121, 124. *See also*
    case; performance
family relations, 72, 97–98, 110–112, 116–
    117, 123–124, 140. *See also* divorce;
    marriage
*fanā*ʿ (self-erasure), 51, 53, 63, 131, 140. *See
    also* self-cultivation
fasting, 1–3, 36, 71, 87, 99, 187n1, 195n3. *See
    also* Ramadan; Ramadan table
fatalism, 30
fatwas, 161, 168
favors: economy of, 110, 127, 135
Ferguson, James, 168, 170, 172–173, 175,
    188n7, 192n2, 194n2, 201n3, 206n31,
    206n35
fieldwork: and anthropologist's entangle-
    ment, 13–14, 81; with Copts, 188n8;
    frustrations and fatigue, 14, 72, 108; at
    khidma, 12, 53–54, 136, 202n9; at Resala,
    9, 13, 81, 108; and secrecy, 12–13, 136,
    202n9; in slums, 14–15, 110; and switch-
    ing sides, 124; at a time of revolution, 11,
    17, 21–22, 24, 182
Flash Hub, 9–10, 171–172
food distribution: history of, 191n21,
    191n24; at *khidmas,* 55–69, 71–72, 136,
    147, 156, 183–184; private, 11–13, 106, 185,
    188n9; as radical, 175, 181; in Ramadan,
    1–2, 106, 187n1; at Resala, 81, 84–89,
    91–99, 109–110; at saint shrines, 8, 55; as
    saintly practice, 195n6; in Sufism, 51–52;

at Tahrir Square, 36, 40; temporality of, 15–16, 40, 169, 183–184. *See also* bread; *khidma;* subsidies

food jihad, 191n24

Free Officers' Coup (1952), 194n20

Freedom and Justice Party, 85, 196n14, 201n6

future-orientedness: and anthropology, 204n3; in development projects, 4, 155–170, 177; in giving, 15–16, 158, 169, 181, 199n20; in protesting, 4, 11, 37, 68, 126, 166–167; in saving, 65, 162–163; in volunteering, 100; in working, 23, 71, 158–159, 165, 199n20; in worrying, 130, 156. *See also* temporality

gated communities, 35, 101, 174. *See also* class differences

Gates, Bill, 70

gender, 53, 85, 129, 193n9

generosity: divine, 6, 57, 63, 136–137, 150, 189n12, 202n5; human, 6, 12, 99, 106, 110–111, 140, 190n21, 195n6, 202n5, 203n12. *See also* blessings

Ghoneim, Wael, 28–29, 183

gift economy/exchange, 8, 76, 136, 142, 148, 201n3. *See also* economy

"giving a man a fish," 72, 85, 168–175. *See also* development; distribution; ethics, of immediacy; neoliberalism

God: as al-Ghani (the Rich), 130; ethnography of, 180, 190n18; God-orientedness, 16, 101, 127; as merciful, 136, 187n1, 189n11, 197n6, 203n15; trading with, 76, 94–97. *See also* divine; hand of God

Gomaa, Ali, 195n8, 205n15

good. *See khayr*

good deeds. *See khayr*

government: as addressee, 15, 62, 99, 110, 115–118, 129; critique of, 29, 73, 112, 174, 177; cutting back on social services, 9, 83, 115, 170; entangled in divine order, 68–69, 108; providing social services, 13, 37, 120, 190n21; spiritual, 62, 196n17; and Sufism, 51, 195n8, 203n2. *See also* bureaucracy; corruption; El-Sisi; mega-aprojects; minimum wage; Ministry of Social Affairs; Morsi; neoliberalism; state

gratitude (*shukr*), 4, 6, 41, 52, 90, 94, 101, 132–136, 148–149, 202n7. *See also* contentment; ingratitude

guests of God, 60, 64, 187n1. *See also* hospitality; *khidma;* Ramadan table

hadith, 2, 12, 196n19; about charity, 2, 12, 50, 69, 79, 95, 169, 200n3; about gratitude, 132; about poverty, 2, 89, 107, 131, 199n17; about work, 71, 144–145, 168–169, 199n20. *See also* Muhammad; Quran

Hafez, Sherine, 35, 193

halal provisions, 59, 138–139

Hanafi, Hassan, 101, 191n23, 199n23

hand of God, 50, 64, 132–133, 185. *See also* divine; generosity

haqq (rightful share), 58, 66–68, 106, 125, 146, 175, 188n10, 206n35; *al-faqīr* (of the poor), 5, 41, 175, 188n10. *See also* justice; rights

Hardt, Michael, 36

hasanāt. See divine, reward

healthcare, 33, 117, 126

hell, 76–77, 89, 95, 99–100, 197n3, 197n6, 199n21, 199n22. *See also* afterlife; divine, punishment; paradise

hereafter. *See* afterlife

Hoffman-Ladd, Valerie, 51, 195n3, 203n14

homeless, 2, 59–60, 73, 131, 147

hope: anthropology of, 204n3; appropriated, 44, 166–167; as expectation, 73, 148; at expense of present, 27, 157–163, 167; and revolution, 9, 21, 29, 38, 174; and spiritual aspiration, 53, 58, 76, 88–89, 95, 100, 134, 136. *See also* afterlife; cynicism; development; disillusionment; future-orientedness; hopelessness

hopelessness, 21, 37. *See also* cynicism; disillusionment; hope

Hosni, Mustafa, 82–83

hospitality, 63, 135–136, 182, 190n21, 195n6. See also *khidma*

houris, 74–75, 197n1. *See also* paradise

human rights, 38, 86, 181. *See also* justice; rights

human, concepts of the, 45, 68, 88, 120, 134–135, 148–149, 175, 181, 207n5

humanitarian reason, 5–6, 108, 151. *See also* nonhumanitarian ethics; suffering

humanitarianism, 5, 23, 42, 125. *See also* compassion; ethics, of giving

hunger: as irrelevant at *khidma*, 64, 147; and religious obligation, 2, 54, 56, 64, 69, 119, 141; and revolution, 33–34, 60, 165; as sacrifice to nation, 164–166; as sign of suffering, 31, 125, 185; as sign of worsening conditions, 60, 112, 164. *See also* Egyptian Food Bank; fasting

imagination, 8, 126, 207n4; in charity work, 8, 58, 76, 95, 99, 182–184, 197n3, 198n12; political, 6, 16, 21, 23, 25, 37, 43, 157, 166, 182–184. See also *al-bāṭin*

Imam Hussain (saint/shrine), 52, 63, 141–144

individualism. *See* responsibility, individual; work ethic

inequality, 3–5, 11, 17, 24, 66, 75, 182–183, 187n3, 199n18. *See also* class differences; equality; injustice; oppression

inflation, 2–3, 12, 112–113, 162, 164–165, 174, 187n2

informal economy, 113, 176–177. *See also* slums

Ingold, Tim, 16

ingratitude, 6, 61, 106, 132–134, 148–151. *See also* contentment; gratitude

injustice, 5, 33, 44, 58, 66, 112, 127, 189n12, 196n17. *See also* inequality; justice; oppression; protests; revolution

intake office, 10, 13, 121–125, 185. *See also* bureaucracy; case; performance

intention (*niyya*): in channeling divine generosity, 63, 144; for God *vs.* for reward, 88, 91, 95–96, 100, 164; integral to charity, 70; unrealistic, 31. *See also* divine, reward; *khayr; li-llāh;* obligation; self-cultivation; self-erasure

International Monetary Fund, 165, 174, 187n4

Intifada, 192n4

invisible realm *(al-bāṭin):* entangled with the visible, 5, 8, 16, 62, 73, 75, 143, 147–

151, 189n12, 201n2. See also *ahl al-bayt;* dreams

Iraq, 192n4, 194n20

Islamic left, 10, 184, 189n13, 191n23. *See also* Abdel Nasser; Mahmoud; socialism

Islamic Revival, 7, 76, 83, 197n6

Islamic State (Daesh), 40

Islamism, 2, 40–41, 74, 85, 160, 165, 184. *See also* Islamic left; Islamic Revival; Muslim Brotherhood; Salafism

Israel, 123, 159

it'ām. See food distribution

jinn (spirit), 148, 203n14

joy of giving, 60–61, 87, 139. *See also* ethics, of giving

Judgment Day, 50, 52, 75, 119. *See also* afterlife

justice: charity's concern for, 11, 16, 41, 66, 68, 180; *vs.* compassion/charity, 5, 15, 24, 66; Islamic concept of, 16, 23, 43, 50, 54, 73, 108, 189n12, 207n5; lack of, 112, 156. *See also* "bread, freedom, social justice"; equality; inequality; injustice; oppression; revolution; social justice

Kefayah movement, 192n4

khayr (good): as activity, 13, 70, 79, 88–89, 188n9, 203n12; difficulties in performing, 13, 111, 163; as expiation and blessing, 58–59, 66–67, 95, 135, 199n19; as exploited, 117, 197n2; God soliciting the, 43, 124, 164; maintaining dependency, 22–23, 82; and the Muslim Brotherhood, 44, 145, 189n10; in public/private, 12, 77, 79, 110; trading with God, 6, 76–77, 88–89, 91, 164. *See also* ethics; *li-llāh;* public giving; secrecy; social justice; trading with God

khidma, 52–69, 129–151; and *ahl al-bayt* (saints), 52–53, 56, 58, 62, 139, 203n12; and divine signs, 7, 63, 137, 203n11; donating to, 13, 58–59, 138–139; expectation-free giving at, 134–136, 140; fieldwork at, 12, 53–54, 136, 202n9; guests at, 59–61, 64, 73, 130, 138–139, 140–141; kind of food given at, 55–56, 59, 138; as nonhumanitarian, 125, 132; physical space of, 52, 54–56, 137–138, 183, 195n4; reconfiguring poverty, 131, 146–149; in Sisi era, 176–178, 183; as site of an Otherwise, 16, 146–147, 181–183; as site of justice, 54–55, 66–68, 73. *See also* dervish; donors; food distribution; hospitality; Sufism

kinship. *See* family relations

kiosk (*kushk*), 114–117, 128, 171, 177, 201n16. *See also* street vendors

Lange, Christian, 100, 190n15, 191n22, 197n3, 197n6, 199n21, 199n23

laziness, 42, 65, 105, 146, 148, 164, 170, 204n2. *See also* work ethic

Lee, Richard, 201n3

li-llāh (for God): in 1919 Egyptian Revolution, 10; defining the Sufi *khidma,* 52; entangling visible and invisible, 158, 189n12; as obligation, 66, 88, 185; as style of charity, 3, 6–7, 56, 76, 88, 100, 106, 133–135, 158. See also *al-hamdu-li-llāh;* intention; *khayr; khidma*

Li, Tania, 173, 188n7

liberalism: and compassion, 4, 45, 197n6; and futurity, 157, 175; and politics, 10, 29–30, 37, 45, 67, 192n4, 196n13; secular, 16. *See also* neoliberalism; secular

liminality, 39, 45. *See also* anti-structure

love of God, 79–83, 139–140, 188n8, 189n11, 203n12, 203n14. See also *li-llāh*

mā'idat al-rahmān. See Ramadan table

Madame Salwa: on deservingness, 105–106, 125; and expectation of gratitude, 134–135; giving to God, 1–6, 8, 15–17, 127, 157, 162–163, 183, 184–185; and investment in/hope for future, 156, 162–163, 169, 174, 182; non-institutionalized giving, 11, 13, 22–23, 147, 171–172, 180–181, 184, 187n1, 188n9; on revolution and Sisi era, 9, 35, 165, 174, 177

magzūb, 147, 203n14

Mahmood, Saba, 140, 193n5

Mahmoud, Mustafa, 190n17, 191n23. *See also* Mustafa Mahmoud Association

Mamluk era, 69, 191n21, 196n17

marriage, 80–82, 91, 99–100, 111, 115, 124, 137, 141, 196n16, 197n2. *See also* divorce

martyrs: of the revolution, 25, 28, 32, 34, 126, 166, 205n18; Western imaginaries of, 74. *See also* houris; paradise; revolution

Marxism, 10, 183, 191n23. *See also* Islamic left

material conditions: and activists' concerns, 11, 32; detachment from, 131, 140, 143, 146–147; 150, 157; and God-orientedness, 9, 101, 181, 202n7; poverty as, 112, 149; and Resala food distribution, 91, 95, 101; and spiritual realm, 8, 12, 54, 69, 73, 125, 135, 198n15

Mauss, Marcel, 4, 8, 75, 142, 181

mawlid, 13, 52, 56, 142–143, 183, 203n13, 203n14. *See also* shrine; Sufism

media, 25, 31, 38, 49, 67, 74, 126, 176, 191n25, 193n5. *See also* Facebook; television; Twitter

megaprojects, 16, 155–156, 158, 161–163, 169, 173–174, 188n4, 190n14, 204n12. *See also* development; sacrifice

Melly, Caroline, 157

microloans, 4, 107, 114, 168, 170–171, 188n4, 200n8. *See also* development

middle class, 5, 131, 163, 188n5, 198n14; activists, 10, 28–30, 35, 38, 126, 165, 193n9; neighborhoods, 1, 78. *See also* class differences; working class

military, 12, 26, 61–62, 160; and charity, 187n1, 205n23; entanglement with neoliberal capitalism, 3, 27, 161, 165–166, 188n4, 204n12; and Tahrir, 25, 179. *See also* coup (2013); Rabaa massacre; security forces

minimum wage, 33, 49–50, 114, 195n1, 196n20. *See also* divine, minimum wage

Ministry of Social Affairs (*shu'ūn*), 115–117, 123. *See also* case; performance

miracle: in charitable contexts, 91–92, 94–95; as manipulation, 105; of neoliberalism, 162, 206n36; by Shaykh Mahmoud, 143–144; of Tahrir, 36; work instead of seeking a, 158–159

Mit Uqba, 14, 109–111, 113, 115, 119, 200n4

Mitchell, Timothy, 206n36

modern/modernity, 35, 70, 101, 109, 194n13, 199n18, 205n15, 205n18, 206n36

Moll, Yasmin, 198n14

Morsi, Mohamed, 2, 22, 26, 67, 155–156, 170, 174, 194n25, 196n13, 201n16, 204n9. *See also* coup; Muslim Brotherhood

mosque: administration, 63, 181; building/ renovating of, 67–68, 84, 141; and community, 43; as refuge, 59, 63, 195n11; as site of distribution, 16, 31, 50–63, 68, 72, 97, 118, 156, 177, 183, 187n1, 195n9. *See also* prayer; shrine

Moumtaz, Nada, 169, 205n26

Moussa, Amr, 67

Mubarak, Hosni: dream about, 151; economy under, 28, 187n4; grievances against, 33, 85, 118; oppression under, 86; protestors in support of, 25–26, 205n18; resignation of, 9, 21, 32, 38, 179; workers' strikes against, 39, 49. *See also* authoritarianism; protests; revolution

Muehlebach, Andrea, 188n8, 199n18

Muhammad, Prophet: choosing poverty *vs.* wealth, 119, 145; closeness to, 2, 61, 95, 140, 146–147; instituting solidarity, 43, 191n23, 195n11; as manifesting divine light, 52–53, 63; revivalist orientation toward, 6–7, 198n9; and the unseen realm, 63, 100, 164, 170. See also *ahl al-bayt;* hadith; Sufism

Muslim Brotherhood: critique of, 23, 26, 29–30, 105, 151, 194n25; in power (2012– 2013), 2, 26–27, 40, 85, 155–156, 174; providing social services, 9–10, 67, 191n21, 191n24, 201n16; and rumors about Resala, 86; in Sisi era, 165–166; on social justice, 29–30, 42–44, 146, 184; and Sufism, 10, 156, 203n2. *See also* al-Banna; al-Qaradawi; Freedom and Justice Party; Qutb; Rabaa massacre

Mustafa Mahmoud Association, 7

nafs (self), 61, 99, 140, 195n10, 202n9. *See also* self-cultivation; self-erasure

Naguib, Nefissa, 191n24

Nasser. *See* Abdel Nasser

Negm, Ahmed Fouad, 32

Negri, Antonio, 36

neighborhood. *See under* Cairo; slums

neighborhood groups (*ligan sh'abiyya*), 39

neighbors: complaining about Resala, 86; of *khidma,* 147; in paradise, 95; as recipient of charity, 2, 66, 117, 119; solidarity among poor, 70, 76, 97–98, 110, 115, 119, 125–126, 135–136; stories of suffering, 2, 14–15, 115, 117

neoliberalism, 3, 44, 187n4, 189n14, 206n36; charity in, 6, 23, 194n23, 199n18; under El-Sisi, 157–158, 161, 174, 187n4, 204n4; and Islam, 9, 158, 168, 198n15, 200n8; and self-sustainability, 4, 172. *See also* "giving a man a fish"; development; economy; El-Sisi; liberalism; work ethic

New (Administrative) Capital, 155, 174, 206n33. *See also* megaprojects

New Preachers, 82–83, 127, 130, 198n14, 198n15. *See also* Hosni

New Suez Canal, 155, 161–162, 169, 204n11, 204n13. *See also* megaprojects

ni'ma. See blessings

nongovernmental organization (NGO): and definition of poverty, 149; and question of deservingness, 125; corruption at, 120, 127; providing social services, 23, 107–108, 110, 115, 119–120, 127, 169; shift to microloans, 4, 84–85, 158–170; state crackdown on, 27, 86, 184. *See also* individual organizations

nonhumanitarian ethics, 5, 125. *See also* ethics; humanitarianism

Nour Party, 80, 85

Nura: and *ahl al-bayt* (saints), 139–143, 149, 203n12; and expectation-free giving, 135–136, 149–150; and God, 136–138, 140, 202n5, 203n15; and *khidma,* 12, 129–130, 132, 136–144, 146–151, 172, 175, 184, 202n9, 203n11; on politics, 151, 156, 182

obligation: to be thankful, 43, 132; each blessing as an, 94; to give, 41, 63, 68, 98, 119, 132, 180–182, 185, 187n2, 189n10, 190n21; national development as an, 161, 170; the poor failing to fulfill their, 71; of social justice, 9; to work, 144–146,

property, private, 132, 146, 189n13, 194n23, 206n36. *See also* capitalism
prophet. *See* Muhammad
Protestantism, 149, 168, 190n16
protests: in the 2011 Egyptian uprising, 9–10, 21–33, 44, 49, 126, 166, 179, 193n11, 194n17; demography of the 2011 Egyptian, 29, 32, 38–39, 193n9, 205n18; in Egyptian history, 35, 49, 194n20; *vs.* everyday charity, 33, 50, 54, 68, 85, 151, 182; against the Muslim Brotherhood, 49, 194n25; as treason, 28, 164–166; as worship, 26, 50. *See also* Battle of the Camel; elections; injustice; oppression; police; social justice; strikes; Tahrir; Tunisia
provisions *(rizq)*, 54, 60, 97–98, 120, 124. *See also* distribution; generosity
public giving, 12, 15, 67, 161, 204n14. *See also* secrecy, ethics of
punishment, divine, 71, 94, 107, 166, 200n1. *See also* hell; suffering

Quran: on almsgiving, 60, 106, 190n21; cited by Mauss, 181–182; and compassion, 189n11; on divine rewards, 94–95, 134, 199n19; on food distribution, 69; listening to/reciting, 54, 144; on making a living, 66, 145; memorized, 82–84; on poverty, 107, 149, 175; on rights and obligations, 41, 108, 134, 181, 188n10. *See also* afterlife; *haqq*
Qutb, Sayyid, 10, 184, 189n10, 191n22, 199n20, 204n2

Rabaa massacre, 86, 105, 126. *See also* coup; El-Sisi; Muslim Brotherhood; military
radical, 10, 16, 54, 69, 146, 172–173, 181, 184
Ramadan: as key season for charitable giving, 1–3, 13, 56, 58, 71, 105–106, 171; producing empathy, 119; as time of community, 70; as time of sacrifice, 160, 165, 170; and *zakāt al-fitr*, 119, 200n12. *See also* fasting; Ramadan table
Ramadan table, 12, 42, 62, 71, 187n1
recipients, 4, 41, 59–61, 92–93, 101–108, 121–125, 129–130, 132–136, 149
reciprocity, 4, 8, 110, 135, 200n5, 202n8. *See also* gift economy; Mauss; triadic giving

reliance *(tawakkul)*, 71, 134. *See also* perseverance
Resala, 74–101; and Amal, 108–110, 114, 117, 119–121, 128; bus lessons at, 87–89, 97–99; fieldwork at, 9, 13, 81, 108; food distribution trip, 77–79, 81–83, 87–89, 91–94, 97–99, 108–110, 133, 280; history of, 83–85, 184; microloans, 114, 170–171, 200n8; Mini-Camp, 89–91, 94–95; paradise at, 74–77, 86, 94–97, 99–101, 136, 182, 197n3; temporality at, 100, 158, 181; and uprising, 85–86, 181; volunteers, 79–81, 90–91, 120. *See also* Abdelazeem; voluntarism
responsibility: government, 37, 117–119, 159, 196n16; individual, 4, 58, 66, 68, 73, 100, 140, 159, 169–170, 189n13. *See also* obligation; sacrifice
revolution: as fleeting, 4, 10, 21, 45, 118, 156, 174, 192n1; at heart of Islam, 10, 24, 191n23; class in the, 29, 32–33, 165, 193n9, 205n18; French, 33; 'loud', against a 'quiet' ethics of giving, 9, 11–12, 22–24, 27, 40, 100, 155, 180–184; of the thieves, 29; opposing an unjust social order, 6, 15, 23, 42, 166; progressive, 22, 40, 192n4; rhetoric of sacrifice in/after the, 166–168, 174, 183; volunteering and, 85–86. *See also* activists; authoritarianism; class differences; counterrevolution; Egyptian Revolutionary Socialists; everyday; hope; martyrs; paradise; protests; sacrifice; social justice; Tahrir; temporality; youth
ridā (contentment), 52, 109, 112, 127, 134, 145. *See also* gratitude; perseverance
rightful share. *See haqq*
rights: *vs.* charity, 5, 41–43; divinely-mandated, 68–70, 73, 134, 188n10, 206n35; human, 38, 86, 181; labor, 22; politics of, 5, 15, 33, 193n12, 206n35; of the poor, 33, 188n10. *See also haqq*; injustice; justice
rizq (provisions), 54, 60, 97–98, 120, 124. *See also* distribution; generosity
Robbins, Joel, 14, 107, 190n18

Sabahi, Hamdeen, 159, 196n13
Sabea, Hanan, 37, 207n2

ultras, 29, 193n10
Umayyad caliphate, 191n21
unemployment, 3, 32, 73, 80, 94, 112, 117,
    198n10. *See also* workers; youth
United Nations, 204n11
Upper Egypt, 31–32, 53, 84, 114, 122, 141,
    182
uprising (2011). *See* bread; "bread, freedom,
    social justice"; Christianity; class differ-
    ences; Facebook; martyrs; Morsi;
    Mubarak; oppression; protests; Resala;
    revolution; Shaykh Salah; slums;
    Tahrir; television; workers
utopia, 11, 25, 35–38, 45, 55, 146, 181, 193n6,
    194n23. *See also* Tahrir

vendors. *See* street vendors
violence: and care, 180; in depictions of
    hell, 199n21; domestic, 128; and ethno-
    graphic portrayal, 107, 175, 184; police,
    9, 25, 36; and revolution, 39, 69; state, 27,
    175–178, 183; structural, 31. *See also*
    injustice; oppression; Rabaa massacre;
    thugs; torture
virtue, 69, 119, 132, 158, 195n6, 200n1. *See
    also* contentment; generosity; persever-
    ance; trading with God
visible, 172; entangled with the invisible
    realm, 5, 8, 16, 62, 73, 75, 143, 147–151,
    189n12, 201n2. *See also* dreams
voluntarism, 23, 84, 90, 199n18. *See also*
    Resala

wages. *See* divine; minimum wage
Wāhid min al-Nās, 34

waqf (endowment), 169, 191n21, 195n11,
    205n26, 205n27
war, 61, 139, 159–160, 190n21, 194n20
wealth: as acceptable in Islam, 132, 145–146;
    as corrupting, 146; as obligation to give,
    108, 119, 183, 190n21; as trial, 112. See
    also *zakāt*
Weber, Max, 168
welfare state, 23, 30, 44, 64, 67–68, 115–116,
    149, 173, 189n14. *See also* social justice
West, imaginaries of, 70, 74, 83, 199n2
Wilde, Oscar, 41, 194n23
Winegar, Jessica, 193n9, 198n16
work ethic, 73, 111, 130, 132, 144–146, 149,
    168. *See also* laziness
workers, 59, 73, 76, 162; in the 2011 upris-
    ing, 26, 33, 39, 49–50, 179, 193n5,
    194n17; efficient, 65–66; in need, 33, 60,
    194n17; as unfitting recipients of char-
    ity, 97. *See also* minimum wage; strikes;
    unemployment
working class, 29, 35, 43, 80, 126, 174,
    188n4, 193n9, 205n18. *See also* class
    differences; middle class
World Bank, 187n4, 206n32

youth, 12, 32, 38, 49, 53, 73, 83, 161, 200n4.
    See also Resala; unemployment

Zaghloul, Saad, 10
zakāt (almsgiving), 30, 119, 122, 184,
    190n21, 200n3, 200n12; al-fitr, 119,
    187n1, 200n12. *See also* donors; *khayr;
    sadaqa*
Žižek, Slavoj, 36, 41, 194n23